THE BEDFORD SERIES IN HISTORY AND CULTURE

Muller v. Oregon

A Brief History with Documents

Related Titles in
THE BEDFORD SERIES IN HISTORY AND CULTURE
Advisory Editors: Lynn Hunt, *University of California, Los Angeles*
David W. Blight, *Yale University*
Bonnie G. Smith, *Rutgers University*
Natalie Zemon Davis, *Princeton University*
Ernest R. May, *Harvard University*

THE BEDFORD SERIES IN HISTORY AND CULTURE

Muller v. Oregon

A Brief History with Documents

Nancy Woloch

Barnard College

BEDFORD/ST. MARTIN'S   Boston ◆ New York

For Bedford/St. Martin's
President and Publisher: Charles H. Christensen
General Manager and Associate Publisher: Joan E. Feinberg
Associate History Editor: Richard Keaveny
Managing Editor: Elizabeth M. Schaaf
Production Editor: Lori Chong
Copyeditor: Barbara G. Flanagan
Indexer: Steve Csipke
Text Design: Claire Seng-Niemoeller
Cover Design: Richard Emery Design, Inc.
Cover Photograph: Woman Working in a Laundry, Lewis W. Hine. Courtesy of George Eastman House.

Library of Congress Catalog Card Number: 95-83525

Manufactured in the United States of America.

5 4 3 2 1
k j

For information, write: Bedford/St. Martin's, 75 Arlington Street, Boston, MA 02116 (617-399-4000)

ISBN-10: 0-312-08586-9 (paperback)
          0-312-12816-9 (hardcover)
ISBN-13: 978-0-312-08586-5 (paperback)
          978-0-312-12816-6 (hardcover)

Acknowledgments

"The Blanket Amendment—A Debate," by Doris Stevens versus Alice Hamilton. Reprinted with permission from *Current History* magazine (August 1924). © 1924 Current History, Inc.

"Do Women Want Protection?" by Harriot Stanton Blatch versus Clara Mortenson Beyer. Reprinted with permission from *The Nation* magazine (January 31, 1923). © The Nation Company, L.P.

Foreword

The Bedford Series in History and Culture is designed so that readers can study the past as historians do.

The historian's first task is finding the evidence. Documents, letters, memoirs, interviews, pictures, movies, novels, or poems can provide facts and clues. Then the historian questions and compares the sources. There is more to do than in a courtroom, for hearsay evidence is welcome, and the historian is usually looking for answers beyond act and motive. Different views of an event may be as important as a single verdict. How a story is told may yield as much information as what it says.

Along the way the historian seeks help from other historians and perhaps from specialists in other disciplines. Finally, it is time to write, to decide on an interpretation and how to arrange the evidence for readers.

Each book in this series contains an important historical document or group of documents, each document a witness from the past and open to interpretation in different ways. The documents are combined with some element of historical narrative—an introduction or a biographical essay, for example—that provides students with an analysis of the primary source material and important background information about the world in which it was produced.

Each book in the series focuses on a specific topic within a specific historical period. Each provides a basis for lively thought and discussion about several aspects of the topic and the historian's role. Each is short enough (and inexpensive enough) to be a reasonable one-week assignment in a college course. Whether as classroom or personal reading, each book in the series provides firsthand experience of the challenge—and fun—of discovering, recreating, and interpreting the past.

Lynn Hunt
David W. Blight
Bonnie G. Smith
Natalie Zemon Davis
Ernest R. May

Preface

Muller v. Oregon lies at a busy juncture where constitutional history, women's history, and progressive politics converge. In 1908 the Supreme Court unanimously upheld an Oregon law that set a ten-hour limit to the workday of women in factories and laundries. The *Muller* decision was a coup for lawyer Louis D. Brandeis, who argued Oregon's case; a green light to reformers who championed protective laws; and a precedent for New Deal labor policies. The decision also sanctioned classification by sex, which spurred a feud among politicized women in the 1920s and split the women's movement for decades thereafter. Single-sex protective laws prevailed until around 1970, when a combination of factors — Title VII of the 1964 Civil Rights Act, a series of court decisions, and the feminist movement — consigned them to oblivion.

The *Muller* case thus involves two major issues that pervade twentieth-century U.S. history: state regulation of private enterprise and sexual equality under the law. The intersection of issues makes the *Muller* case a pivot in several historical dramas and, in recent years, a focus of conflicting interpretations.

For more than half a century, *Muller v. Oregon* enjoyed (and in many ways still enjoys) an overwhelmingly positive press. Historians of the early twentieth century have long found the campaign for labor standards, which *Muller* advanced, one of the Progressive era's most durable legacies. In constitutional history, the *Muller* decision represents a timely gain in the progressives' drawn-out battle against the "legal fiction" of freedom of contract — a triumph bracketed by two crushing defeats, *Lochner v. New York* (1905) and *Adkins v. Children's Hospital* (1923). Brandeis biographers, finally, see the *Muller* case as the high point of Brandeis's career as a lawyer and celebrate the success of the famous "Brandeis brief," which served to circumvent legal formalism and co-opt conservative justices. In the past few decades, however, a focus on gender has undercut, reversed, or at least modified the favorable spin on *Muller*. Feminist revisionism has two prongs. First, feminist legal historians find

vii

the *Muller* decision a setback in women's progress toward legal equality. Second, recent work in women's history has reshaped the context in which *Muller* emerged by moving women from the margins to the center of progressive reform. Well-off, educated women of the early twentieth century — a female reform network that promoted such measures as protective laws and mothers' pensions — created precedents that came to fruition in the 1930s and thereby laid the foundations of the welfare state. But this remarkable achievement, current studies suggest, came at a price: The policies effected by the women's reform network sustained gender distinctions that worked to women's disadvantage.

The recent focus on gender has raised (or revived) many questions about women's role in progressive reform in general and the battle for protective laws in particular. Were single-sex protective laws, like Oregon's ten-hour law, *primarily* an effort to compensate for women's disadvantages in the labor market *or* the linchpin of a larger plan to attain wage-and-hour laws for all employees? Did protective laws in fact improve the lives of women workers and, if so, which workers, under what circumstances, and for how long? Did the women's reform network that supported protection secure its own niche in public affairs more than it empowered women workers? Were leading proponents of protective policies, such as Florence Kelley and her colleagues in the National Consumers' League, misguided in their defense of sexual difference, in their "maternalist" stance, and in their commitment to the family wage? Did they promote, in effect, patriarchal assumptions? Were their opponents in the National Woman's Party of the 1920s, in contrast, captives of laissez-faire individualism and tools of conservative legal strategies? In what ways, moreover, did the legal process and constitutional questions determine reformers' options and tactics?

Such questions reverberate through any discussion of *Muller v. Oregon,* which generates its own deluge of questions. Was Brandeis's involvement with the *Muller* case, for instance, a bonus or misfortune for women workers? Could Brandeis have pursued an alternative strategy? Is "social science" evidence a risky basis for constitutional decisions? Did the Court's decision in *Muller* reflect humane considerations or sexist assumptions? Did it defy the *Lochner* decision or reinforce it? In what ways, moreover, did the *Muller* opinion diverge from the Brandeis brief? Did the "social facts" that Brandeis presented pave the way for a new "legal fiction" of female dependence? Alternatively, was the Brandeis brief irrelevant, and would the justices have reached the same decision without it? Finally, how can *we* fairly assess the roles of the protagonists in the *Muller* case? Did Muller's lawyers present a cogent argument for sexual equality or a rationale to preserve employers' power? Have the reformers who prepared Oregon's defense been betrayed over time by developments they could not anticipate and shifts in attitudes they could not foresee? Were there fundamental flaws in their arguments and strategies? Or did they become enmeshed in a nexus of obstinate problems that defied resolution for decades to come and emerge in public policy questions even today?

This book is a consideration of *Muller v. Oregon* and its ramifications in twentieth-century history. Part One, the introductory essay, explores the origins of the case, the issues it involved, and its impact from the Progressive era to the 1990s. Part Two, the documents section, covers 1895 to 1941, a crucial period in the battle for modern labor standards. Documents include major court decisions, the lawyers' briefs in the *Muller* case, and arguments over single-sex protective laws from the women's movement of the 1920s. The combination of essay and documents is designed to explore the questions suggested here and to provoke debate about the problems embedded in *Muller*. Above all, this book seeks to recreate the particular context in which *Muller v. Oregon* arose — to focus attention on the early decades of this century, on the controversial roles of progressive reformers, on political strategies that both succeeded and failed, and on the complex antecedents of contemporary public policy.

ACKNOWLEDGMENTS

I am indebted to my outstanding publisher, Bedford Books. I owe special thanks to Chuck Christensen and to editors Sabra Scribner and Niels Aaboe for commissioning this project and seeing it through, and to production editor Lori Chong and copyeditor Barbara Flanagan for their excellent work on the manuscript. I have profited immensely from the stimulating reviews of Eileen Boris, Paul Clemens, Robert Johnston, Kathryn Kish Sklar, and Melvin I. Urofsky, for whose contributions I am profoundly grateful. I am similarly grateful for the advice and help of friends and colleagues — David Farber, Richard Pious, Rosalind Rosenberg, Ann Schofield, Deborah Valenze, and Susan Ware. I am indebted to Richard and Elizabeth Davis at the Center for the History of Freedom at Washington University in St. Louis, and to Raymond Grew, Sergio Luzzatto, and Claire Messina for their company while this book was in progress. To my husband, Isser Woloch, many thanks for living with *Muller* and the spirit of argument it fosters. I am especially grateful, finally, to my distinguished colleague Herb Sloan, for generously sharing his library, office, and expertise. None of the people mentioned here, of course, are responsible for any errors I may have made.

Nancy Woloch

Contents

APPENDICES

Muller v. Oregon

A Brief History with Documents

"Entering Wedge":
Muller v. Oregon and
Its Legacy

Introduction

In January 1908, the Supreme Court considered the case of Curt Muller, owner of a Portland laundry that had kept a woman employee at work overtime. Convicted of violating an Oregon law of 1903 that barred the employment of women in factories and laundries for more than ten hours a day, Muller challenged the constitutionality of the law, which, he claimed, violated his right to freedom of contract under the due process clause of the Fourteenth Amendment. Representing the state of Oregon, lawyer Louis D. Brandeis argued that freedom of contract could be curbed by the state to protect the health and welfare of its people. In a lengthy brief, the famous "Brandeis brief," he presented a barrage of "facts" to show the relationship among long hours, worker health, and public welfare. Overwork, the brief contended, "is more disastrous to the health of women than of men, and entails upon them more lasting injury." Furthermore, "the deterioration is handed down to succeeding generations" and "the overwork of future mothers thus directly attacks the welfare of the nation." Six weeks later, the Court unanimously upheld the Oregon law. "As healthy mothers are essential to vigorous offspring," declared Justice David J. Brewer, "the physical well-being of woman becomes an object of public interest and care in order to preserve the strength and vigor of the race."[1]

To progressive reformers, *Muller v. Oregon* was a momentous triumph. Three years before, their campaign for protective laws had been thwarted by the ominous decision in *Lochner v. New York* (1905), in which the Supreme Court rejected a ten-hour law for bakery workers. The Oregon case, which legitimized maximum-hours laws for women workers, was a turning point. By gaining acceptance for "sociological jurisprudence" — consideration by courts of social and economic data — the Brandeis brief opened a channel through which new protective laws could be steered; by winning protection for women in industry, reformers inched closer to a broader goal, protection by the state of all workers. Their drive to curb industrial abuse ultimately led, in the New Deal, to

3

federal laws that provided maximum hours, minimum wages, and other parts of the progressive agenda. A long trail of scholarship, launched by the progressives themselves, applauds their achievements, among which the Brandeis brief and the *Muller* decision loom large. Well into the 1960s, *Muller v. Oregon* seemed to be a "judicial landmark unscarred by criticism."[2]

More recently, however, *Muller*'s stock has plummeted. Fueled by the feminist movement of the 1960s, a new generation of analysts points to another facet of the *Muller* decision: It embedded in constitutional law an axiom of female difference. Women, said the Brewer opinion, could be treated as a class in different ways than men. Protective laws that treated women workers as a separate class remained in effect for six decades, until toppled by a legal revolution in the 1960s and 1970s. Moreover, the principle of sex as a valid basis of classification served as a rationale for discriminatory laws in other fields from family law to criminal law. To feminist critics, the progressive achievement in *Muller v. Oregon* has come to represent a colossal mistake. The *Muller* decision now seems a repository of retrograde ideas that harmed women more than they helped and consequently impeded the arrival of sexual equality. "Beyond any doubt *Muller* opened the door to gender bias in protective legislation," writes historian Joan Hoff in one of the more temperate critiques. "In retrospect . . . it is possible to question the long-term wisdom of the Brandeis approach in *Muller*."[3]

Muller v. Oregon thus leads a double life in constitutional history — as both a step forward on the road to modern labor standards and a step backward away from sexual equality. Why did the struggles for workers' rights and women's rights collide? The answer to this question spans the twentieth century, for the *Muller* case had both complex origins and long-term consequences. The story opens around the turn of the century, when progressive reformers sought remedies to problems posed by industrialization. We turn first to the campaign for protective laws, the goals and tactics of reformers, and the progressive strategy of the "entering wedge" — the use of sex-specific laws to gain a foothold from which to pursue a larger legislative agenda.

1

The Rise of Protective Laws

In the late nineteenth century, factories invaded American cities, industrialization changed the nature of work, and women surged into the labor force. By 1900, five million women earned wages; one-fourth held jobs in manufacturing, where they constituted 17 percent of employees. Women crowded the labor pool in the industries that hired them, mainly clothing, textile, and food production; they formed the bulk of the workforce in cotton mills, garment shops, canning plants, and commercial laundries. According to government surveys, women in industry were mainly, though not exclusively, young, single, and either immigrants or daughters of immigrants. Typically unskilled or semiskilled and transient (few expected to spend their lives in the workforce), they earned about half the pay of men in industry. Plentiful in supply, limited in occupational choice, concentrated at the bottom rungs of the industrial ladder, and often intermittently employed, women workers lacked bargaining power. Spontaneous or sporadic protests, even if successful, rarely led to permanent labor organizations. Overall, "women inhabited a distinct and separate labor market, one characterized by low pay, low skill, low security, and low mobility," historian Leslie Woodcock Tentler reminds us. "In the world of work, sex, before all else, established the boundaries of opportunity."[1]

Women's disadvantaged status in the workforce played a major role in the progressive campaign for labor reform. Through legislation, reformers hoped to improve the lives of all industrial workers — to limit hours, raise wages, improve factory conditions, and promote occupational safety. By World War I, their efforts had led to scores of state protective laws — child labor laws, maximum-hours laws, minimum-wage laws, fire and safety laws, and workmen's compensation laws. A portion of such laws applied to men but, except for workmen's compensation, almost always to men in special circumstances. Maximum-hours laws, for instance, might affect men employed by state agencies or on public works projects (jobs in which the state itself was the contractor); or in trades that involved public safety, such as railway work; or in hazardous work such as mining. Attempts to regulate male labor in other fields, or in general, however, never evoked a groundswell of popular or legislative support and invited defeat in the courts. So did laws that empowered labor unions, to which judges were especially hostile.[2]

Roadblocks to laws that affected men in industry pushed protective laws for women and children to the front of the reform agenda, where, progressives hoped, they would clear a path for more "general" laws. Suspicious of the latter, lawmakers proved receptive to the former. As one reformer observed, the "hard-boiled legislator has a soft side when it comes to women workers."[3] By the turn of the century, twenty-eight states had passed laws to regulate child labor, and over the next fifteen years most states enacted at least some type of law to regulate women's hours, wages, or working conditions.

Maximum-hours laws for women workers made the greatest headway, along with child labor laws. Protection for women and for children often went together, as in the earliest ten-hour laws, passed in New Hampshire, Maine, Pennsylvania, and Ohio in the 1840s and 1850s. Such laws lacked provisions for enforcement. In 1874, Massachusetts, the first state with extensive industry and a large female workforce, passed a law that limited the work weeks of women and minors to sixty hours; at first, employers could not be prosecuted unless they "willfully" violated the law, but an amendment of 1879 closed this loophole. In Illinois in the early 1890s, reformer Florence Kelley fired the opening round of the progressive campaign: She drafted and promoted a law that banned child labor and provided an eight-hour day and forty-eight-hour week for women and teenagers in workshops and factories. Enacted in 1893, this pioneer statute included apparatus for enforcement; indeed, Kelley led the team of factory inspectors that enforced it. Although the Illinois Supreme Court overturned the limit on women's hours two years later, other states, including Oregon, passed similar measures or improved earlier ones. By 1908, when Curt Muller's case reached the U.S. Supreme Court, twenty states had maximum-hours laws for women in manufacturing, most of them ten-hour laws.[4]

Maximum-hours laws, significantly, did not ensure that women in manufacturing worked *shorter* days than men did. Rather, if enforced, as was not always the case, such laws reduced the very long hours that women had labored in the most exploitative trades, such as laundries — twelve- or fourteen- or even sixteen-hour days in rush periods — to a level closer to that of the typical male industrial worker. At the turn of the century, the average work week was fifty-seven hours and falling. Workdays in sawmills, steel mills, and bakeries remained long, but skilled men in trades with strong unions, such as construction or cigarmaking, worked fifty hours a week or less.[5]

As maximum-hours laws spread, states passed other types of protective laws for women workers. Some laws improved the conditions of work: They regulated industrial homework (piecework done in workers' residences) or required chairs, meal breaks, or rest periods. Several states, led by Massachusetts in 1890, prohibited night work, which, a reformer explained in 1913, caused "destruction of homelife; impossibility of properly caring for home and children; lack of restraining influence." Other laws limited the occupations that women could enter. Although the California Supreme Court upset an 1881 law that banned women from work in places that sold alcoholic drinks, restrictive measures emerged elsewhere. New York, for instance, in laws of 1899, 1906, and 1913, barred women and children from jobs in factories that operated polishing and buffing wheels, from mines and quarries, and from core-making (a fume-producing part of the iron-molding process) and foundries. Finally, as the push for protection reached its peak, reformers pressed for minimum-wage laws for women workers, a far more controversial type of statute. Still, between 1912 and 1923, fifteen states plus the District of Columbia enacted such laws. To propel protective laws through legislatures, progressive reformers formed pressure groups, which, like the industrial system they sought to improve, divided along gender lines.[6]

THE CAMPAIGN FOR PROTECTION

Drawn from the ranks of the urban middle class (typically the upper middle class), progressive reformers sought to ameliorate the ills of industrialization; they strove variously to curb corporate excess, control monopoly, end government corruption, democratize electoral procedures, and bridge the gap between social classes. Whatever their goals, they shared a number of qualities. Embarked on a quest for order, progressives valued reason, expertise, efficiency, and professionalism; impelled by moral purpose, they championed education, investigation, a spirit of experiment, and a cooperative ethic. Suspicious of privilege but wary of conflict, they turned class perceptions into political posture. Labor reformers reflected all aspects of the progressive mentality.[7]

In 1906, progressive professionals formed a pressure group, the American Association for Labor Legislation (AALL), spearheaded by two economists at the University of Wisconsin, John R. Commons and his student John B. Andrews. The AALL membership comprised journalists, academics, lawyers, and "social workers" (the progressive rubric for women active in charity, welfare, or reform) plus reform-minded legislators, factory inspectors, bureaucrats, and other state employees. By 1911, the AALL had two thousand members (mainly men), a New York headquarters, annual conferences, and a hefty journal, edited by Andrews. Proud of its chosen role as middleman between manufacturers' groups and labor unions, the AALL focused its efforts on "general" laws such as workmen's compensation. A women's committee reported on progress with women's labor laws.[8]

Middle-class women and their organizations — a female reform network — led the campaign to protect women workers. Around the turn of the century, the huge General Federation of Women's Clubs (GFWC, founded in 1890) shifted its goals from self-improvement to civic concerns and soon endorsed laws to protect women and children in industry. The National Women's Trade Union League (NWTUL, founded in 1903), which rose to prominence in New York's massive shirtwaist strike of 1909, strove both to spur unions among women workers and to attain protective laws, often as a substitute for unionization, which proved difficult to achieve. Under the auspices of the NWTUL, which welcomed working-class members (along with upper-class "allies"), working women joined the protectionist chorus — although NWTUL spokeswomen of working-class origin were typically no longer workers.[9]

Most important was the National Consumers' League (NCL, founded in 1898), led by its dynamic general secretary, Florence Kelley, who had engineered Illinois's pioneer eight-hour law in 1893. A counterpart to the AALL, the NCL strove to improve the conditions of women workers in stores and factories. "Investigate, record, agitate" was its motto. A longtime socialist, Kelley assumed a pivotal role: She forged a link between male and female supporters of protective laws; embraced large-scale goals for protection of all workers; pursued protectionist goals with relentless drive; and galvanized support among women's constituencies, such as clubwomen, whose "maternalist rhetoric" wielded pressure on civic leaders, lawmakers, judges, and public opinion. When "weighty women's groups advocated new measures on behalf of children, and for the sake of women as actual or potential mothers," scholar Theda Skocpol contends, "their demands were hard for legislators to ignore."[10]

Did socialist Kelley, a sophisticated politician, co-opt the "maternalist" clubwomen? Yes and no. Concerned about exploited women and children, clubwomen did not necessarily support Kelley's broader plans to protect labor in general. Still, when it came to women, members of the women's reform network shared a common agenda: to save the home from the contamination of industry (by bans on industrial homework, for instance); to defend women who lacked the support of men (by such measures as mothers' pensions — funding for children in families without male breadwinners); and overall, to safeguard the interests of women and children, at home or in the workforce, if they were forced to enter it. To the women's network, motherhood *was* a priority. As a reformer declared in a 1910 study of women workers, "The woman is worth more to society in dollars and cents as the mother of healthy children than as the swiftest labeler of cans."[11]

Progressive reformers, in fact, endorsed two distinct rationales for women's labor laws, often simultaneously. The first rationale, implicit more than explicit, was strategic: Laws to protect women workers — the type of measure that legislators and judges were most likely to approve — would serve as an "entering wedge" for protective laws for all workers. They would set precedents on which reformers could capitalize. Moreover, laws that covered only women also affected men who worked in the same industries. In Massachusetts textile mills, for instance, limits on women's hours also cut men's hours; the brief tenure of Illinois's 1893 law, Florence Kelley noted, had shortened hours for all workers in Chicago stockyards. Men "who wished reduced hours of work for themselves," she pointed out in 1905, might gain them "indirectly" if they worked in a trade with a large female labor force. Women's labor laws were thus not merely a worthy end in themselves but also served as a means to achieve a larger goal: the protection of all employees from industrial abuse.[12]

Reformers had a specific model for the "entering wedge" strategy: England's factory laws. Since the start of the nineteenth century, Parliament had passed laws to limit working hours in mills and factories, first those of young apprentices, then of all child workers, and then of women. Successive factory laws (of 1802, 1819, 1831, 1833, 1842, 1847, 1850, 1853, 1864, and on and on into the twentieth century) became more stringent, to cut out loopholes, and broader in scope, to cover more types of work. They also included models of night work laws; laws that excluded women and children from dangerous work, as in mines; and, eventually, minimum-wage laws. One impact of the factory acts, by the mid-nineteenth century, was to limit hours for male employees in textile mills, where men, women, and children worked together. In industries with all-male labor, such as mining, unions and collective bargaining shortened workdays.[13]

The English model could not be easily replicated across the Atlantic. The American federal system hampered enactment of a national protection policy, since each state acted independently. American laws, moreover, were subject to judicial review, as Parliament's acts were not. Still, in England, with its long string of factory acts and teams of factory inspectors, efforts to protect women and children led to far-reaching state regulation of industry, and progressives hoped to follow suit.

A second, more explicit, rationale for protective laws for women workers rested on the difference between women and men in the workforce. Laws based on difference were compensatory. They were intended to help women "overcome the disabilities arising from their unequal power in the workplace and in society," points out historian Kathryn Kish Sklar, "and to help them fulfill maternal responsibilities." Many "disabilities" rested on circumstance. Reformers contended, for instance, that women were (next to children) a particularly needy class of workers. Often young and temporary, they were crowded into low-level, low-paid jobs; if overburdened mothers, they combined factory work with obligations at home; in either case, since unorganized (not members of labor unions), they were easy prey for greedy employers. Or, as a clubwoman claimed in 1910, women were "almost as helpless as the children in obtaining redress from oppression." Another facet of difference involved innate attributes: Women were physically weaker than men and they were actual or potential mothers — points that gained currency after the *Muller* decision. Of course, the "sexual difference" rationale and the "entering wedge" strategy clashed; the first undercut the second. If protective laws compensated for sex-linked disabilities or disadvantages, their extension to men was unnecessary. Reformers found this contradiction irrelevant; in terms of tactics, women's labor laws (like laws that curbed the hours of miners, railway workers, and state employees) were effective steps toward the protection of all workers. More to the point, women's labor laws were one of the few steps possible, for reformers had narrow options and faced substantial obstacles.[14]

Organized labor was one such obstacle. Until the 1890s, the labor movement had been the main proponent of protection, specifically of the eight-hour workday. Thereafter, labor support became problematic. The American Federation of Labor (AFL, founded in 1886), an association of unions that represented skilled workers, almost entirely male, gave nominal support to maximum-hours laws for women and children but rejected such measures for men in general, and in particular for its own members, who favored more effective tactics such as organization and collective bargaining. AFL leader Samuel Gompers explained this stance concisely in his testimony before a federal commission in 1914:

The AF of L is in favor of fixing the maximum number of hours of work for children, minors, and women. It does not favor a legal limit of the workday for adult men workers. The unions have very largely established the shorter workday by their own initiative.

Clearly, too, the unions lacked confidence in the type of state intrusion that protective laws represented and especially feared the courts, which did all they could to repress unions. Or, as Gompers put it, "The AF of L has apprehension as to the wisdom of placing in the hands of the government additional powers which may be used to the detriment of the working people." Finally, the AFL distrusted minimum-wage laws, which, it suspected, might be maximum-wage laws. Self-interest prompted union support for women's maximum-hours laws in another way, too. The AFL feared that low-paid women workers would take men's jobs; laws restricting women's hours would make women less desirable employees and perhaps exclude them from the workforce entirely. Overall, the AFL sought both to stave off the prospect of low-paid female competition *and* to reject the weakness and dependence that legal protection implied. Organized labor was therefore a wild card in the campaign for protective laws, though state federations, acting independently, might offer support to reformers (and the AFL rank and file defiantly endorsed workman's compensation laws, which Gompers at first opposed but later supported).[15]

While the AFL impeded *some* of the reformers' goals, an embattled contingent of employers opposed *all* of them. The business community resisted state interference with the economic system and endorsed the theory of laissez-faire: Business worked best, in the view of business owners, if left alone. According to employers, protective laws violated property rights, imposed unneeded "paternalism," and paved a path to socialism. Foes of protection swiftly mobilized. After the passage of Illinois's eight-hour law in 1893, Chicago manufacturers took the lead. The Illinois Manufacturers Association spurred the formation of kindred groups, which in 1895 formed the National Association of Manufacturers, whose members often belonged as well to local chambers of commerce and specialized business associations. Like reformers, employers subscribed to an "entering wedge" theory, but in reverse: They feared that laws that shortened the workday for women in industry would lead to more damaging measures, such as state control of working conditions for all workers.[16]

Employers had important allies in the fight against protection: their lawyers. "Able lawyers have, to a large extent, allowed themselves to become adjuncts of large corporations," Louis D. Brandeis wrote in 1905. Corporate lawyers shared with their clients a vested interest in laissez-faire. At state and local bar associations, they denounced "despotism of the majority," incursions on property rights, and efforts to impede the freedom of business to maximize profits. As Justice Brewer, who later wrote the *Muller* opinion, told the New York Bar Association in 1893, judges needed support "to restrain the greedy hand of the many filching from the few." Employers and their lawyers lobbied against protective laws in state legislatures and, when that failed, challenged the laws in court. Through their challenges, they shaped the nature of protection and the campaign to achieve it.[17]

CONSTITUTIONAL ISSUES

Challenges to protective laws followed a pattern that took hold in the 1890s. Opponents of protection relied on the doctrine of "freedom of contract," that is, the right of employers and workers to negotiate wages, hours, and working conditions. Such a right was guaranteed, employers claimed, under the due process clause of the Fourteenth Amendment, which says that no state shall "deprive any person of life, liberty, or property without due process of law." Proposed and ratified after the Civil War to protect the civil rights of newly freed southern blacks against the infringements of the ex-Confederate states, the amendment now served the needs of employers who wanted to preserve their own liberty from legislatures. *Liberty* and *property* were the key words. "The privilege of contracting is both a liberty and a property right," explained Justice Benjamin Magruder of the Illinois Supreme Court in 1895, on overturning the state's eight-hour law. "Liberty includes the right to acquire property, and that means and includes the right to make and enforce contracts." Labor, moreover, *was* property, Magruder continued, which a worker had a right to sell to an employer (foes of protection often framed their arguments in terms of the employee's rights). Laws that regulated labor thus interfered with property rights and violated the Constitution.[18]

"Freedom of contract" was not a long-established constitutional right but rather an innovative one. Its roots lay in Justice Stephen J. Field's dissent in the *Slaughter-House Cases* (1873). Field asserted the judiciary's obligation under the due process clause of the Fourteenth Amendment to protect citizens' rights against hostile state action. Thereafter, corporate lawyers urged the courts to use the Fourteenth Amendment to protect private property from legislative regulation. Their efforts spurred a conservative shift in jurisprudence that featured a new interpretation of the due process clause. Once solely a "procedural" safeguard that encompassed a citizen's right to obtain a lawyer or to call witnesses, the due process clause became "substantive," a guarantee of rights against legislative infringement. From there it was just a short leap to freedom of contract. The conservative judicial revolution of the 1890s, writes legal historian Arnold M. Paul, "vastly expanded the scope of judicial supremacy."[19] It also held great promise for business.

Substantive due process emerged in the states, where legislatures had tried to curb abusive labor practices. In *In re Jacobs* (1885), for instance, which upset a state law banning tenement cigarmaking, the New York Court of Appeals (the state's highest court) cited the cigarmaker's due process right "to live and work where he will" and asserted the power of the courts to "determine what is reasonable." Reference to freedom of contract swiftly followed, first in two 1886 cases in Pennsylvania and Illinois that involved the payment of wages in scrip, or certificates for the purchase of goods in company stores. In both instances, state laws had banned this manner of payment. State courts overturned the laws, which, they declared, were "an insulting attempt" to subvert workers' rights and bar them from freely contracting with their employers. A decade later, in *Allgeyer v. Louisiana* (1897), a case that involved not labor law but a law to regulate insurance contracts, the Supreme Court confirmed the right of freedom to contract. Thereafter, employers found extensive use for it to battle protective laws.[20]

Supporters of protection vehemently challenged the doctrine of freedom of contract, which, they claimed, was hardly sacrosanct but rather a recently revealed (or concocted) "right." Legislatures and courts, they pointed out, had traditionally modified contract rights, as in the case of usury laws, which protected the borrower, the weaker party to the contract. Not only was freedom of contract a dubious doctrine, its critics argued, but it was a "legal fiction," since employers and employees did not operate from positions of equal strength. In real life, reformers repeatedly explained, workers lacked the power to determine the conditions of their employment. "The worker in fact obeys the compulsion of circumstance," wrote Josephine Goldmark of the NCL in 1912. "The alternative is to work or to starve. To refuse means to be dismissed. Modern industry has reduced 'freedom of contract' to a paper privilege, a mere figure of rhetoric." Finally, critics charged, freedom of contract could deprive legislatures of *their* freedom to represent constituents. The word *liberty* in the Fourteenth Amendment was "perverted," said Justice

Oliver Wendell Holmes Jr. in 1905, when it was used to "prevent the natural outcome of a dominant opinion."[21]

Still, as the Supreme Court had conceded in *Allgeyer* in 1897, freedom of contract was not absolute but was subject to state regulation. To forge exceptions to freedom of contract, reformers relied on the ancient "police power" of the state: Any sovereign power can overrule individual rights or property rights to preserve the health, safety, and welfare of the people. The police power was the crux of the issue, for both foes and friends of protection agreed that the state had such a power; they differed only as to its extent. In each instance, therefore, it was up to the court to decide how far the police power would stretch, that is, to judge the nature of an alleged threat to the public welfare and the reasonableness of the law to curtail it. *Reasonableness* was the key word. Did a legislature have reasonable grounds to believe that a law would remedy a specific hazard to health and welfare? What was reasonable? As historian Melvin I. Urofsky points out, "The police power at any time was essentially what the courts declared it to be."[22]

The court's view of "reasonableness" applied to another issue, too. Employers often opposed protective laws as "class legislation" that arbitrarily singled out a category of people for favor or disfavor; such legislation, they claimed, violated the Fourteenth Amendment's equal protection clause, which says that no state shall "deny to any person within its jurisdiction the equal protection of the law." Was a particular law a genuine "health and welfare" law, judges asked, or an illegitimate "labor law" that sought to promote the interests of a particular group? States' attorneys had to convince judges that the classification in question was reasonable and not arbitrary.[23]

The constitutional issues set the ground rules for court encounters, or, rather, the rules evolved as the game was played. To employers, the police power had to be narrowly construed; to reformers, industrial conditions provided ample hazards to justify its use. To employers, freedom of contract was an endangered right; to reformers, it was a legal fiction, an excuse to secure employers' power. Each side sought to amass precedents on which future decisions could rely, and each suspected the other of ulterior motives, for which legal maneuvers were just a pretext. From the 1890s into the 1920s, state and federal courts mediated a series of contests between corporate lawyers and states' attorneys. Although reformers denounced the courts as bastions of laissez-faire, most protective laws survived judicial review. Before 1908, maximum-hours laws were the crux of contention. The decisions in maximum-hours cases suggest the arguments that would emerge in *Muller v. Oregon.*

HOURS LAWS AND THE COURTS

The first challenge to a maximum-hours law in a state court involved the Massachusetts law of 1874 providing a ten-hour day and a sixty-hour week for women and minors in manufacturing. In *Commonwealth v. Hamilton Manufacturing Co.* (1876), the state Supreme Judicial Court upheld the law under the police power, without further explanation. The court denied that the law limited a woman's "right to labor as many hours per day or per week as she may desire," but rather provided that she could not work continuously for more than the maximum hours in a factory.[24]

But two decades later, just as freedom of contract came into play, reformers met a major setback. In *Ritchie v. People* (1895), the Illinois Supreme Court rejected the eight-hour provision affecting women in the law of 1893 because, the court said, it violated the Fourteenth Amendment. First, it was class legislation ("it discriminates against one class of employers and employees and in favor of all others"); second, it interfered with freedom of contract, deprived women of that freedom, and had no direct relation to public health or safety. The state's claim that the law promoted public health, said Justice Magruder, was based not on "the nature of things done, but on the sex of the persons doing them." A restriction based solely on sex, he declared, was arbitrary and unreasonable. Indeed, there was "no reasonable ground . . . for fixing upon eight hours in one day as the limit with which woman can work without injury to her physique." The *Ritchie* court then forged an important link between freedom of contract and women's rights. Justice Magruder cited several Illinois laws: an 1867 law that guaranteed a woman's right to work overtime; an 1872 law that precluded barring a person from an occupation because of sex; and an 1874 law that entitled married women to sue and be sued. Pointing to the expansion of women's right to contract, he contended that "the mere fact of sex will not justify the legislature in putting forth the police power of the state for the purpose of limiting her rights."[25]

The first decision to apply the due process clause to women, the *Ritchie* ruling posited freedom of contract against sex discrimination; it cited "women's rights" in order to deny women in industry what reformers saw as workers' rights. Florence Kelley, who had been instrumental in the passage of the eight-hour law in Illinois, voiced dismay that the Fourteenth Amendment could be used in such a manner. "The measure to guarantee the Negro freedom from oppression has become an insuperable obstacle to the protection of women and children," she declared.[26] Her dismay was well founded. Issued a year after the Pullman strike —

a boycott of Pullman railway cars by the American Railway Union that resulted in violence and was quelled by federal troops — the *Ritchie* decision was an antilabor decision by a conservative court. It also embodied a special irony. Two decades earlier, the same Illinois court had rejected Myra Bradwell's application to join the bar: "God designed the sexes to occupy different spheres of action," the court had declared. When the U.S. Supreme Court upheld Bradwell's rejection in *Bradwell v. Illinois* (1873), Justice Joseph P. Bradley, in a concurring opinion, expressed a similar sentiment. Meanwhile, Myra Bradwell had promoted the state law of 1872, cited by Justice Magruder, that enabled women to enter all occupations. The *Bradwell* decisions, legal theorist Frances E. Olsen contends, were examples of "false paternalism" because they injured Myra Bradwell, just as the *Ritchie* decision exemplified "false equality" because, in 1895, it injured women workers in factories. Depending on the context, Olsen shows, both equal treatment and special treatment held potential for harm.[27]

The *Ritchie* decision could not be appealed,[28] and, since it was not a federal ruling, it did not stop other states from passing more maximum-hours laws for women or state courts from upholding them. By 1895, twelve states had enacted such laws, though most were weak or unenforceable; between 1895 and 1908, nine states, including Oregon in 1903, passed stronger laws. More immediately, three years after *Ritchie*, the Supreme Court expanded the police power, endorsed an exception to freedom of contract, and handed reformers a major victory.

The victory came in *Holden v. Hardy* (1898), when the Court upheld by 7 to 2 an eight-hour law for miners in Utah. In the majority opinion, Justice Henry B. Brown argued that the Utah law was not class legislation. Rather, it involved the legislature's view "that a limitation is necessary for the preservation of the health of employees, and there are reasonable grounds for believing that such determination is supported by the facts." The facts included the history of the mining industry, the dangers of mining, and the enactment of similar protective laws in other states. According to *Holden v. Hardy*, the health of workers was part of "public welfare" and justified protection. Nor did the law violate freedom of contract, because employer and worker "do not stand upon an equality." Unequal bargaining power could justify the use of the police power. The decision legitimized hours laws for miners and employees who worked with dangerous machinery. By 1916, fourteen states limited miners' hours, and scores of regulations curbed workdays in smelters, glassworks, sawmills, railway work, and many other trades in which men were employed.[29]

At the turn of the century, state courts in Pennsylvania, Nebraska, and Washington upheld women's hours laws. Just as the *Ritchie* decision had linked freedom of contract with sexual equality (however disingenuously), the new decisions linked the police power to ways in which women differed from men. Women, like children, said the decisions, constituted a special class that needed protection, as men did not. A lower court in Pennsylvania led the way when it upheld a state law that limited the work of women and minors to twelve hours a day and sixty a week. Citing precedents that upheld hours limits for public employees, railroad workers, and miners, the court in *Commonwealth v. Beatty* (1900) defined the distinctive nature of women workers: their weaker physiques and their roles as potential mothers. "Surely an act which prevents the mothers of our race from being tempted to endanger their life and health by exhaustive employment can be condemned by none save those who expect to profit by it," said the Pennsylvania court. "If such legislation savors of paternalism it is in its least objectionable form." Overlong hours of work ("unreasonable and dangerous employment"), the court concluded, "injuriously affects" the health of women "and hence the interests of the state itself."[30]

Two years later, state supreme courts in Nebraska and Washington sustained ten-hour laws for women workers in manufacturing, stores, hotels, and restaurants. In *State v. Buchanan* (1902), the Washington court, like that in Pennsylvania, cited women's weaker physical condition and their roles as "the mothers of succeeding generations" to invoke the police power. In *Wenham v. State* (1902), the Nebraska Supreme Court, too, justified the police power on the grounds of "physical limitations":

> Certain kinds of work, which may be performed by men without injury to their health, would wreck the constitutions and destroy the health of women, and render them incapable of bearing their share of the family and the home. The state must be accorded the right to guard and protect women as a class, against such a condition; and the law in question, to that extent, conserves the public health and welfare.

The *Wenham* court, however, also stressed women's distinctive circumstances in the workforce. Women had always "to a certain extent been wards of the state," it declared. In recent years, they had been "partly emancipated from their disabilities. But they have no voice in the enactment of the laws by which they are governed, and can take no part in municipal affairs." Moreover, the employer and the male employee were "practically on an equal footing," but not so the employer and the female worker. Few occupations were open to her; her "field of remunerative labor" was restricted; and she faced competition for those jobs available to her. Under such circumstances, the court said, "[t]he employer who seeks to obtain the most hours of labor for the least wages, has such an advantage over them that the wisdom of the law, for their protection, cannot well be questioned." (Eight years earlier, in 1894, the same Nebraska court had rejected a "general" eight-hour law for "mechanics, servants, and laborers.")[31]

The state cases at the turn of the century suggested that the *Ritchie* decision posed no threat to women's hours laws in other states. But suddenly, in 1905, reformers faced a major setback. In *Lochner v. New York* (1905), the U.S. Supreme Court struck down, 5–4, a state ten-hour law for bakery workers, who were men, and thereby set the challenge that Oregon's lawyers would have to meet in 1908.

THE BAKESHOP CASE, 1905

Joseph Lochner, the proprietor of a nonunion bakery in Utica, New York, violated an 1896 law that limited hours of work in bakeries and confectioneries to ten a day and sixty a week. State courts upheld the law three times as a health measure under the police power. Baking, said the state's highest court, was an unhealthy trade and led to respiratory diseases. The Supreme Court majority (including Justice Brown, who had written the liberal *Holden v. Hardy* opinion) disagreed. According to Justice Rufus W. Peckham's majority opinion, New York had not proved its contention that overlong hours endangered either bakers or the public. The law therefore arbitrarily violated freedom of contract:

> Clean and wholesome bread does not depend upon whether the baker works but ten hours per day or only sixty hours a week. . . . The act is not, within any fair meaning of the term, a health law, but is an illegal interference with the right of individuals, both employers and employe[e]s, to make contracts regarding labor upon such terms as they may think best, or which they may agree upon with the other parties to such contracts. Statutes of the nature under review, limiting the hours in which grown and intelligent men may labor to learn their living, are mere meddlesome interferences with the rights of the individuals.

Baking was no more unhealthful than many other occupations, the Court argued, for "almost all occupations more or less affect the health." If baking could be regulated by the state, then "[n]o trade, no occupation, no mode of earning one's living, could escape this all-pervading power." Moreover, according to the *Lochner* majority, the New York law was class legislation that treated bakers, who were "equal in intelligence and capacity to men in other trades," as if they were different. Finally, the law represented an unwelcome and suspicious trend. Legislative interference with "the ordinary trades and occupations . . . seems to be on the increase," the Court observed, and "many of the laws of this character, while passed under what is claimed to be the police power for the purpose of protecting the public health or welfare, are in reality passed from other motives."[32]

In short, the Constitution guaranteed workers the right to labor as long as they chose, and the state could not abridge that right without proving that intervention was necessary for the public welfare. In this case, the state had failed to meet the burden of proof. To the *Lochner* majority, the New York law was not a health and safety law but rather an illegitimate "labor law" (enacted by those with "other motives"). Reformers, who suspected the motives of the majority, applauded the dissenting opinions. Justice John Marshall Harlan contended that "employers and employees in such establishments were not upon an equal footing" and that the Court lacked the power to challenge the legislature. Harlan also cited numerous authorities to show that long hours of labor in bakeries damaged workers' health, thereby providing something of a precedent for the Brandeis brief of 1908. Justice Oliver Wendell Holmes Jr. discerned a conservative bias: "This case is decided upon an economic theory which a large part of the country does not entertain." The Constitution, he wrote, was not intended "to embody a particular economic theory, whether paternalism . . . or *laissez faire*," nor was it the Court's role to impede a state from experimenting with a new "truth."

A close call (one justice seemed to change his mind at the last minute), *Lochner* remains an exceptional case. Unlike most maximum-hours cases, it involved not only men but unions. Bakers' unions in New York, which had organized some firms but not others, promoted the 1896 law to affect nonunion bakeries and thereby secure their own gains. To the *Lochner* majority, the case concerned union power, not public welfare.[33] Still, the *Lochner* case shows how difficult it was to stretch the police power to cover men. In his brief for New York, the state's attorney general, Julius M. Mayer, lamely struggled to link bakers' hours to public welfare: Bakers with skin diseases and tuberculosis might communicate their diseases to the public, he argued, and night work deprived bakers of sunlight, which injured their health. Lochner's lawyer, Henry Weismann, in a far stronger brief, claimed that bakers were no less healthy than other workers. (In the 1890s, Weismann had played a role in the bakers' union and in the campaign for the 1896 law, but he had suddenly switched sides, joined the bar, and bought a bakeshop.) The brief for Lochner also included some statistical tables on the mortality rates of occupations and excerpts from English medical journals on health standards in bakeries: Ironically, the first social science evidence offered in a brief to the Supreme Court served not to defend a protective law but to discredit it.[34]

To reformers, *Lochner* was a disaster, only to be followed by another calamity. In *People v. Williams* (1907), New York's Court of Appeals rejected a night work ban for women and children. A factory inspector had found women at work beyond the permitted hours in a New York City bookbinding shop. Convicted in a lower court, the proprietor triumphed in two appellate courts for much the same reason Lochner had won: The lawyers for the state had not proved *why* women could not work at night. Although they had argued that "women are physically weaker than men" and had referred to women's roles as "mothers of the race," they had not shown the relevance of these attributes to night work. "In order to sustain the reasonableness of the proviso," said the appellate court, "we must find that owing to some physical or nervous differences, it is more harmful for a woman to work at night than for a man to do so. We are not aware of any difference, and . . . none such has been pointed out." The law was therefore not within the police power. Indeed, it injured "female citizens" by "denying them equal rights with men in the same pursuit." New York's highest court, the Court of Appeals, sustained the decision.[35]

The cases on maximum-hours laws from 1895 to 1907 set the stage for *Muller v. Oregon* and provided the lawyers who argued it with guidelines. In the state cases on women's hours laws, decisions that upheld the laws stressed factors that distinguished women from men, such as their disabilities in the workforce or their roles as "mothers of the race." In cases where protective laws sank, lawyers for the states had failed to convince judges that the laws at issue were connected to public health and welfare. It was *Lochner*, above all, that dominated recent precedents. As the *Lochner* decision declared, "[T]here must be some ground, reasonable in and of itself, to say that there is a material danger to the public health or to the health of the employees, if the hours of labor are not curtailed." The case on which all depended, to reformers, involved an Oregon law enacted on February 19, 1903, which required that "[n]o female be employed in any mechanical establishment, or factory, or laundry in this state for more than ten hours a day" and imposed penalties for violations.

2

"The Facts of Common Knowledge"

1908

On September 4, 1905, Labor Day, an overseer at the Grand Laundry in Portland, Oregon, Joe Haselbock, required an employee and labor activist named Emma Gotcher (Mrs. E. Gotcher, in the legal records) to work overtime in violation of the Oregon ten-hour law of 1903. Two weeks later, in the Circuit Court of Multnomah County, the state of Oregon launched criminal charges against the owner of the laundry, Curt Muller. For his defense, Muller hired William D. Fenton, a prominent Portland lawyer whose clients included the American Steel and Wire Company and Standard Oil. Fenton also served as general counsel for the local lines of the Southern Pacific Railroad, in which capacity he had recently feuded with Oregon's labor commissioner over a proposed law to limit railroad workers' hours.[1]

Fenton's argument in the circuit court (the same argument that he would carry to the Supreme Court) relied on the recent *Lochner* decision: He contended that the Oregon law violated Muller's right to contract freely with his workers and was thus an unconstitutional use of the police power. It was also class legislation that did not apply equally to other workers. The circuit court judge tilted toward Muller. As recent expansion of women's rights had "almost annihilated any distinction between the sexes," he wrote, there was little "real distinction" between the laws that regulated the hours of a baker in New York and those of a laundress in Oregon. Still, averse to rejecting the legislature's work, he sustained the law, found Muller guilty of a misdemeanor, and fined him ten dollars. The laundry owner then appealed to the Oregon Supreme Court, where, in 1906, he lost again. Oregon Chief Justice Robert Bean upheld the law on the basis of *Holden v. Hardy,* plus the recent decisions in Nebraska and Washington that sustained similar hours laws for women workers. When Muller decided to take his case to the U.S. Supreme Court, Portland laundry owners financed his appeal.[2]

The second decision against Muller in 1906 drew attention beyond Oregon. Should Muller appeal, reformers feared, the Supreme Court might follow the *Lochner* precedent, upset the Oregon law, and cripple the movement for worker protection. In July 1906, Florence Kelley of the National Consumers' League went to Portland to confer with local reformers who had promoted the 1903 law as well as a recent child labor law. From then on, the NCL and Kelley became major players in Curt Muller's case.

FLORENCE KELLEY, THE NCL, AND THE "RIGHT TO LEISURE"

By 1906, Florence Kelley held a prominent place in progressive reform. Her career had begun to accelerate in 1891, when she became a resident at Hull House, Chicago's pioneer social settlement. Like Jane Addams and others in the settlement's inner circle, Kelley was the daughter of a politician. Her father, William Darrah "Pig Iron" Kelley, a longtime Republican congressman from Philadelphia, had supported radical Republican policies in Reconstruction and the eight-hour day. Like other Hull House residents, too, Kelley was a college graduate (Cornell, 1882). Atypically, she was divorced and a mother. After Cornell, Kelley had studied law and government in Zurich, where she married a Polish-Jewish socialist medical student, had three children, and translated works of the German socialist Friedrich Engels, which she hoped to make available to American workers. "The Americans are so little enlightened that they revile and repudiate everything that bears the name of Socialism," she wrote to Engels in 1886. When Kelley's family returned to New York in the late 1880s, her marriage collapsed and she fled to Chicago with her children.[3]

While at Hull House, Kelley studied law at night at Northwestern University, where in 1894 she earned a degree. She also drafted the Illinois maximum-hours law of 1893, led a campaign of women's groups to enact it, and, as chief factory inspector, headed the staff of twelve that enforced it. When an Illinois employer challenged the law, Kelley and her colleagues wrote the brief to defend it, which posited, among other arguments, the damage caused by overwork to women's reproductive lives. The *Ritchie* decision of 1895, which Kelley denounced thereafter as "sinister" and "antisocial," destroyed much of her achievement. But her appointment in 1899 as the NCL's general secretary in New York gave

Kelley a national platform from which to promote the goals that had failed in Chicago.[4]

At the turn of the century, the NCL carved out a special fief in the world of reform. Consumers' leagues had erupted in the 1890s as if by spontaneous combustion. The first league arose in New York, under the impetus of Josephine Shaw Lowell, activist in social welfare and founder of the Charity Organization Society. Lowell was concerned with the long hours, low wages, and imperiled morals of young women store clerks, who worked overtime in rush seasons without extra pay. To end this abuse, the league compiled a "white list" of department stores that dealt "justly" with their clerks (blacklists were illegal) and sought legislation to limit clerks' hours. Consumers' leagues quickly spread to other cities — Brooklyn, Boston, Philadelphia, Chicago — and local leagues expanded their concerns from store clerks to child labor to women factory workers. In 1898, when the NCL, an umbrella group, began, its goal was to guarantee that goods were produced and sold under proper working conditions. Through the NCL and its affiliates, the consumer (a gender-free term but presumably female) entered pressure-group politics.[5]

Under Kelley's leadership, the NCL blossomed: In 1901 there were thirty local leagues; three years later, in 1904, there were sixty-four leagues in twenty states. Kelley was a dynamo. Assailing child labor, tenement sweatshops, low wages, and long hours, she became, in the words of her colleague Josephine Goldmark, "a guerilla warrior . . . in the wilderness of industrial wrongs." Shifting its focus from "white lists" to labor law, the NCL helped local leagues promote new laws by sending emissaries (often Kelley) to legislative hearings and offering statistical data and expert advice. In a single year, 1903, when the Oregon Consumers' League was formed, Kelley addressed 111 meetings in fifteen states. She also inspired college students such as Frances Perkins (the future secretary of labor in the New Deal), a student at Mount Holyoke College, where the NCL formed a collegiate chapter. To Perkins, Kelley's speech in 1902 "first opened my mind to . . . the work which became my vocation."[6]

Perkins's experience was not unique: The NCL served as a training ground for other women in public affairs, among them Mary W. Dewson (head of the Democratic Party's Women's Division in the 1930s) and Jeanette Rankin (in 1916 the first woman elected to serve in Congress), who worked first as Kelley's colleagues. A most devout trainee, at the outset, was Josephine Goldmark, a Bryn Mawr graduate of 1898 and a tutor in English at Barnard College, who began volunteer work as Kelley's aide. In 1903, she became publications secretary of the NCL and chair of its Committee on the Legal Defense of Labor Laws. Her younger sister Pauline was an officer of the New York Consumers' League; an older sister, Alice, had married lawyer Louis D. Brandeis in 1890.[7]

With Kelley at the helm, the NCL further defined its distinctive role. Unlike the AALL, it cultivated activist, grass-roots chapters in the states, which made it more effective as a pressure group. From its headquarters on Henry Street in the United Charities Building, where two progressive periodicals, *The Survey* and *The Outlook,* were published, it adeptly promoted its causes in these and other journals. Unlike the huge General Federation of Women's Clubs or the giant Women's Christian Temperance Union, the NCL took pains to secure the patronage of men and nominal male leadership. Its president from 1899 to 1915 was John Graham Brooks, a Cambridge writer and reformer who was part of the committee that appointed Kelley. Economics professors at major universities served as honorary officers, which underscored the NCL's quasi-professional, social science aura. The league also nurtured the support of elite families, whose members were named to the boards of the NCL and local leagues. Finally, although the NCL represented a relatively small contingent of activists — a few thousand well-off women at the start plus the collegiate members, token professors, and some legal advisers — Florence Kelley's dynamism and expertise vastly increased its leverage.[8]

Kelley promoted her protectionist goals in *Some Ethical Gains in Legislation* (1905), a book published just as the Supreme Court issued the *Lochner* decision. Assaulting freedom of contract, Kelley posited a countervailing right, the "right to leisure," to which, she asserted, all workers were entitled. Such a right, of course, did not exist on paper — rather, she explained, it was "a human right, in process of recognition as a statutory right." Its most "virile" form was the movement to curb employees' hours. Workers, Kelley contended, deserved to share in the gains arising from improved machinery and productivity. Skilled workers, such as cigarmakers, she noted, had already achieved a shorter day through trade unionism and collective bargaining. Kelley was interested in "the weakest and most defenseless of workers": children, young girls, and "the mass of unskilled working women as unorganized and defenseless as the children themselves."[9]

Such workers could attain the right to leisure only through statute, Kelley contended. But protective laws, she argued, were preferable in any case to labor protest or collective bargaining. Indeed, without such laws, workers would strive "to attain by strikes what they had failed to achieve by statute." Strikes, Kelley claimed, were precarious, "never final," and limited to well-organized trades; they aided only "those most able to make favorable terms for themselves," which excluded women, children, and unskilled or feeble men. Moreover, Kelley asserted, protective laws would aid employers, by reducing the struggle between labor and management. Had the 1893 law in Illinois been upheld, she insisted, strikes could have been averted. Indeed, if the protective laws already enacted had been enforced, "the multitude of men, women, and children affected by them would be so far reaching, that relatively little would be left to the trade agreement," that is, to collective bargaining. This was a slap at the AFL.[10]

The main obstacle to worker protection, Kelley argued, was the conservative judiciary, as exemplified in the *Ritchie* and *Lochner* decisions. She ended her book with some questions: "How can the courts be enlightened and instructed concerning conditions as they exist?" she asked. "How can the gradual, cumulative effect of working conditions, and of living conditions, be made obvious to the mind of the judges composing the courts of last resort?" The answer, it turned out, lay not in new talk of "rights" but in a new tool of argument. In retrospect, Kelley's question seems like Brandeis's cue.[11]

When the Oregon Consumers' League notified NCL headquarters in New York of Curt Muller's appeal in October 1907, the NCL sought a lawyer to argue Oregon's case. According to Goldmark, Louis D. Brandeis was Kelley's choice; she admired him for "his outspoken enmity against concentration of wealth in the hands of the few." But at the Oregon attorney general's request, the NCL board arranged for Kelley to call on Joseph Choate, leader of the New York bar, onetime president of the American Bar Association, and former ambassador to England. Choate had successfully argued against the federal income tax before the Supreme Court in 1895. When Kelley and Goldmark went to see him, he seemed puzzled about their request. " 'A law prohibiting more than ten hours a day in laundry work,' he boomed. 'Big strong laundry women. Why shouldn't they work longer?' " In Goldmark's indignant account, the two women then rejected Choate and the next day asked Brandeis to take the case. Kelley had "tried one so-called eminent lawyer after another," recalled Felix Frankfurter, an NCL lawyer who later served on the Supreme Court, "and despairingly she found that no eminent lawyer would care to argue such a case. There was no money in it. From their point of view it was a dubious social policy."[12]

The meeting with Brandeis on November 14, 1907, Goldmark claimed, "gave a revolutionary new direction to judicial thinking, indeed to the judicial process itself." To Kelley, who had seen the *Ritchie* case negate her work, Brandeis seemed like "a champion to fight her battle in the court."[13]

LOUIS D. BRANDEIS AND THE "LIVING LAW"

"I really long for the excitement of the contest," Brandeis wrote as a young man to his brother; his longing was amply gratified. After graduating from Harvard Law School in 1875, Brandeis worked for a year in St. Louis and then began a practice in Boston with a law school friend. The firm prospered, and by the 1890s he earned over $50,000 a year, more than ten times the income of most lawyers; corporate clients valued his informed counsel and instinct for winning strategies. Imbued with progressive ideals, Brandeis also sought to defend the public interest. In the first decade of the twentieth century, he challenged corrupt streetcar franchises, fought for lower utility costs, battled the insurance companies, and devised a plan for savings bank life insurance.[14]

By the 1890s, Brandeis had joined a dissenting group of lawyers of progressive bent. Inspired by Oliver Wendell Holmes Jr., who would join the Supreme Court in 1902 and who criticized the law's lack of responsiveness to "the felt necessities of the time," the dissenters attacked the philosophy of "formalism" that dominated late-nineteenth-century courts. Formalists saw the law as a system of logic and deductive reasoning. Invoking precedent and extracting general principles from previous cases, lawyers applied the logic of the law to the issue at hand. To formalists, said Felix Frankfurter, a Brandeis protégé, legislation was "a kind of interloper in the harmonious symmetry of the common law." The dissidents took another approach, variously labeled "sociological jurisprudence" or, later, "legal realism." Laws should not be judged as an exercise of logic, they contended, but on the basis of the conditions from which they arose. Society was changing and the law had to keep pace. Unlike formalists, with their emphasis on logic, the dissidents turned to experience; they replaced deduction with induction. Their concern with the concrete, the details, the "facts," and the lives of ordinary people gave them much in common with literary realists of the era, like novelist Theodore Dreiser; with the journalism of muckrakers, like Lincoln Steffens; with new work in photography, like that of Jacob Riis and Lewis Hine; with the pragmatic philosophy of William James and John Dewey; and with the realist school of painting that emerged around the turn of the century.[15]

Two of Brandeis's essays convey his approach to the law. In a 1905 speech to the Harvard Ethical Society, in which he assailed the lawyers' roles as "adjuncts of large corporations," Brandeis proposed an alternative. He saw lawyers as mediators: They should assume a stance of independence between the wealthy and the people, prepared to curb the excesses of either. Brandeis asserted *his* independence by working without fee on behalf of the public and even repaid his own firm for the time he gave to public service.[16]

A decade later, after the phenomenal success of the Brandeis brief, Brandeis linked his vision of the lawyer's role to the practice of sociological jurisprudence. In the essay "The Living Law," he explained that "the law has everywhere a tendency to lag behind the facts of life." Legal institutions had not kept pace with the "rapid development of our political, economic, and social ideals." Brandeis attacked the tendency of courts to overturn the work of state legislatures, which represented the people; the use of the Fourteenth Amendment to block reform; and legal formalism, as in the 1895 *Ritchie* case, in which judges reasoned from "abstract conception." And he mourned the shift from the "all round" lawyer, or general practitioner, to the specialist, the corporate lawyer, who lacked "broad knowledge of present day problems" and whose "vast areas of ignorance" distorted his judgment. The lawyer, said Brandeis, needed a "diversified clientele" that provided him with "an economic and social education." He had to be familiar with economics, sociology, and politics. Judges, similarly, should be trained "to perform adequately the function of harmonizing law with life."[17]

Most important, Brandeis believed in "the facts." No law, he contended, "written or unwritten, can be understood without full knowledge of the facts out of which it arises, and to which it is to be applied." To ascertain the "facts" of a case, Brandeis explored the context in which a problem arose, the remedies provided by existing laws, and the experience of other states or countries with the same or similar problems. Such explorations involved mastery of economic and sociological data. The Oregon case presented an opportunity to follow this method and bring the law into harmony with life. When approached by Kelley and Goldmark, Brandeis stipulated that he would take the case (without fee) only if invited to represent Oregon by the state attorney. That is, he wanted to be a major player, not merely the submitter of an *amicus curiae* ("friend of the court") brief on behalf of the NCL. Oregon officials agreed to his terms. At this juncture, Brandeis decided what sort of case to pursue.[18]

Did he have a choice? According to some recent commentators, Brandeis faced two options. First, he might challenge *Lochner* directly; that is, he might convince the Court that all industrial jobs, even allegedly nonhazardous jobs, endangered workers' health if performed for more than ten hours a day. This was a high-risk option. Since Justice Brown of the *Lochner* majority had left the Court, there was a chance that his replacement would side with Oregon. If the case for Oregon failed, however, the movement for protective laws could be irretrievably damaged. Alternatively, instead of refuting *Lochner,* Brandeis could capitalize on the small window of opportunity that the *Lochner* decision provided; that is, he could convince the Court that the ten-hour law was a reasonable exception to freedom of contract because it affected only women.[19]

Brandeis either chose the second, more promising option or never considered any other. As Ann Corinne Hill points out, reformers had gone for the "whole loaf" in *Lochner* and failed; in *Muller,* they "acted to win back half the loaf." According to Philippa Strum, Brandeis's recent biographer, clearly the Court would not abandon freedom of contract. But without discarding *Lochner,* a lawyer could show that the Oregon law was connected to public health and welfare. Brandeis chose, therefore, to distinguish the case of the women from that of the bakers, to prove that the Oregon law fell within the police power, and to offer data linking long hours, workers' health, and public welfare. Such data would have to concern sexual difference. Unlike the "grown and intelligent men" who were bakers in New York, the data would show, women workers were a special class that needed the protection of the state.[20]

THE BRANDEIS BRIEF

As soon as Brandeis took the NCL assignment, wrote Josephine Goldmark, he demanded "facts" — data on the impact of women's working hours by "anyone with expert knowledge of women's labor, such as factory inspectors, physicians, trade unions, economists, social workers." As head of the NCL committee on labor law, Goldmark recruited ten researchers, including her sister Pauline and Florence Kelley, who served as "readers, translators, copyists, typists." Scouring the resources of Columbia University and the New York Public Library, the research team unearthed the reports of English factory commissions and medical commissions; translated sources from western Europe; and amassed information from states with women's hours laws. In each source, they sought statements about the dangers of long hours and the benefits of shorter ones, or, as Goldmark put it, "We would contrast evil and good."[21]

In two weeks, the researchers had collected the data for the 113-page Brandeis brief, a joint endeavor that bore the imprint of its coauthors, Brandeis and Goldmark — and no doubt that of Florence Kelley, whose *Ritchie* brief of 1895 contained a precursor of the Brandeis argument in *Muller*. Unlike a traditional brief, an argument based on precedent — that is, on citations from relevant court decisions — the Brandeis brief cited the testimony of nonjudicial authorities: doctors, academics, factory inspectors, sanitary inspectors, legislators, bureaucrats, and other investigators. Among this medley of experts, the brief relied most heavily on English sources, such as the reports of British factory inspectors from as far back as the 1830s; parliamentary debates over successive factory laws; and Beatrice Webb's *The Case for the Factory Acts* (1901), a collection of essays by women reformers in defense of English protective laws. A prominent source of American data was the Massachusetts Bureau of Labor Statistics, started in 1869 and directed by Carroll D. Wright, later the first head of the U.S. Bureau of Labor Statistics; the bureau had been collecting data on women workers since the 1870s. Spanning six decades, the Brandeis brief was a historical documentary.

At its start, Brandeis offered two pages of legal argument, the only concise part of the brief. Citing *Lochner*, Brandeis explained that a law restricting freedom of contract must have " 'a real or substantial relation to the protection of the public health and the public safety' "; that " 'when the validity of a statute is questioned, the burden of proof, so to speak, is upon those' who assail it" (that is, on Muller and his lawyers); and, finally, that the Oregon law must be sustained unless the Court found "no 'fair ground, reasonable in and of itself, to say that there is material danger to the public health . . . or to the health . . . of the employees (or to the general welfare), if the hours of labor are not curtailed.' " The data to follow, said Brandeis, constituted "[t]he facts of common knowledge of which the Court may take judicial notice."[22]

The second and far longer part of the brief, "The World's Experience," presented the dangers of long hours and the benefits of shorter hours. A running argument supported by quotations, the brief contended that overwork "is more disastrous to the health of women than of men," not only because of "the speed and hazard of modern industry" but mainly because of women's "special physical organization." Long hours, testified experts from America and Europe, caused many ailments, ranging from indigestion, anemia, insomnia, and headaches to lead poisoning, misshapen joints, and tuberculosis. The overlong day also affected "childbirth and female functions." It led to pelvic disease, menstrual problems, miscarriage, premature births, infant mortality, and enfeebled offspring.

" 'Women's ill health and drudgery in a factory may affect her progeny in a way that the statistician cannot estimate,' " a physician explained in 1895. " 'It is well known that like begets like,' " asserted the Massachusetts Bureau of Labor Statistics in 1871, " 'and if the parents are feeble in constitution, the children must also inevitably be feeble.' " Long hours not only injured women as individuals, the Brandeis brief contended, but through their offspring or potential offspring hurt the entire community. As one of the experts, a member of the French Senate in 1891, asserted: " '[I]t is not only of the women that we think; it is not principally of the women, it is of the whole human race. It is of the father, it is of the child, it is of society.' "[23]

The brief then shifted to the advantages of a shorter workday. When hours were reduced, argued Brandeis and Goldmark, succeeding generations showed "extraordinary improvement in physique and morals" and "the tone of the entire community is raised." Observers reported the benefits that ensued from the curtailed day of ten hours (or longer, as in some instances cited). The head British factory inspector in 1859, for instance, was unable to find " 'a crooked leg or a distorted spine as the result of factory labor' " since hours were reduced. Shorter hours, said the inspector for Upper Bavaria in 1905, gave the young unmarried working woman " 'the opportunity to learn the art of home-making [upon which] the health, welfare, and prosperity of her whole family will depend.' " The brief also tried to anticipate and refute critics' objections. Would maximum-hours laws injure employers? Definitely not. Curbed hours increased efficiency, raised productivity, reduced costs, and improved the quality of goods, as experts from Canada, Germany, Belgium, England, France, Massachusetts, Connecticut, Wisconsin, and New York attested. What about those trades that depended on long workdays in rush seasons? "Foresight and management" would curb the need for irregular hours. Did employers concur? A 1904 study of women in the printing trades reported that some employers " 'admit candidly enough that legislation enables them to be more humane . . . than they could otherwise afford to be.' " Would the shorter workday harm the woman worker — by "contracting the sphere of her work"? One of the essays in the 1901 book that Beatrice Webb edited offered a cogent reply: " 'Where women can be employed, their labor is so much cheaper than that of men that there is no chance of their being displaced.' " Low pay would protect women's jobs! (The essay, in fact, attributed women's low wages to their "industrial incompetence," but this the brief omitted.)[24]

Finally, the Brandeis brief turned to the particular hazards of labor in commercial laundries (a late-nineteenth-century development), which depended on power-driven machinery. Here women worked at mangles, large machines with revolving, heated iron cylinders; at starching tables; and with ironing machines, which resembled mangles. "'The work is not the light and often pleasant occupation of sewing or folding,'" a British authority explained in 1902. "'It is not done sitting down.'" Long hours of upright labor, factory inspectors reported, amidst steam and heat, caused varicose veins, leg ulcers, rheumatism, bronchitis, and "'all forms of internal disease aggravated by standing for long hours.'" Gas jets poisoned those who worked with irons; exhaustion spurred bad habits and ruined morale; and girls were "'worn out while still young.'" To limit hours in such establishments, as in factories, Brandeis and Goldmark argued, was not an "'arbitrary discrimination.'"[25]

At the end of the brief, after one hundred pages of "facts" spanning six decades, Brandeis again slammed the burden of proof back into his opponents' court, with a triple negative: "It cannot be said that the Legislature of Oregon had no reason for believing that the public health, safety, or welfare did not require a legal limitation on women's work in manufacturing . . . to ten hours in one day." In short, the state legislature had acted reasonably in limiting women's hours, Brandeis asserted, and the lawyers for Muller would be unable to prove otherwise (as indeed was the case).[26]

Oregon's lawyers also submitted another, more conventional brief, signed by state officials and Brandeis, no doubt in case the Court rejected the novel Brandeis brief. The backup brief cited legal precedent, called the insistence on freedom of contract "gilded sophistry," and denied that the Oregon law was class legislation. Unlike the Brandeis brief, which avoided mention of woman suffrage, the second brief argued that women were disadvantaged because they lacked the vote. (Oregon would enfranchise women in 1912.) Unlike the Brandeis brief, again, the second brief conceded at the outset that the ten-hour law might "work a hardship" on individuals. But the "welfare of the individual" mattered less, Oregon's lawyers contended, when "placed in the balance against the welfare of the state at large." It was the Brandeis brief, however, that captured the spotlight, and it is toward that brief that contemporary commentators direct their attention.[27]

Recent critics of the Brandeis brief find much to decry in both method and message. Modern readers, they point out, are unlikely to accept the opinions and observations of nineteenth-century commentators as reputable, verifiable "facts." They are not scientific facts, Judith A. Baer contends. There are no controls, she points out; there is no consideration of independent variables. (Among the general population, for instance, the same proportion of women might have suffered the ailments that beset women in factories; or poverty, not factory work, might have caused such ailments.) Much of the evidence presented in the brief applies, or could apply, to overworked men as well as to overworked women, critics assert. The expertise of the authorities cited is often questionable, as is the relevance of their remarks. Strikingly, the views of women workers rarely appear (we hear only from several bookbinders and printers of the 1870s, but not from laundry workers of 1908). Overall, to modern readers, much of the hastily compiled brief seems a "hodgepodge," a miscellany of quotations severed from their original contexts. The main objection of recent critics to the Brandeis brief, of course, is its very argument — its stress on sexual difference and sex-linked deficiency. The brief treats all women as mothers or potential mothers; it either conflates the needs of families and society with those of women or prefers the former to the latter; and it depicts women as weak and defective. As Nancy Erickson contends, the brief stresses not the hazards of work but the vulnerabilities of the workers.[28]

If the brief is so open to attack today, what was its appeal in 1908? First, to turn-of-the-century Americans, including, we must assume, the justices, the opinions of experts *were* "facts." Social science was young, and the Progressive era valued expertise. Moreover, whatever their defects to modern critics, the "facts" in the brief suggested that Oregon legislators had reason to act as they did when they approved the 1903 law — which was *all* that Brandeis needed to prove. Second, the affinity then prevalent for evolutionary concepts legitimized a concern with women's reproductive roles that, though suspect to readers now, carried weight at the time. The "future mothers" argument of the Brandeis brief, in short, had an aura of "scientific" clout. But it was probably a traditional aspect of the brief that made it convincing. In particular, to Brandeis's contemporaries, female difference *was* "common knowledge." That women were weaker than men needed no scientific proof. As Brandeis later told his law clerk Dean Acheson, the brief should have been entitled "What Every Fool Knows." In short, as David J. Bryden points out in a recent article, the Brandeis brief told the justices what they already knew.[29]

Perhaps most important, finally, the Brandeis brief — like the triple negative at its conclusion — was unanswerable. There was no way that Muller's lawyers could have responded with contradictory "facts" (to show, for instance, that long hours of work did not harm women, or that women and men had the same amount of physical strength, or that overlong hours had no impact on the incidence of infertility or infant mortality). Bryden asks: Could Muller's lawyers have disparaged the "facts" of the Brandeis brief? In a 1915 case that involved a similar brief by Brandeis and Goldmark, opposing counsel tried this very tactic; they decried the historical method of the brief ("The 'Facts' are not up to date," they claimed; the brief "concerns itself mainly with old conditions"). But their assault failed. Such an attack in 1908 would have been difficult, if not hopeless, Bryden contends, because there was no way to undo the mind-set that made the Brandeis brief plausible. "To refute Brandeis's facts would have been a great challenge," Bryden argues, "to refute the ethos that made the facts intuitively persuasive would have been impossible."[30]

Muller's lawyers chose another course. In a thirty-two-page conventional brief, citing precedent, lawyer William Fenton and his associate presented an equal rights argument.

THE BRIEF FOR MULLER

The brief for Muller argued that women, like men, were entitled to "the equal protection of the laws" under the Fourteenth Amendment. Muller's lawyers contended that the Oregon law was class legislation; that it was not a valid exercise of the police power; that it violated freedom of contract, which was "both a liberty and a property right"; and that the legislature could not deprive women of liberty and property "under the pretense of exercising the police power." They also argued that the kind of work the law restricted was not dangerous to health or morals; that there was no reasonable connection between hours limits and public health, safety, or welfare; and that the reasoning behind the law "would lead to ultimate state socialism."[31]

But the main thrust of the brief for Muller was its equal rights argument — an updated version of the argument's antecedent in the 1895 *Ritchie* decision. All women, argued Muller's lawyers, were "persons and citizens" and "as competent to contract with reference to their labor as are men." They then chipped away at the premise of female difference with an avalanche of propositions, counterexamples, and rhetorical questions. "What conditions of employment exist in a laundry that . . . do not apply alike to a healthy man?" asked the brief. "It is difficult to imagine any employment that may be dangerous to women employees that would not be equally dangerous to men." Why should a woman working in a laundry be treated differently under the law from a man working in a bakery? "The health of men is no less entitled to protection than that of women," said Muller's lawyers. Had the law applied only to "all persons of white color," they pointed out, no one would find the classification reasonable. Moreover, why were women's hours limited only in factory work and not in other occupations, such as nursing and stenography? What if the worker were a widow who "had the care of a family of dependent children"? Was she not entitled to contract for longer hours? What about the single woman worker? Was it not dubious policy to limit her rights because "in the distant and remote future the possible children which she may bear will need the protection of this statute"? What "magic" was there in the limitation of precisely ten hours? Why not six hours? The brief concluded with an equal rights peroration and a warning about legislative interference:

> The question involved is far-reaching. If such legislation may be sustained and justified merely because the employe[e] is a woman, and if such employment in a healthy vocation may be limited and restricted in her case, there is no limit beyond which the legislative power may not go. Women, in increasing numbers, are compelled to earn their living. They enter the various lines of employment hampered and handicapped by centuries of tutelage and the limitation and restriction of freedom of contract. Social customs narrow the field of her endeavor. Shall her hands be further tied by statute ostensibly framed in her interests, but intended perhaps to limit and restrict her employment, and whether intended so or not, enlarging the field and opportunity of her competitor among men? The extortions and demands of employers, if any such exist, should not be made the cover under which to destroy the freedom of individual contract and the right of individual action. It is respectfully submitted that the judgment of the Supreme Court of Oregon should be reversed.[32]

Since the feminist upsurge of the late 1960s, the brief for Muller has gained admirers; it seems to anticipate contemporary equal rights arguments, the rudiments of which had also been used to thwart the eight-hour law in Illinois in 1895. Was William Fenton's stance in favor of equal rights for women a cynical ploy, another demand for "false equality"? Or did corporate lawyer Fenton have some prescient insight into the logic of sexual equality? Both of the above, in fact, are reasonable propositions. Clearly, the equal rights argument in the Muller brief was a legal maneuver: William Fenton, counsel to businessmen, used the premise of sexual equality as a tool to preserve employers' power (just as Brandeis used the "facts" about sexual difference to curtail it). At the same time, arguments for freedom of contract and sexual equality were natural allies; they were branches of the same tree, individualism. The thrust of the nineteenth-century movement for women's legal rights involved expanding women's freedom as individuals, specifically their freedom of contract, as in the campaign for married women's property rights (or, as in Myra Bradwell's case, the right to practice law). To women who strove for rights as individuals, as to employers, the Fourteenth Amendment was crucial. The specter of protective laws now forced employers and their lawyers to develop an affinity for sexually egalitarian ideals, even before those ideals won a vocal following among women. The budding romance between the business class and women's rights — and between conservative lawyers and egalitarian feminists — would soon play a larger role in the controversy over protective laws.

When Brandeis and Fenton presented their cases to the Supreme Court in January 1908, each had cause to expect success. In 1905, when rejecting New York's bakeshop law, the Court had been almost equally divided, and Justice Brown of the *Lochner* majority had retired. His replacement, William Moody, at fifty-four the youngest member of the Court, had been Theodore Roosevelt's attorney general and a trust-buster. Did this augur well for Oregon? Could Brandeis count on retaining the *Lochner* dissenters? What about the age of the justices? Most had been born in the 1830s and 1840s. The next year, then President William Howard Taft, who would join the Court in 1921, described the justices in unflattering terms ("pitiable," "almost senile," "does no work," "so deaf that he cannot hear"). Justices Brewer and Harlan, said Taft, "sleep through all the arguments." Was this aged body ready to move with the times and, if so, in which direction? Would the justices accept Brandeis's unprecedented attempt to harmonize law with life? Would they prefer Fenton's advanced contentions about sexual equality? Most important, would they recognize the Oregon law as the "entering wedge" that it was (an argument that William Fenton had in fact failed to make)?[33]

JUSTICE BREWER'S OPINION

On February 24, 1908, a unanimous Supreme Court upheld the Oregon law. Associate Justice David J. Brewer, a staunch conservative, spoke for the Court. Brewer had long defended the "sacred right" of private property, denounced state interference in the economy, and especially opposed labor protest. In *In re Debs* (1895), he had written the Court's unanimous opinion upholding an injunction against the leaders of the 1894 Pullman strike in Chicago. Subsequently, he had dissented in *Holden v. Hardy* and supported the *Lochner* majority. His opinion in *Muller,* however, more than gratified reformers.

First, Brewer praised Brandeis's unusual brief and even mentioned the lawyer by name, a rare event in judicial opinions. The Court, said Brewer, noticed the course of legislation as well as expressions of opinion from nonjudicial sources. In his brief, Louis D. Brandeis had provided "a very copious collection of all these matters, an epitome of which is found in the margin." (The marginal note listed all the laws that Brandeis had cited and credited him with presenting excerpts from over ninety reports.) Justice Brewer rejected the view that "a consensus of present public opinion" could decide constitutional questions. He conceded, however, that "a widespread and long continued belief" about a question of fact was "worthy of consideration." In a graceful phrase, Brewer accepted the new type of argument that Brandeis had presented: "We take judicial cognizance of all matters of general knowledge."[34]

Moving on to the constitutional issue, Justice Brewer accepted the broadest argument in the Brandeis brief: Women's overwork injured the general welfare. Oregon's lawyer had shown "[t]hat woman's physical structure and the performance of maternal functions place her at a disadvantage in the struggle for subsistence," especially "when the burdens of motherhood are upon her." Even when they were not, day after day of prolonged work on their feet had "injurious effects" on women's bodies, "and as healthy mothers are essential to vigorous offspring, the physical well-being of woman becomes an object of public interest and care in order to preserve the strength . . . of the race." This section of the opinion suggests that Brandeis had convinced the Court of a valid link between "means" (the law) and "ends" (health and welfare), as New York had failed to do in *Lochner*.

Brewer then seized the moment to present his own (or the Court's) views on women's nature and to explain why women constituted a special class. Woman had always been dependent on man, he wrote. Even if legislation expanded her personal and contractual rights, "there is that in her disposition and habits of life which will operate against a full assertion of those rights. She will still be where some legislation to protect her seems necessary to secure a real equality of right." Woman was thus "properly placed in a class by herself, and legislation designed for her protection may be sustained, even when like legislation is not necessary for men and could not be sustained." Indeed, such legislation was "designed to compensate [woman] for some of the burdens which rest upon her" and was necessary to "protect her from the greed as well as the passion of man." Most important, legislation that protected woman by limiting her contractual powers was "not imposed solely for her benefit, but also largely for the benefit of all." Citing the remarks of one of the experts in the Brandeis brief, Brewer reiterated (in a footnote) that women's physiology, maternal function, and homemaking role were "'so far-reaching that the need for such reduction [in hours] need hardly be discussed.'"

The Brewer opinion contained several significant points, each laden with implications. First, the Court's concession that it was open to persuasion by "opinions" from nonjudicial sources opened the door to sociological jurisprudence, to the type of argument — the "facts" — with which the Brandeis brief abounded. The Court's concession, in reformers' eyes, portended changes in the lawyer's role. As Brandeis would assert in 1916, the lawyer had to inform judges of "social facts." The Court's new tolerance of such facts suggested that protective laws had brighter prospects. By achieving a hearing for the "facts," Brandeis had carved out a potential path for upholding such laws; he had found a way to elude freedom of contract.[35]

Second, despite the concession on "social facts," in no way did the Court refute the *Lochner* decision, abandon its zeal for freedom of contract, or discard its aversion to class legislation. On the contrary, the *Muller* decision reinforced the *Lochner* decision by reiterating that "like legislation is not necessary for men and could not be sustained." Brandeis had provided the basis for an *exception* to freedom of contract, but he had not at all changed the terms of the debate. The *Muller* decision, therefore, did not signify a major change in judicial policy. The Court retained its distaste for "general" protective laws that affected men, to say nothing of its hostility to labor unions. In 1908, the very year of the *Muller* decision, it declared the boycott an illegal combination in restraint of trade in *Loewe v. Lawler,* also known as the Danbury Hatters' case, and, in *Adair v. United States,* used the due process clause of the Fifth Amendment to upset a federal ban on yellow dog contracts (promises by workers not to join a union) on railroads.[36]

Third, like the Brandeis brief, the Brewer opinion treated all women as mothers or potential mothers; it justified protection because women were physically weaker and "bearers of the race" and it reiterated that legislation to protect women workers was enacted not solely for their benefit but for the benefit of society. Like the Brandeis brief, the opinion conflated the welfare of women and that of society, but even more than the brief (which devoted much space to women workers as individuals) the opinion stressed public welfare over women's welfare. Felix Frankfurter praised this tilt in emphasis. The Brandeis brief, he contended in 1916, had not only forced the Court to consider "a realistic study of the industrial condition" but had shifted the Court's focus from the impact of laws on individuals to "community interests . . . the human values of the whole community."[37]

Finally, the Brewer opinion moved beyond the arguments of the Brandeis brief to sanctify a principle of immutable sexual difference. In relatively few words, Justice Brewer condensed a host of ideas, none of them advanced in the Brandeis brief, about women's inherent and permanent state of dependence: (1) Women, said Brewer, were by nature dependent persons, and even legal rights (including the right to vote) would not change their nature. (2) Innate psychological differences ("disposition and habits of life") barred women from asserting whatever legal rights they attained. (3) Compensatory laws were needed to enable women to function as equals ("to secure a real equality of right"). (4) Protective laws, while acceptable or even "necessary" for women, were unacceptable for men. Here, leaving the "facts" of the Brandeis brief behind, Brewer presented a timeless portrait of the "dependent woman."

The idea of female exceptionalism conveyed in the Brewer opinion was so widely held at the turn of the century, among both women and men, that few disputed it. To contemporaries, the Brewer opinion seemed altruistic, humane, and democratic: It extended the disabilities widely discussed in nineteenth-century middle-class women's culture to the working class; far from catering to fears of "race suicide," as conventionally understood (meager population growth among the middle and upper classes), it included working-class women in the future of "the race." And it lifted respect for motherhood to a judicial plateau. Appreciation of the Court's altruism contributed to the almost unanimous praise for the *Muller* decision in 1908. Headlines in the press announced: "Decision Favors Women" and "Supreme Court Holds Women Above Men." Editorials applauded Justice Brewer's efforts "that the race may be preserved, that the health, vigor, and soundness of posterity be assured." Suffragists, too, praised the decision on the grounds that it would not hamper women's fight for the vote, which, the *Woman's Journal* noted, Justice Brewer supported. Editor Alice Stone Blackwell, for instance, who complimented Louis D. Brandeis and Florence Kelley, found nothing in the decision "incompatible with political rights for women." A scattering of criticism barely dented *Muller's* reputation.[38]

Still, any ripple of opposition to *Muller* that arose in the women's movement is salient. In March 1908, the *Woman's Journal* published a letter from a group of New York women who decried Justice Brewer's decision as "unjust and humiliating to women; as tending to sex slavery; as opposed to economic freedom, and as inimical to the best interests of present and future generations." This startling critique generated no further discussion in print, though editor Blackwell had earlier mentioned "some differences of opinion among suffragists." A full-scale debate among women over single-sex protective laws, already in progress in England, would not emerge for more than a decade. Meanwhile, the triumphant NCL widely circulated the Brewer opinion along with the Brandeis brief. Were Florence Kelley and her colleagues deterred by Justice Brewer's firm dismissal of protection for men? Not at all, as we shall see. Did they appreciate Brewer's concern for "a real equality of right" and for laws that would "compensate" women for at least some of their "burdens"? Undoubtedly they did. It is also possible, however, that the specifics of the Brewer opinion mattered less to NCL leaders than winning the case.[39]

Only in the past generation, in the light of a revolution in "common knowledge" (about sexual equality), has an extensive and forceful attack on the *Muller* decision erupted. Recent analysts of the *Muller* case (that is, since the 1970s) assail both Brandeis's arguments *and* Brewer's opinion. To what extent was Brandeis responsible for the "dependent woman" in the Brewer opinion? Did the Brandeis "facts" provide a springboard to a new legal fiction? Critics suggest that Brandeis overshot the mark by making a stronger case for female exceptionalism than was necessary to win the case for Oregon. Judith A. Baer contends that Brandeis should have made more modest arguments about women's distinctive circumstances as industrial workers rather than provide ammunition for a decision based on immutable difference. Deborah L. Rhode argues that reformers should have challenged *Lochner* directly. Nancy S. Erickson suggests that the arguments Brewer selected from the Brandeis brief (that women needed protection and that they were "bearers of the race") appeared in the state's brief as well: The "facts" were thus irrelevant and the Brandeis brief unnecessary![40]

The brunt of the recent criticism, however, falls on Brewer. Critics point out that Brandeis had presented a range of arguments (as indeed was his job) and that Brewer chose only the most extreme, those that emphasized immutable difference. Baer contends that Brewer indulged in "judicial overkill"; by stressing physical and "quasi-permanent" differences between the sexes, rather than situation-based differences, he provided the basis for restrictive as well as protective laws. (Other analysts, such as Alice Kessler-Harris, reject the distinction between the two types of laws as illusory; *all* protective laws were potentially restrictive.) Lise Vogel points out that Brewer's opinion was not too different from Justice Bradley's concurring opinion in *Bradwell v. Illinois* (1873), which found distinctions between the sexes to be divinely ordained;

Brewer left divinity out, but the eternal differences, now physical and psychological, remained. To Frances E. Olsen, the "altruism" of the Brewer decision was linked to hierarchy. Although the case might have "seemed to exalt women," she points out, "it effectively degraded them by treating the asserted differences as evidence of women's inferiority." To many critics, women were not unqualified beneficiaries of the decision: Men, children, and families were the beneficiaries. Susan Lehrer brings employers into the equation. The *Muller* decision, she suggests, represented a mediation between the needs of families and those of employers for women's services, a compromise between women's productive and reproductive capacities.[41]

The concept of mediation is a useful one, for Justice Brewer's opinion not only catered to contemporary views about female difference but offered something to *both* reformers and employers. Progressives saw the decision as a major victory, in which they recouped at least some of the losses of *Lochner,* and as a precedent for further protective measures. Opponents of protection, however, had little to regret, for Brewer had conceded very little. The decision explicitly excluded male workers — over 80 percent of the industrial labor force — and therefore seemed unlikely to inflict severe injury on employers. By linking protection to female frailty, it may have even alleviated some employers' fears. Those who depended on women workers might in fact appreciate ten-hour laws; comply with them without problem; evade them; or, in some instances, find alternative sources of labor. (Curt Muller, for example, switched first to Chinese employees and then hired the deaf and mute.) In any case, laws that protected women and children, as a business journal conceded a few years later, did not "seriously infringe upon industrial liberty."[42]

Both foes and friends of protection, in short, had something to appreciate. Still, for modern readers, questions of interpretation remain. Did Brandeis outmaneuver the justices by appealing to their conservative views on gender roles? Or, in their effort to compensate for women's disadvantages, had reformers in fact ensured yet further disadvantage?

3

From *Muller* to *Adkins*
1908–1923

After the *Muller* case, the NCL's status in reform circles skyrocketed. The league now had a paramount purpose: to promote and defend protective laws. The acclaimed Brandeis brief served as a publicity device; lawyers, colleges, reform organizations, and state commissions asked for copies of it, and the NCL published and distributed it. With funds from the Russell Sage Foundation, Josephine Goldmark pursued new research on worker fatigue, and, as the states passed new protective laws, she and Brandeis collaborated to defend them. The era after *Muller* became a golden age of Brandeis briefs, which mushroomed in size as the data mounted. The goals of the briefs expanded, too, to include maximum hours for men in industry and the minimum wage for women. Only in 1923 did the reformers' campaign run into a major snag.[1]

NEW BRANDEIS BRIEFS

Muller v. Oregon had widespread repercussions. Between 1908 and 1917, nineteen states and the District of Columbia enacted women's hours laws, and the twenty states that already had such laws enhanced them, by lowering the hour limit or extending the laws to affect women in nonfactory jobs, such as in stores (for instance, New York) or in hospitals (for instance, California). Although challenged by employers and in one case by an employee, the new laws all survived. In the state courts as in the Supreme Court, Brandeis briefs worked like sledgehammers. In 1909, Illinois enacted a second women's hours law, this time for a ten-hour limit, a less stringent version of the eight-hour limit of 1893. When a paper box manufacturer challenged the law, Brandeis and Goldmark produced a six-hundred-page brief, which included new data that Goldmark had collected. The Illinois Supreme Court upheld the ten-hour law, thus reversing the 1895 *Ritchie* decision, which Florence Kelley had steadily denounced. For Kelley, *Ritchie v. Wayman* (1910) was a personal triumph.[2]

The second *Ritchie* case also launched a slew of victories. In 1910, challenges to women's hours laws arose in Virginia, Michigan, and Louisiana; state courts upheld all the laws. In 1912, women's hours cases arose in Ohio, California, Washington, and again in Illinois, which had broadened its law to cover women store clerks. Brandeis, with Goldmark, helped to prepare the Ohio brief and argued the case before the state Supreme Court. The California eight-hour law of 1911 covered not only women in factories but student nurses in hospitals, other hospital employees, and pharmacists, one of whom challenged it. Brandeis joined California's attorney general to defend the law. In California and Ohio, as elsewhere, protection triumphed.[3]

So did a New York law banning night work, which fast became the most disputed part of the reformers' agenda. The New York law, which barred women from work in factories, including print shops, from 10 P.M. to 7 A.M., was challenged by a print shop, the Schweinler Press, that had violated it. Although New York's attorney general prepared a brief, Brandeis and Goldmark added four hundred pages to it. The brief stressed such factors as the hazards of travel at night, the problem of sleep in daytime, the ill effects of lack of sunlight (an argument made to no avail in New York's *Lochner* brief), and night work's impact on home life, such as "neglect of household duties during the day." In an energetic response, Schweinler's lawyers attacked the historical thrust of the Brandeis briefs ("the 'Facts' are not up to date") and argued that women workers opposed night work laws. New York's brief contended (quoting the state's Factory Investigating Committee in 1913), however, that "'ignorant women can scarcely be expected to realize the dangers not only to their own health but to that of the next generation.'"[4]

The New York Court of Appeals upheld the night work ban in *People v. Schweinler Press* (1915), which reversed the *Williams* decision of 1907. "Impairments caused by exhaustion or even weariness must be repaired by normal and refreshing sleep," said the court. Moreover, the night work ban protected the workers' future children, "who will almost inevitably display in their deficiencies the unfortunate inheritance conferred upon them by physically broken-down mothers." The U.S. Supreme Court refused to hear an appeal. Night work bans represented a small but crucial tilt in protective policy. The demand for such laws was in fact pragmatic: Night work laws were needed, Josephine Goldmark had explained in 1912, to *enforce* maximum hours laws for women workers. But the burden of compliance shifted to employees. Night work bans afflicted two types of working women in particular: those whose vocations required work at night (women printers in New York, for instance, claimed that night work laws threatened their livelihood) and working mothers, who, according to contemporary surveys, constituted the bulk of night workers.[5]

Even as protective measures assumed an overtly restrictive cast, reformers pursued their broader strategy to attain "general" laws. In *Muller's* wake, Florence Kelley exuded confidence. "Henceforth," she declared in the *Woman's Journal* in 1908, "both men and women need only show a clear relation between their working hours and their good or bad health in order to get hours legislation sustained by the Supreme Court." But what about men in trades that the courts had thus far viewed as nonhazardous? The challenge after 1908 was to show that overwork in industry endangered men in general as well as women. While preparing the original Brandeis brief, Goldmark had collected data on men that Brandeis had excluded, and she had continued her research. In 1912, the Russell Sage Foundation issued the result of her work. A huge book, *Fatigue and Efficiency* contained two conflicting halves. The second half was a composite brief in defense of maximum-hours laws for women workers plus the *Muller* decision. In the first half, Goldmark presented "a new basis for labor legislation."[6]

FATIGUE AND EFFICIENCY

The new basis was science. Revealing the hazards of overwork, *Fatigue and Efficiency* made a scientific plea for a shortened workday for *all* workers. Goldmark used case studies in physiology to show the impact of overwork on the human body, male or female. Full of charts, numbers, and references to "methods of the laboratory," *Fatigue and Efficiency* explained how chemical impurities collected in the blood and how overwork could cause disability or death. Fatigue, in short, was toxic — "a fatigued person is a poisoned person" — and a killer. Rest, in contrast, detoxified. Professor Frederic Lee, a physiologist at Columbia University, whose research on toxicity had been cited in the original Brandeis brief, wrote a preface to the book. His work and kindred studies proved, said Goldmark, that "the need for the short workday rests upon a scientific basis."[7]

In the tradition of the Brandeis brief, Goldmark rebutted potential critics. What about the cost to employers, for instance? English factory inspectors reported that manufacturers profited in the long run from hours laws, Goldmark argued; the shorter workday promoted efficiency, generated vigor, and raised output. Could workers handle more free time? Goldmark was sanguine. Although "cynics prophesied mere drunken idleness and rowdyism, fairer observers found a kind of regeneration." English mill operatives, once sunk in "physical and moral degradation," now engaged in gardening, sewing, evening schools, outdoor summer evenings, and " 'endearing trivialities of home life.' " What about those who claimed that men and women deserved equal rights in the job market? Goldmark found this "specious" argument an obstacle to labor laws:

> Superficially viewed, the great movement to obtain for women, in all fields, rights from which they have been debarred, might appear inconsistent with the efforts to protect one sex as contrasted with the other, but this is a fundamental misconception. It ignores the fact that the protection of health has never been held a bar to the efficacy of men as citizens. . . . Why, then, should similar restrictions — wider and more inclusive for women — operate against their dignity or value as citizens? Their physical endowments and special functions make the protection of their health even more necessary than the protection of men's health.

To Goldmark, science justified hours laws for *all* workers, but women remained a more vulnerable class. She concluded: "Shortening the workday is something that legislation can effect for women and children today, for men doubtless in the future."[8]

For Harvard Law School professor Felix Frankfurter, four years later, the future had arrived. "Science has demonstrated that there is no sharp difference in kind as to the effect of labor on men and women," he wrote in 1916. There was only a difference in "degree"; both sexes needed protection, albeit for different reasons:

> [O]nce we cease to look upon the regulation of women in industry as exceptional, as the law's graciousness to a disabled class, and shift the emphasis from the fact that they are *women* to the fact that it is *industry,* and the relation of industry to the community which is regulated, the whole problem is seen from a totally different aspect.

Convinced that "the groundwork of the Lochner case has by this time been cut from under," Frankfurter prepared to defend a 1913 Oregon law that limited the hours of all industrial workers. Upheld by the Oregon Supreme Court in 1914, it was on its way to the U.S. Supreme Court.[9]

BUNTING V. OREGON (1917)

The Oregon law of 1913 provided a maximum ten-hour day for all industrial workers but allowed employees to work overtime for another three hours if their employers paid them time and a half. Franklin Bunting, owner of a flour mill, was convicted of violating the law; his mill had employed a man over thirteen hours without overtime pay. Bunting's lawyers charged that the law was not a ten-hour law but a "thirteen-hour law designed solely for the purpose of compelling the employer . . . to pay more for labor than the actual market value thereof." On behalf of Oregon, Brandeis and Goldmark produced a 1,021-page brief on the ill effects of overwork. When Brandeis joined the U.S. Supreme Court in 1916, Frankfurter assumed the role of NCL counsel, added a preface to the brief, and argued the case. "With women, you could talk about maternity, motherhood, the next generation, and so on," Frankfurter recalled in his memoir. "Well, you couldn't talk about maternity in the case of men workers."[10]

What could you talk about? A counterpart to the *Muller* brief, the *Bunting* brief presented the case for a shorter workday for men. First it cited the many laws that already limited men's hours in mines, sawmills, blast furnaces, railroads, telegraph offices, and other workplaces. Then, using Goldmark's data from *Fatigue and Efficiency,* the brief presented "facts and statistics" to show the impact of overwork on worker health and thus on American "vitality, efficiency, and prosperity." Health was "the foundation of the state," declared the brief. "No nation can progress if its workers are crippled by overexertion." Overwork, however, "undermines vitality and lays the foundation for many diseases." Prolonged hours of factory labor injured eyes, ears, and nerves; induced premature old age and degenerative ailments; caused industrial accidents, especially in the "penultimate hours of work"; and led to moral degeneration ("After excessive labor, the overtaxed worker is left stupefied or responds most readily to coarse pleasures and excitement") and desire for drink. The shorter day, in contrast, curbed intemperance, helped Americanize the foreign-born, developed morals and intelligence, and fostered an educated electorate. "If democracy is to flourish," declared the brief, "the education of the citizen . . . must be a continuous process to enable men to understand great issues as they arise, to discuss them and reach decisions upon them." According to the *Muller* brief, the overwork of women injured the unborn; according to the *Bunting* brief, the overwork of men sabotaged the democratic process.[11]

In his preface to the brief, Frankfurter stressed the new evidence about the toxicity of industrial work. "In the last decade science has given us the basis for judgment by experience to which, when furnished, judgment by speculation must yield," he contended. The type of danger revealed in *Holden v. Hardy,* "the poisoning of the human system by long hours," was neither exceptional nor peculiar to mining, but was "now disclosed to be of far wider and deeper applicability," Frankfurter argued. "[T]he considerations that were patent to miners in 1898 are today, to a greater or lesser degree, throughout the industrial system." It was *industry* that was dangerous![12]

In oral argument, Frankfurter pressed Oregon's contention that the state law of 1913 was an hours law, not a wage law. Justice James C. McReynolds, he recalled, kept interrupting him ("Ten hours! Ten hours! Ten! Why not four?"). The majority opinion in *Bunting v. Oregon* (1917), written by Justice Joseph McKenna, devoted much attention to this subsidiary question: Was the state law a wage regulation in disguise? No, said the Court. But the *Bunting* decision neither accepted nor rejected Frankfurter's argument about the hazards of industry. Instead, it quoted the conclusion of the Oregon Supreme Court that the law was not arbitrary because "the custom in our industries does not sanction a longer service than ten hours per day." The Oregon law was reasonable, in short, because the ten-hour day *already existed in Oregon.*[13]

By affirming the Oregon law, the *Bunting* Court had tacitly (or *sub silento*) overruled the *Lochner* decision, or so it seemed. The decision thus fulfilled the reformers' long-sought goal: It extended protection to men in all kinds of industrial jobs. According to the progressive plan, *Bunting* should have inspired other states to limit the working hours of men. But none did. For a landmark decision, *Bunting* was a nonstarter. What went wrong? Economist Elizabeth Brandeis, the younger of Louis D. Brandeis's two daughters, later offered some cogent answers. First, the Oregon law was a very weak general-hours law; second, the opinion "scarcely provided a firm precedent for stronger laws." Third, and perhaps most important, "the general public was never particularly interested in hours legislation for adult men." Organized labor clearly preferred "direct trade union action," and the unions, said Brandeis, had a point. Laws that limited men's hours were difficult to enforce ("Inspection has rarely proved an entirely effective instrument"). Finally, workingmen "lured by overtime pay are altogether apt to connive with employers in violating hours laws." With *Bunting,* the "entering wedge" strategy produced a precedent without impact.[14]

Yet another factor contributed to *Bunting's* apparent impotence. By 1917, reformers themselves had veered into another crusade: the battle for the minimum wage.

"A LIVING WAGE"

The concept of the minimum wage reflected models elsewhere: New Zealand (1894), Australia (1896), and, most recently, England (1906) had enacted minimum-wage laws that affected both men and women in industry. In the United States, reformers targeted only women. The NCL initiated studies of women's wages in 1907; in 1908–09, on a European trip, Florence Kelley discussed the issue with Beatrice Webb; in 1910, she included the minimum wage as part of the NCL's long-term plans; in 1911, the NWTUL came on board; and in 1912, in response to the reformers' efforts, Massachusetts enacted a minimum-wage law for women workers. The law lacked enforcement provisions, but in 1913, eight more states passed minimum-wage laws. A few laws set minimum wages; most established commissions that were empowered to do so. An Oregon law of 1913, for instance, drafted by the NCL and AALL and promoted by the Oregon Consumers' League, established an industrial welfare commission, defined its powers, and provided for the setting of a minimum wage, maximum hours, and standard conditions of labor, as well as penalties for violation.[15]

Following the NCL lead, Oregon reformers justified the minimum wage as a measure to protect women workers "from the economic distress that leads to impaired health and efficiency" and especially from employer exploitation. "In any justly and reasonably organized society each industry should support the people who are employed in it," declared Rev. Edwin V. O'Hara, a crusader in the Oregon Consumers' League and soon head of the state's Minimum Wage Board. "An industry which fails to do so is a parasite upon its employees and their homes." Caroline J. Gleason, a recent graduate of the University of Minnesota, who reported on women's wages for the Oregon Consumers' League, found that "in Portland $10 a week is the least on which the average girl can support herself decently" and that "the average girl in every occupation, except office work, receives wages which are inadequate to her support." The Industrial Welfare Commission prescribed a nine-hour day, a fifty-six-hour week, a lunch break, and minimum wage of $8.64 a week for women workers in Portland factories and laundries. (Minimum wages set by state commissions typically failed to cover the basic living costs determined by surveys.)[16]

To the NCL, the minimum wage for women workers was a needed companion to maximum-hours laws (without such a wage, some women workers with curtailed hours suffered loss of income). The women-only law, moreover, was another "entering wedge"; like hours laws, reformers hoped, wage laws for women would set a precedent that could be extended to men. In a 1912 article, Florence Kelley advocated a minimum wage for all workers, so that men could support their dependents, and spoke warmly of "conserving the family and the home with the man as its economic support." The NCL stalwarts — Brandeis, Frankfurter, Kelley, and Goldmark — urged that the Oregon law of 1913 apply to men as well, but the Oregon reformers refused to press for such a broad measure.[17]

Even in its single-sex guise, however, the minimum wage evoked far more antagonism than did hours laws; legislators resisted it and labor distrusted it. To the AFL, which had endorsed maximum hours for women, the minimum wage would vitiate collective bargaining and, more ominously, might lead to — or *be* — a maximum wage. "The same law may endeavor to force men to work for a minimum wage scale," AFL leader Samuel Gompers contended, "and when government compels men to work for a minimum wage that means slavery." In several states, such as Massachusetts, reformers won labor support in their minimum-wage campaigns, but usually suspicion exceeded approval.[18]

To employers, the minimum wage was an unprecedented danger, far more insidious than maximum-hours laws, which rarely involved serious costs (especially since they were difficult to enforce and were often violated). Government tampering with wages, however, would cut into profits and undercut control. Wage fixing, said employers, was as illegitimate as price fixing. States might regulate the *conditions* of labor, they conceded, but to determine its *cost* was another matter (the *Bunting* Court had made this very point). Moreover, the minimum wage reflected not the value of the work but the alleged "need" of the worker. Finally, to its foes, the minimum wage was "redistributive" — it promoted the welfare of one class (workers) at the expense of another (employers). "This sort of legislation is a new expression of the paternalistic and socialistic tendencies of the day," charged Rome G. Brown, the lawyer who challenged the 1913 Oregon law. "It savors of the division of property between those who have and those who have not, and the leveling of fortunes by division under government supervision."[19]

The Oregon law spurred the first test case of the minimum wage. A paper box manufacturer, Frank Stettler, applied for an injunction against the enforcement of the law; he claimed that the Industrial Welfare Commission assumed powers belonging to the legislature. One of Stettler's workers, Elmira Simpson, also sued the state because, she claimed, if the state imposed the $8.64 minimum wage, she would lose her $6 a week job. That is, employer Stettler — or any other employer — could decide that employee Simpson — or any other employee — was not worth the minimum wage and fire her. In 1914, the Oregon Supreme Court upheld the minimum-wage law. It was "common knowledge," said the court, that low wages demoralized the public and the individuals concerned. The Oregon court issued the *Stettler* decision on the same day that it announced the *Bunting* decision, a heady triumph for reformers.[20]

When Stettler appealed to the Supreme Court, Brandeis and Goldmark prepared a brief to defend the minimum wage. The *Stettler* brief argued for a "living wage" — enough money to cover basic living costs plus a small sum for recreation and saving. In the tradition of the *Muller* brief, it discussed the extent of the problem, that is, the hazardous impact of low wages on health and morals; presented the effectiveness of the remedy; and sought to rebut potential critics. The minimum wage, said the brief, would not lead to "wholesale dismissal of women workers and their replacement by men." Nor would it injure employers. On the contrary, it would stimulate efficiency; "introduce new machinery, new methods of management and organization"; improve workers' health and vigor; and thereby increase output. Finally, it would enable "the enlightened employer to pay higher wages without fear of underbidding by competition."[21]

The authorities cited in the *Stettler* brief included the familiar sources of the *Muller* brief — the opinions of advocates abroad, reaching back to the English factory inspectors of 1833. But the *Stettler* brief also included many recent studies from state industrial welfare commissions about the financial plight of women workers and the positive impact of the minimum wage. This new type of twentieth-century evidence — from social workers, bureaucrats, and academics — offered statistics (which the *Muller* brief lacked) to show that many workers, notably women, were underpaid, underfed, poorly housed, and unable to buy medical care. Brandeis and Goldmark melded the new data with the popular *Muller* argument about women's roles as mothers of the race:

> It is a matter of common knowledge, universally accepted, that when the health of women has been injured in industrial work, not only is the working efficiency of the community impaired, but the deterioration is handed down to succeeding generations. The health of the race is conditioned upon preserving the health of women, the future mothers of the republic.[22]

Instead of reaching a decision in 1914, when arguments were first presented, the Supreme Court let the Oregon minimum-wage cases stew for three years. When Brandeis was appointed to the Court in 1916,

Frankfurter added to the brief and reargued it. Brandeis withdrew from deliberations since he had prepared the case. In 1917 the Court rendered a split decision in the *Stettler* and *Simpson* cases, which traveled together, and no written opinion. The 4–4 vote allowed the law to remain unchanged.[23]

The close call in *Stettler* should have sent a warning signal to reformers. But the minimum wage for women workers had now become a lively women's cause. The NCL devoted all its resources to the battle and unleashed, in addition, the powerful apparatus of the General Federation of Women's Clubs (GFWC). Theda Skocpol finds that one or more women's groups — the NCL, GFWC, or NWTUL — campaigned for the minimum wage in at least twelve of the fifteen states (plus the District of Columbia and Puerto Rico) where it was enacted. Yet the minimum wage seems to have succeeded more as a cause than in practice. The states that enacted minimum-wage laws were not among the most industrialized states; the wages set by state commissions never reached subsistence levels; and in the five states that set the level of minimum wages in their laws, inflation soon undermined the wages imposed.[24]

Nineteen seventeen was at once a banner year for reformers and a turning point. World War I brought a sea change in political climate that affected the campaign for protection. In one respect, reformers won a major coup. In 1920, under pressure from the NCL and other women's groups, Congress established the Women's Bureau in the Department of Labor. The outgrowth of a wartime "Women-in-Industry Service," created by the federal government in 1918, the new bureau was a close cousin to the NCL, whose interests it represented and whose functions it assumed — to investigate the conditions of women workers and promote their welfare. Protective laws, said reformer Mary Van Kleeck, former head of the Women-in-Industry Service, would set a precedent for laws to "remove the evils of industry which affect either men or women workers." The Women's Bureau inherited the NCL's dual goals: protection of women in industry *and* a "family wage" for men, so that women would not be forced into factories in the first place.[25]

Other signposts of the World War I era, however, suggested new problems for reformers. First, vocal opposition to protection arose among working women: New York's women printers and streetcar conductors protested state laws that curtailed opportunity. During the war, women had taken jobs on New York's street railways as conductors, ticket agents, and ticket collectors. After the war, the railway employees union promoted a law to limit women's hours and ban work after 10 P.M., and in May 1919, over half of the fifteen hundred women street railway employees lost their jobs. Women printers in New York protested the state's night work ban. "We are forced to compete with the worker who is not restricted as we are," a widowed printer contended. The remnant of women railway workers won exemptions from protection, as did, eventually, the printers. But the organizations they founded formed the nucleus of a workers' equal rights campaign: The Women's League for Equal Opportunity (1915) and the Equal Rights Association (1917) urged an end to protective laws.[26]

A second sign of trouble for reformers followed the ratification of the Nineteenth Amendment, which granted women the vote, in 1920. Suffragist Alice Paul now revamped the National Woman's Party (NWP), the militant wing of the suffrage movement that had picketed the White House in 1916 and had pressed for a federal suffrage amendment. The goal of the NWP, Paul announced, would henceforth be legal equality, notably the liberation of married women from common-law restrictions. In 1921, Paul proposed a "blanket bill" to bar sex discrimination in federal law and similar bills on the state level, which would of course void protective laws. When the NWP began to draft an equal rights amendment (ERA), it made several attempts to add a "saving clause" to exempt protective laws, but each effort failed. As NWP member and lawyer Gail Laughlin argued in April 1921, "If women can be segregated as a class for special legislation, the same classification can be used for special restrictions along any other line which may, at any time, appeal to the caprice or prejudice of our legislators."[27]

To Florence Kelley, a member of the NWP until 1921, Alice Paul offered only "empty phrases about equality of opportunity." In Kelley's view, NWP members served as "tools (consciously or unconsciously) of the worst exploiters." To Paul and the NWP, however, woman suffrage represented a first step toward sexual equality from which further gains would follow. The minimum-wage issue catalyzed a split between two strategies for change, two factions of politicized women, and two colliding sets of goals: labor standards and equal rights. The first clash involved a case that was moving through the federal courts.[28]

"THE HEART OF THE CONTRACT," 1923

In 1918, after an NCL campaign, Congress enacted a minimum-wage law for the District of Columbia. As in the Oregon minimum-wage cases, two challenges arose. An employer, Children's Hospital, sought an injunction against the District of Columbia Minimum Wage Board to restrain it from imposing the minimum wage. Willie Lyons, a twenty-year-old elevator operator at the Congress Hotel, protested the minimum wage because she wanted to keep her job (which paid $35 a week plus meals); when the board forced the hotel to pay the minimum wage, which was higher, Lyons was dismissed.[29]

The District of Columbia Supreme Court upheld the law in June 1920, as did the District Court of Appeals in June 1921. It was well known, said the majority opinion, that a working woman needed "a sufficient wage to supply her with necessary food, shelter, and clothing" and if she were required to settle for less, her health would suffer. In a dissenting opinion, Justice Van Orsdel assaulted "the tendency of the hour to socialize property rights under the subterfuge of the police regulation." But the District's law was not yet secure. Justice Robb, a conservative who had missed the 1921 appeal because he was sick and had been replaced by another judge, returned to the bench and in October 1921 insisted on a new hearing ("a procedure unique in the history of the court," Florence Kelley told *Survey* readers). This time, the foes of the minimum wage prevailed. Justice Van Orsdel, who now wrote the majority opinion, issued in November 1922, pointed to the dangers of wage fixing, the violation of freedom of contract, Willie Lyons's loss of her right to earn a living, and "paternalism in the highest degree." The minimum wage meant, he said, that "the most industrious worker must share his living with his indolent, worthless neighbor."[30]

The next year, *Adkins v. Children's Hospital* and its companion case, *Adkins v. Lyons,* reached the Supreme Court. Unlike earlier cases on protective laws, these cases concerned a federal law (Congress legislates for the District of Columbia) and therefore involved the due process clause of the Fifth Amendment, which applies to the federal government, not the parallel clause of the Fourteenth, which applies to the states. There were other changes, too. New appointments of justices during the war or soon after had produced a more conservative Court. The NCL team, which represented the District of Columbia's Minimum Wage Board and its head, Jesse Adkins, had changed as well. When Josephine Goldmark moved on to study the nursing profession, Mary W. Dewson replaced her and, with Felix Frankfurter, prepared the brief for the *Adkins* cases. An experienced social worker and social scientist, Dewson had done extensive research on women workers for the commission that proposed the minimum wage in Massachusetts. Her 1,138-page brief, the longest of the NCL "Brandeis" briefs, not only cited recent data, mainly from minimum-wage commissions, but conveyed a modernized reform argument that emerged in the 1920s.[31]

The contentions of the *Adkins* brief often resembled those of the *Stettler* brief. "The dangers to the health of women from low wages are twofold: lack of adequate nourishment and lack of medical care in illness," Dewson wrote. These created a "descending spiral into the regions of destitution." Again, as in earlier Brandeis briefs, "the deterioration is handed down to succeeding generations." But in the *Adkins* brief, the dependent woman of the *Muller* brief gave way to an updated counterpart who provided for herself and others: "[T]he bulk of the girls living at home, work to support themselves, not for extra spending money"; many women supported "aging parents or other dependents." The *Adkins* brief, historian Sybil Lipschultz contends, reflected the revised ideas of women reformers in the 1920s: "It argued for the minimum wage not primarily to protect women's health or the future of the race but to redress women's economic disadvantage." Dewson selected material that stressed women's roles as breadwinners who supported others — aged parents, disabled husbands, dependent children — or who had themselves been deserted, divorced, or separated. Women needed a "living wage" not because they were dependent but because they were independent; and, in some cases, others depended on *them*.[32]

Dewson, in short, had modernized the *Muller* and *Stettler* arguments to suit the 1920s ideal of "economic independence." The woman worker of the *Adkins* brief was disadvantaged by social and economic circumstances, not by innate, sex-linked attributes. But as the argument became more modern, it assumed new risks. Employed men, like independent or breadwinner women, also supported themselves and others. Women's case was distinctive only insofar as they earned less.

The opposing argument in the *Adkins* case, for Children's Hospital and Willie Lyons, was made by the brothers Wade H. Ellis and Challen Ellis, to whom the advent of Alice Paul and the NWP must have seemed a providential gift. Since the *Muller* case, reformers had cited hundreds of experts; now the opposition had an expert of its own. Alice Paul, who had conferred with Challen Ellis about the wording of an ERA, supplied him with NWP literature, which his brother cited in oral argument. The affinity between freedom of contract and women's rights that had first emerged in the *Ritchie* decision of 1895 and had reappeared in William Fenton's brief for Muller now blossomed again. "Challen Ellis helped forge the critical link between equal rights for women and the liberty of contract principle," historian Joan G. Zimmerman writes. "Paul's talk of rights provided the Ellis brothers with a way to revive an old doctrine in the new guise of equal rights." This interchange, she shows, also affected

Alice Paul. "For Paul, legal formalism would be, not a barrier, but an avenue to achieving the reforms she sought for women."[33]

In his argument before the Supreme Court, Wade Ellis presented the positions of the NWP and other equal rights groups against "discrimination or restriction based upon sex" and used the arguments for sexual equality to denounce the single-sex minimum wage. "Can it be that the women of the country favor such laws, and especially for them alone?" Ellis asked.

> In my own investigations I have found an overwhelming sentiment just the other way. All over the country today thoughtful and progressive women are contending for industrial equality which follows as a natural and logical sequence to political equality. . . . The women of this country . . . want, and they deserve equal rights with men. They believe in self-reliance, independence, and character. And they believe that the right to make their own bargains will result ultimately in better pay, a finer sense of self-respect and a higher quality of citizenship. They are learning from experience that minimum wage laws are not discriminations in their favor but discriminations against them.

Then Ellis challenged the "entering wedge" strategy. "Where will this legislation lead?" he asked. In his view, it was "perfectly obvious that if the state or the nation . . . may fix the wages of women, they may fix the wages of men." Had not *Bunting* followed *Muller?* Still, once again, the reformers were defending a law for women on the basis that distinctive circumstances — "considerations of her life and morals" — made the law necessary. "I submit that such an alleged distinction is unreal and fanciful," Ellis charged. In the hundreds of pages of extracts in the Dewson/Frankfurter brief, he contended, "there is scarcely the slightest hint anywhere of a distinction between men and women." All the authorities cited in the brief, Ellis pointed out, "believe in the minimum wage for both men and women."[34]

In a 5–3 decision (Brandeis again withdrew because his daughter Elizabeth was an officer of the District of Columbia Minimum Wage Board), the Court failed to sustain the minimum-wage law. Justice George Sutherland, who had joined the Court in 1922, wrote the majority opinion. As senator from Utah, Sutherland had opposed Brandeis's confirmation in 1916, and before his own appointment he had, like Challen Ellis, advised Alice Paul on the drafting of an ERA. To Sutherland, the minimum wage struck "at the heart of the contract." Revolutionary changes in women's status had brought "the ancient inequality of the sexes" and the differences between men and women "almost to the vanishing point," he wrote. Now that women had the vote, they were no longer a dependent class, excluded from freedom of contract, but equal to men. Nor was there a link between morals, health, and the minumum wage; the evidence offered by Frankfurter and Dewson in their lengthy brief was only "mildly persuasive" (although, as David J. Bryden points out, that should have sufficed to uphold the law). Finally, Sutherland revived the *Lochner* decision, whose death, it seemed, had been misreported. "Subsequent cases in this court have been distinguished from that decision," he declared, "but the principles therein have never been disproved."[35]

"Most ominous part of the opinion," Frankfurter telegraphed Kelley on April 23, 1923, "is suggestion that the Muller doctrine has been supplanted by the Nineteenth Amendment." The *Adkins* decision, he later wrote, gave "the industrially subnormal woman-earner the constitutional right to starve."[36]

The *Adkins* decision was another crucial turning point. Although it upset only the District of Columbia's minimum-wage law, it had a stultifying effect in the states, where minimum-wage laws seemed doomed. Moreover, as Joan G. Zimmerman points out, it posited an "equal woman" who did not exist: Women in industry had no more freedom of contract in 1923 than they did in the nineteenth century. The newly won right to vote had been used as a hatchet to deny new voters a living wage; woman suffrage, it appeared, did not come without cost. Finally, the *Adkins* decision sabotaged reformers' plans to extend the minimum wage to all workers; the "entering wedge" strategy had backfired. But the *Muller* decision survived intact. Although it had been "supplanted," as Frankfurter contended, in regard to the minimum wage, it was also confirmed: Differences between the sexes, Sutherland explained, still legitimized regulations that applied solely to women. Hence, maximum-hours laws, night work bans, and occupational restrictions limited to women remained in place.[37]

This became clear in 1924 when the Court upheld a New York law that barred women's work in restaurants in large cities after 10 P.M. A restaurant owner in Buffalo had challenged the law. In *Radice v. New York* (1924), citing *Muller,* the Court affirmed that the night work ban was in the interest of women's health and public welfare. Ironically, Judith A. Baer observes, freedom of contract for women workers had been "sustained in a situation where it did not exist and curtailed in a situation where it did exist."[38] False paternalism (which deprived New York waitresses of high tips at night) and false equality (which denied Washington, D.C., workers a "living wage") could coexist.

The *Adkins* decision evoked a torrent of adverse commentary in law journals, a sign of the growing hold of legal realism. Some critics proposed constitutional reform: an amendment that required a larger Supreme Court majority to strike down laws. "An eighteenth-century Constitution cannot, without change, be fitted to these twentieth-century conditions," declared George Gorham Groat in the *Yale Law Journal*. Most law review contributors reargued the case, usually (but not always) on the losing side. In the *California Law Review,* Barbara N. Grimes reiterated the gist of the reformers' argument, which Justice Sutherland, in her view, seemed to have missed:

> Minimum wage legislation is not and was not predicated upon political, contractual or civil inequalities of women. It is predicated rather upon evils to society resulting from the exploitation of women in industry, who *as a class labor under a tremendous economic handicap.* The problem is one of economic fact, not of political, contractual, or civil status.

Supporters of *Adkins,* however, found a flaw in the reformers' case: If economic hardship was the criterion for the minimum wage, then men met this criterion as well. "[I]t is difficult to see how a low or high wage can affect women as a class to a greater extent than men," wrote the commentator in *Law Notes.* "Good wages are as conducive to health in men as in women, and poor wages would be equally detrimental to both classes." One analyst of the case, in the *Harvard Law Review,* eschewed reargument for numerical analysis. In all the votes ever cast on the minimum wage in state and federal courts, wrote Thomas Reed Powell, thirty-two judges favored it and nine were opposed. But five of those nine were on the Supreme Court in 1923. Had the case been heard earlier (as it might well have been), Powell contended, the vote would probably have been 5 to 3 to uphold the law. The *Adkins* decision was an accident![39]

Recent commentary on the *Adkins* case suggests another type of accident: The legal system pitted two groups of women activists against one another and, to their detriment, involved both factions with *lawyers.* (To be sure, several of the leading women involved, like Florence Kelley, *were* lawyers — Alice Paul, for instance, attended law school in Washington while the *Adkins* case was in progress — but their priorities lay elsewhere.) Sybil Lipschultz contends that social feminists — women reformers who clustered in the NCL, NWTUL, and settlement work — underwent important changes in the 1920s; that Florence Kelley and her allies strove for "industrial equality" for working women (which meant "equality through difference"); and that the minimum-wage campaign best exemplified the new egalitarian spirit. But Frankfurter and other lawyers close to the NCL, she posits, did not share the shift in attitude: "The social feminists were saddled with lawyers who basically believed in women's inferiority and who read proposals for highlighting women's differences as formulae for inequality." Joan G. Zimmerman, who examines ties between Alice Paul and the lawyers on the other side, points to equally unfortunate consequences. "By formalizing Paul's talk of rights, Sutherland had co-opted Paul's view and narrowed it to serve the most conservative economic and legal interests," she contends. "The litigation that culminated in the *Adkins* decision propelled Kelley and Paul toward different, incompatible kinds of arguments."[40]

After the *Adkins* decision, in December 1923, Alice Paul proposed to Congress her final version of the ERA: "Men and women shall have equal rights throughout the United States and every place subject to its jurisdiction." The legal battle for the minimum wage continued in the courts, but the argument over protective laws now spun out of the judicial system and into the women's movement, where it flourished for almost half a century.

4

Legacy: Labor Law, Women's Politics, and Protective Policies

The Progressive era left an uncertain legacy: As of 1923, scores of protective laws survived, but the minimum wage — and reformers' plans to expand it — faltered. A half century later, single-sex protective laws had been discarded, but the labor standards for which progressives strove were in place. Two legal revolutions, in the 1930s and the 1960s, effected this double reversal; the "entering wedge" strategy succeeded in the long run, though not without long-term impact on women workers and women's politics. Post-*Adkins* milestones include the feud over protection that split the women's movement in the 1920s and after; New Deal measures that regulated the wages and hours of men and women workers; a sudden shift of federal policy on sex discrimination in the 1960s; and the consequent death of protective laws for women workers. As single-sex protection expired, the once-high reputation of *Muller v. Oregon* swiftly sank.

THE WOMEN'S MOVEMENT IN THE 1920s

Dissension over protective laws shaped the post-suffrage women's movement. Although the vast majority of women's organizations — including the NCL, NWTUL, GFWC, and the new League of Women Voters — opposed the ERA and defended protective laws for women workers, as did the Women's Bureau, the small but determined NWP kept up a persistent challenge and occasionally gained ground. The 1920s set the terms of debate.

To ERA supporters, sex-specific protective laws defined women as weak and dependent, classified them with minors as wards of the state, limited them to low-level jobs, curtailed their earning capacity, and penalized the ambitious — those who competed with men for work. "Labor men wanted protective laws for women only so that they could steal women's jobs under cover of chivalry," charged the NWP journal *Equal Rights* in 1929. To the ERA's foes, protective laws served a compensatory, equalizing function; they brought "the women's standard up a little towards the standards of men." To discard them would wipe out years of progressive gains, sanction exploitation, and keep women in "industrial slavery." To reformers, the ERA represented the interests of a professional elite that had no knowledge of women in industry; it enjoyed the backing of the business class ("powerfully organized exploiting employers of women and children," said Florence Kelley); and it was pernicious, insane, diabolical, and reactionary — in the words of Mary Anderson of the Women's Bureau, "a kind of hysterical feminism with a slogan for a program."[1]

Both factions claimed that, ideally, protective laws should be "extended" to men, but such claims were now shaky, and on the NWP's part, after *Adkins,* disingenuous. The possibility of extending wage and hours laws to men in industry — when the AFL opposed such an extension, when legislatures failed to endorse it, and when the Supreme Court (with a boost from Alice Paul) had just rejected the minimum wage — was extremely remote. Other sex-specific laws, such as night work bans and occupational restrictions, were even less likely candidates for extension to men, at least without abolishing *all* work after 10 P.M. (a prospect that in fact appealed to reformers), plus a long list of jobs and sectors of industry. An ERA, as reformers claimed, meant the death of protection. But on the reformers' side, the "entering wedge" strategy (which had always embodied contradictions) faltered. If protection *were* extended to men, explained reformer Clara Beyer, an officer of the District of Columbia Minimum Wage Board at the time of *Adkins,* "women would be left without the safeguards which are peculiarly necessary to their well-being." Clearly, since protective laws were compensatory, their extension to men would be counterproductive. Beneath the dispute in the women's movement lay an insoluble dilemma: Were women fundamentally different from men or equal to men, or, if both, where did the advantage lie? This question pitted the interests of strivers, go-getters, and bourgeois professionals against the interests of the least advantaged — those with less skill, less clout, and no alternatives. To the *Nation* in 1928, the "sex struggle" and the "class struggle" were on a collision course: "The rub comes when the two struggles overlap."[2]

External problems compounded the internal feud in the women's movement: Both factions faced a hardening political climate in which options for change ebbed. During the 1920s, the ERA made no progress, but social welfare measures fared little better; the women's movement had inherited the Progressive-era battle for labor standards just as progress had become futile. Florence Kelley turned her efforts to an amendment to ban child labor, which the states failed to ratify, and to another favored project, the Sheppard-Towner Act, which Congress passed in 1921. The first federally funded health care law, Sheppard-Towner provided matching funds for mother and child welfare clinics in rural areas; it was an "entering wedge" for universal health care coverage. But the American Medical Association opposed government interference in the medical field, and Congress repealed the law in 1929. Similarly, employers stepped up their campaign against the minimum wage. During the 1920s, minimum-wage laws fell in Arizona, Arkansas, Kansas, and Wisconsin. By 1930, the six such laws that remained in place were, to varied degrees, unenforced or ineffective.[3]

Under these circumstances, assessment of the impact of maximum-hours laws began. In 1928, the Women's Bureau published a five-hundred-page report on the impact of such laws. Surveying five industries in nine states, the bureau (hardly a disinterested party) narrowed its inquiry to one main question: Did the laws lead to the replacement of women by men? This was a loaded question, since three of the industries (paper box, hosiery, and garment production) relied on female labor in a sex-segregated market; in the others (boots and shoes and electrical products), female minorities performed specific types of work; in all cases, low pay protected women's jobs. The bureau, accordingly, found that hours limits did not decrease female employment or curb opportunity; indeed, by banning overtime, it claimed, the limits increased openings for other women workers. Night work bans and exclusionary laws, the report conceded, "restricted women's opportunities in a small number of cases." But among women who held jobs when hours laws went into effect (another loaded proviso), "Not one woman found that such legislation had handicapped her or limited her opportunity in industry."[4]

In a review of the report, economist Elizabeth Faulkner Baker stressed the role of some sixty thousand women workers, whom, she claimed, the bureau had "largely overlooked." Such workers entered occupations dominated by men, labored on "little industrial frontiers," served to "make way for the many to follow," and were "cramped or cut off" by protective laws. Baker's critique reflected her own study of 1925, an analysis of protective laws in New York State; her conclusions diverged in part from those of the Women's Bureau. Enforcement of hours laws in New York, Baker contended, had been dismal. She told a sad story of exhausted inspectors, recalcitrant employers, gross violations, bungled prosecutions, dismissed charges, inadequate penalties, unpaid fines, and cowed employees, who, out of "ignorance, indifference, or fear" of dismissal, hesitated to complain about abuses. New York's night work laws, easier to enforce, failed for other reasons: "Many of the women themselves are not in sympathy with being deprived of work at night." The shorter workday, Baker asserted, depended on worker organization, more humane employers, and a shrinking labor pool. Maximum-hours laws, she concluded, were an advantage in industries where women predominated (the industries where most women workers were employed). Here, protective laws for women were "likely to protect both men and women." (Subsequent research generally confirms that in the 1920s, maximum-hours laws provided benefits to the majority of women affected.) But in trades in which women were a minority, Baker contended, protective laws curtailed opportunity:

> In occupations or industries where men greatly predominate, protective laws for women are likely to prohibit rather than protect their employment, or in other words, to relieve men of the competition of women. . . . For these minorities of women, legislation based only upon sex is of doubtful value.

Baker's sympathies clearly lay with "the significant minority who have emerged from the mass into a more self-reliant position."[5]

By 1933, all but six states had enacted maximum-hours laws, which, according to Elizabeth Brandeis, applied to "virtually all types of work in which women workers engage," save domestic service and agricultural labor; sixteen states banned women from night work. Now, in combination, the Depression of the 1930s and Franklin D. Roosevelt's New Deal effected a revolution in the history of protection.

PROTECTION TRIUMPHANT: THE NEW DEAL AND AFTER

The New Deal represented a triumph for the social reform wing of the women's movement. Veterans of the NCL, the NWTUL, and the 1920s battles finally gained a chance to influence public policy, promote protective laws, and effect the progressive agenda. Florence Kelley died in 1932, but NCL and NWTUL alumnae dominated the circle surrounding Eleanor Roosevelt, a vocal supporter of protection who had been trained for public life in the Women's Trade Union League of New York and the League of Women Voters; these veterans of progressive reform wielded pressure from posts in the Women's Bureau, the Department of Labor, and the Democratic Party. Labor Secretary Frances Perkins commented that she did not feel personally chosen for her job but that "it was the Consumers' League who was appointed and I was merely the symbol that happened to be at hand." Denouncing the NWP opposition ("Some of these hard-boiled females seem to forget the virtues of generosity and sympathy for the underprivileged," said Mary W. Dewson, who headed the Women's Division of the Democratic Party), New Deal officeholders upheld the "right to differ."[7]

They also promoted progressive social policies. The Social Security Act of 1935 and its amendments provided unemployment compensation, old age pensions, care for the disabled, and aid to dependent children (a substitute for the mothers' pensions of the Progressive era). The short-lived National Recovery Administration codes of 1933 regulated hours and wages for men and women workers. Finally, the Fair Labor Standards Act (FLSA) of 1938 provided minimum wages, maximum hours, and overtime pay rules for men and women involved in the production of goods for interstate commerce, as well as a ban on child labor. To NCL veterans, like Frances Perkins, the FLSA was *their* achievement, not that of organized labor. "Everybody claimed credit for it," Perkins recalled. "The AF of L said it was their bill. . . . The CIO (Congress of Industrial Organizations) claimed credit for its passage." But, in her view, "the President and I . . . thought we had done it."[8]

Simultaneously, hard times gave the minimum wage a sudden boost. During the 1930s, fourteen states passed minimum-wage laws for women workers. Since *Adkins,* the Supreme Court had steadily rebuffed the minimum wage; it upset an Arizona law in 1925, an Arkansas law in 1927, and a New York law in 1936. But President Roosevelt's landslide victory in the 1936 election and his Judicial Reorganization bill of 1937 suddenly reversed the Court's direction. The president's bill proposed, among other items, to increase Supreme Court membership from nine to as many as fifteen, if justices who reached the age of seventy refused to retire. Faced with this "court-packing" threat, the justices expeditiously shifted gears and began to approve New Deal measures. In the landmark decision *West Coast Hotel v. Parrish* (1937), they upheld by 5 to 4 a 1914 minimum-wage law for women in Washington State. (Twice sustained in the state courts, the law was identical to the Oregon law of 1913 that had just squeaked by a divided Court in *Stettler.*)[9]

Elsie Parrish, a chambermaid in the Cascadia Hotel in Wenatchee, Washington, had sued to recover the difference between the wage she received and the minimum wage established by Washington's Industrial Welfare Commission ($14.50 for a forty-eight-hour week). Upholding the law, the Supreme Court now discarded freedom of contract. Citing *Holden,* it referred to the "inequality in the footing of the parties," a principle that was "peculiarly applicable in relation to the employment of women in whose protection the state has a special interest." Here, the majority opinion repeated a chunk of the *Muller* decision and denounced managerial greed: "What can be closer to the public interest than the health of women and their protection from unscrupulous and overreaching employers?" Overruling the *Adkins* decision, the Court declared the minimum wage for women workers constitutional.[10]

Four years later, the Court followed up with a companion decision. In *United States v. Darby* (1941), the justices upheld the minimum-wage provisions of the 1938 FLSA, which affected both men and women, with a terse sentence: "[I]t is no longer open to question that the fixing of a minimum wage is within the legislative power." As in *Bunting,* most of the *Darby* opinion dealt with another issue: whether hour and wage regulations fell under the interstate commerce clause (they did). Thus, with no fanfare and no Brandeis briefs, the Supreme Court upheld the minimum wage for men; and, once again, as in 1917, the "entering wedge" strategy worked. The single-sex minimum wage played a vital role in its success. "Attention to gender differences," historian Alice Kessler-Harris points out, "had kept alive the possibility that all workers deserved state protection."[11]

Darby was a turning point: With the FLSA, the machinery of modern labor law cranked into place, and subsequent amendments steadily expanded its power. The federal government could now fulfill goals that progressives had long envisioned: It could impose health and safety standards, end child labor, regulate industrial homework, and enforce wage and hours laws for male and female employees. But the law's immediate impact on wages, hours, and women workers has to be qualified. First, the FLSA, which excluded employees in agriculture and domestic service, covered just a segment of industrial workers. It affected only about a quarter of workers in the 1930s (it would affect almost half in the 1950s and, by the end of the 1970s, would reach about 90 percent). Second, states did not at once enact minimum-wage laws that covered men and would not start to do so until the mid-1950s. Finally, although the Supreme Court had discarded the rationale for single-sex state protective laws, the laws themselves remained and affected women workers in factories, stores, and offices. State maximum-hours laws for women workers combined with the FLSA now provided a particular type of handicap. For men in industry, under the FLSA, the limit on hours represented the point at which overtime pay began. For women, however, maximum-hours laws barred both overtime and promotion to jobs that might require it. This outcome defied reformers' intentions. Time-and-a-half pay, they hoped, would make overtime expensive for employers, decrease its incidence, shorten hours for all workers, and spread jobs around. But employers preferred to pay overtime rates rather than hire and train new workers. Thus, women's labor laws imposed disadvantages unanticipated by their proponents.[12]

The need for labor during World War II and the massive entry of women into defense work led to the suspension of many protective laws "for the duration." After the war, the laws returned in force, including night work bans, exclusion from jobs deemed immoral or hazardous, limits on the weight a woman worker could lift, and maximum-hours laws that barred overtime and hence curbed opportunity. The Progressive era had left a legacy of restrictions, and *Muller* provided a precedent for new laws that prevented women from competing for jobs with returning veterans. In 1945, for instance, Michigan passed a law that prohibited women from obtaining licenses as bartenders unless they were the wives or daughters of male tavern owners — a measure supported by the International Union of Hotel and Restaurant Employees and Bartenders. Two women who owned bars and their daughters, whom they employed, contended that the law violated their Fourteenth Amendment rights. But in *Goesaert v. Cleary* (1948), the Supreme Court upheld the Michigan law. Bartending by women, said Justice Frankfurter (appointed to the Court in 1939), might give rise to "social and moral problems." Denying that the law had been impelled by "an unchivalrous desire of male bartenders to monopolize the calling," he found nothing in the change in women's social and legal position to "preclude the states from drawing a sharp line between the sexes."[13]

Just as the Supreme Court spoke on *Goesaert,* the female workforce entered an era of rapid modernization, in which trends that had been building up incrementally since the 1920s accelerated: The woman wage earner became older, married, and middle class. After World War II, women surged into white-collar work — office, sales, and service jobs. In 1960, when the median age of women employees was forty-one, twice as many women worked as in 1940; twice as many women held sales or clerical jobs as industrial jobs; married women constituted over half the female labor force; and 30 percent of wives earned wages, compared to 9 percent in 1920 and 15 percent in 1940. When the Kennedy Commission on the Status of Women convened in the early 1960s, it took such changes into account. Chaired by Eleanor Roosevelt and led by the head of the Women's Bureau, Esther Peterson, the commission met to advise the president on policies that concerned women — and, the Women's Bureau hoped, to terminate the annoying issue of the proposed ERA.

The main business of the commission transpired in its Committee on Civil Rights, which sought a means to achieve equality for women while keeping protective laws in place. Lawyer Pauli Murray of Yale devised a solution: The committee urged challenges to sexually discriminatory laws (but not protective laws) under the Fifth and Fourteenth amendments. To win such challenges, Murray proposed a "Brandeis-type brief" on women's changing roles. The Committee on Labor Laws also confronted the problem of protection, though with less unity. By the 1960s, historian Cynthia Harrison points out, many of those committed to protection "were willing to acknowledge that some of the more restrictive and rigid rules did more harm than good"; other regulations, most agreed, should be "extended" to men and kept in place in the interim. But maximum-hours laws remained a stumbling block. In its final report, the commission recommended ambiguously that in cases where hours laws remained the best attainable protection, they should be "maintained, strengthened, and expanded"; that women with administrative, executive, and professional jobs should be exempted; and that premium overtime pay for both sexes was the best way to shorten the workday. The report also urged an amalgam of changes, such as the extension of the FLSA to cover small-business employees, equal pay for comparable work, tax deductions for child care, and paid maternity leaves. Sexual equality, the commission hoped, could be achieved without an ERA.[14]

Toward this end, the Women's Bureau supported the Equal Pay Act, which Congress passed in 1963 — the first federal law against sex discrimination in employment (a similar bill had failed in 1946). Persons performing the same work (not comparable work), said the law, had to receive the same pay. Like the FLSA, which it amended, the new law left many types of work uncovered, and it did not impel employers to hire women in the first place. But it represented the Women's Bureau goal: to combat sex discrimination without disrupting protection.[15]

What state protective laws were in effect in the 1960s? Minimum-wage laws, once the most controversial part of the progressive agenda, had surged to the fore; in the 1950s, pressured by unions and the Women's Bureau, many states began to enact or extend such laws to cover men and women, and the process accelerated in the 1960s. In 1955, of thirty-three minimum-wage laws in twenty-nine states and four jurisdictions, only ten covered men; by 1968, out of forty-one such laws, only ten protected women alone, and three of those were inoperative. Maximum-hours laws, however, affected mainly women: Of forty-two maximum-hours laws in the 1960s, thirty-nine covered women only. Restrictive and exclusionary laws had expanded: By 1968, twenty-six states barred women from mining, bartending, or other jobs deemed hazardous to health or morals; eleven states imposed limits on the weight women could lift; nineteen states prohibited or regulated night work; and seven states prohibited work for periods before or after childbirth. When challenges arose, a rare occurrence, the courts found sex to be a "valid basis for classification" and cited *Muller*. Sex as a valid basis of classification, moreover, extended to laws affecting education, welfare, family life, criminal conduct, and other areas; courts continued to rely on the *Muller* principle to provide differential treatment in licensing for occupations, for example, or to exclude women from juries ("Woman is still regarded as the center of the home and family life," Justice Harlan wrote in a 1961 opinion supporting differential treatment for jury selection). These were the circumstances in 1964, when an unexpected event suddenly turned the ground rules upside down.[16]

PROTECTION DISMANTLED: TITLE VII AND AFTER

Ironically, the most important legislation connected to feminist revival in the 1960s preceded it and occurred seemingly by accident. In the summer of 1964, Congress considered a new civil rights bill. Title VII of the bill prohibited discrimination in employment on the basis of race, color, religion, or national origin. Democratic Representative Howard W. Smith of Virginia (whose motives remain obscure) proposed an amendment to add discrimination on the basis of sex. The controversial amendment, which threatened protective laws, delayed passage of the bill. Organized labor, the Women's Bureau, and most women's organizations opposed it. But the Johnson administration, though at first reluctant, supported it, as did women in Congress, including two NWP members, Democratic Representative Martha Griffiths and Republican Senator Margaret Chase Smith. Enacted by Congress, its provision against sex discrimination intact, the Civil Rights Act of 1964 barred classification of workers in ways that would deprive them of opportunity, called for "affirmative" efforts by employers to provide opportunity to groups that had suffered discrimination, and established an enforcement agency, the Equal Employment Opportunity Commission (EEOC). A loophole made it legal to hire on the basis of sex (or religion or national origin, but not race) in instances where it was a bona fide occupational qualification.[17]

Would Title VII of the 1964 Civil Rights Act, which took effect in 1965, invalidate protective laws for women workers? At the outset, the answer was far from clear. The new law merely revived the argument over protection. The EEOC narrowed the field of contention in 1966 when it announced that "beneficial" laws (regulating the minimum wage, over-time pay, rest periods, or physical facilities) had to apply to both men and women; the rest of single-sex protective laws (maximum-hours laws, night work bans, weight-lifting restrictions, and exclusionary laws) would be left to litigation in the states. The United Auto Workers (UAW) and a nascent group of feminists, who had joined forces in the National Organization for Women (NOW) in 1966, claimed that protection was dead. To the UAW, protective laws, based on "stereotypes," were "undesirable relics of the past." Other unions and many women's organizations, loath to cede the progressive legacy, claimed that differences between the sexes "amply justify existing legislation." Maximum-hours laws and weight limits, they contended, aided the lowest-paid, least-organized workers and served a "valid protective purpose." The NCL fought to the end. "While men may also require protection from overtime hours," argued its representative, "as a group their need is often less than women, who usually spend more time on family and home responsibilities." To one expert in industrial relations, the needs of unionized women in 1968 depended on whether they competed with men or earned secondary incomes:

> In industries . . . where men and women work on many of the same jobs, and where women who are primary wage earners share with men the desire to get as much overtime pay as possible, women workers . . . will be restive under restrictive legislation. On the other hand, where the majority of women members are secondary earners, where they are young and have school-age children, where their jobs are insulated to some considerable degree from competition with men, and where night work or overtime work is a rare exception, they will probably feel no burdensome restrictions flowing from the legislation and may, indeed, actually welcome the limits it sets on their employment.

The rationales of the Progressive era, now updated and modified, had considerably less punch.[18]

At the end of the 1960s, finally, a combination of state action, EEOC guidelines, and litigation began to reverse a half century of protective laws. Court decisions did most of the work. Unlike the cases of the Progressive era, in which employers challenged protective laws, this time workers demanded equal opportunities under Title VII, either as individuals or in class action suits. Several cases paved the way. In *Rosenfeld v. Southern Pacific* (1968), a rejected applicant for an agent-telegrapher's job with a railroad challenged a California ten-hour plus weight-restriction law. The law, said a federal district judge, was preempted by Title VII, and in 1971 the Ninth Circuit affirmed the decision. In *Weeks v. Southern Bell* (1969), the first Title VII case to reach an appellate court, the Fifth Circuit reversed a Georgia decision in a similar case in which a rejected applicant for the job of switchman with a telephone company had challenged a state law. "The promise of Title VII is that women are now to be on an equal footing," declared the Fifth Circuit; the employer had the burden of proving that "all or substantially all women would be unable to perform safely and efficiently the duties of the job involved." After *Weeks,* state and federal courts invalidated every protective law challenged under Title VII. In the first Title VII case to reach the Supreme Court, *Phillips v. Martin Marietta,* for instance, a worker sued her employer for discriminating against her because she had preschool-age children. Here, the Fifth Circuit in 1969 had sided with the employer, but the Supreme Court in 1971 rejected the "sex-plus" argument.[19]

Striving to keep pace with the courts and impelled in particular by the *Rosenfeld* district court decision, the EEOC declared in 1969 that "prohibitory" laws (maximum-hours laws, night work bans, weight-lifting limits, and occupational exclusions) that were "originally promulgated for the purpose of protecting females have ceased to be relevant" and "tend to discriminate rather than protect." Meanwhile, the states took action. Delaware, for instance, had repealed all laws in violation of Title VII in 1965. In twenty-one states, by 1973, attorneys general declared that prohibitory laws did not apply to workers covered by Title VII. By 1974, all states but Nevada had repealed maximum-hours laws for women workers. At the same time, sex discrimination suits based on the equal protection clause of the Fourteenth Amendment began to reach the Supreme Court. Starting with *Reed v. Reed* (1971), lawyer Ruth Bader Ginsburg argued a series of such cases; in *Reed* she successfully challenged an Idaho law that gave preference to fathers in the administration of children's estates. In *Frontiero v. Richardson* (1972), Ginsburg won for a woman air force officer the benefits for her spouse that a man in the same job would have been granted automatically. The laws at issue in *Reed* and *Frontiero,* Ginsburg contended, stereotyped men as "breadwinners" and women as "dependents." The decline of protection and the rise of "equal protection" worked in tandem.[20]

The era of protective laws for women workers thus ended, in spurts and gasps, at some indefinite point in the early 1970s, just as Congress approved an equal rights amendment, which the states would fail to ratify by 1983. What happened to *Muller v. Oregon?* As protective laws fell, the courts chipped away at the substance of *Muller,* sometimes solely to distinguish the case at hand from that of 1908. "In *Muller,* the statute was upheld in part because it was thought to be a necessary way of safeguarding women's competitive position," the Ninth Circuit explained in 1971, as it toppled a maximum-hours law. "Here the statute is attacked on the ground that it gives male employees an unfair economic advantage over females." In other instances, the *Muller* decision absorbed heavier blows. "No judge today would justify classification based on sex by resort to such openly biased and wholly chauvinistic statements as this one made by Justice Brewer," declared the California Supreme Court the same year, as it upset a ban on women bartenders; classification based on sex, it argued, had imposed a "stigma of inferiority and second-class citizenship." The issue that most clearly brought aspects of *Muller* into play, however, turned out to be pregnancy-related discrimination.[21]

In 1978, Congress passed the Pregnancy Discrimination Act. Employers of fifteen or more persons, said the law, may not treat pregnancy more or less favorably than other temporary, nonoccupational disabilities. Five states, however, went further and enacted maternity leave legislation. A California law provided that employers must grant pregnant workers up to four months of unpaid leave with job security. In 1982, a California worker, Lillian Garland, sued the bank that employed her for her right to resume her old job under the state law. The employer claimed that the law, which provided special treatment for pregnant women, was invalidated by the federal Pregnancy Discrimination Act, which banned special treatment. The case divided feminists. All agreed that Garland deserved her job back, but they differed on how the law should ensure this result. According to NOW and the American Civil Liberties Union (ACLU), the bank could obey both laws only by providing disability leave for *other* workers as well as pregnant women. According to this argument, pregnancy was analogous to other disabilities, and any form of "special" treatment was undesirable. Other feminists, however, plus the local ACLU chapter, argued that a degree of special treatment was needed to achieve equal results and that pregnancy was a real sexual difference. This position stressed that equal treatment can yield unequal results and that strict equality, with no room for difference, held hidden disadvantages.[22]

In *California Federal Savings and Loan Association v. Guerra* (1987), the Supreme Court upheld the state law, but the controversial decision merely fueled the equal/different conflict that had erupted. Needed to resolve the dispute was, paradoxically, a gender-neutral form of pregnancy policy. In 1990, Congress passed such a policy, the Family Leave Act, which provided unpaid leave to workers with family obligations. President George Bush vetoed the act; granting such a leave, he claimed, should be voluntary on the part of employers. President Bill Clinton signed a new Family Leave Act in 1993. The new law enables workers to take four-month leaves for their own disabilities or to care for family members, such as new infants, sick children or spouses, or aged parents. In this instance, the state pregnancy law served as an "entering wedge" for a broad-based, gender-neutral policy that fulfilled feminist demands. "Family leave" deconstructs pregnancy into two components, disability and care for others, both of which can be stretched to include the nonpregnant. Although the family leave policy imposes costs on employers, it does not involve heavy costs. However, as scholar Lise Vogel points out in a recent study, family leave provides only meager benefits to its recipients, far less than the paid maternity leaves that workers receive in European states (and that the Kennedy commission recommended in 1963).[23]

Another aspect of pregnancy policy, which involved *Muller* directly, emerged in the *UAW v. Johnson Controls* case of 1991. Women employees at a battery manufacturing company and their union, the UAW, challenged the company's fetal protection policy, adopted in 1982, as a violation of the Pregnancy Discrimination Act. Because battery manufacturing involves exposure to lead, which entails health risks to any fetus carried by a pregnant employee, the company barred all women from jobs involving actual or potential lead exposure, except in cases where infertility was medically documented. Was the company's policy a legitimate bona fide occupational qualification, as the employer claimed, or did Title VII, amended by the Pregnancy Discrimination Act, forbid a sex-specific fetal protection policy? The company contended that its policy was "facially neutral" because its purpose was "benign," and a federal appeals court agreed. The workers and the UAW, however, charged that the classification of all women as "capable of bearing children" as a criterion for exclusion was a form of sex discrimination. The Supreme Court concurred that the company policy violated Title VII, and in the majority opinion, citing *Muller,* Justice Harry A. Blackmun rejected it:

Concern for a woman's existing or potential offspring historically has been the excuse for denying women equal employment opportunities. . . . It is no more appropriate for the courts than it is for individual employers to decide whether a woman's reproductive role is more important to herself and her family than her economic role. Congress has left this choice to the woman as hers to make.[24]

With *UAW v. Johnson Controls,* the story of *Muller v. Oregon* seems finally to have ended.

MULLER REVISITED

"Intellectual progress usually occurs through sheer abandonment of questions together with both of the alternatives they assume," John Dewey wrote in 1909. "We do not solve them. We get over them." Neither of the questions that arose in *Muller v. Oregon* proved simple to "get over." The legal revolution of the New Deal finally resolved one fundamental question — whether the state can impose basic labor standards. Critics of the *Muller* case take such standards for granted. Recent politics, however, suggest that government's power to regulate business and industry, like other aspects of the welfare state, remains vulnerable to assault and potentially reversible. The second question that arose in *Muller* — whether the law can treat women as a separate class — spurred another legal revolution in the 1960s, after decades of contention. A major paradox of modern feminism, as Nancy Cott has shown, is the tension between equality and difference, which pervaded the debate among politicized women for much of the twentieth century and shows hardy resilience. One form the tension has taken recently among feminists, for whom such issues are far from settled, is a debate about "equal treatment" or "special treatment" in public policy.[25]

Supporters of strict egalitarianism, or "equal treatment," point to the hazards of recognizing sexual difference in law. Any classification based on difference, they contend, even to remedy disadvantage or provide a benefit, will stigmatize those who are classified as different and increase disadvantage. The history of protective laws serves as an example. Seemingly advantageous measures, like maximum-hours laws in 1908, had consequences that their proponents did not envision; moreover, any recognition of difference, as NWP lawyer Gail Laughlin pointed out in 1921, can be used for whatever purposes "appeal to the caprice or prejudice of our legislators." According to the strict equality argument, any accommodation to sexual difference, even in the instance of unpaid maternity leave, has the potential to be punitive. Benefits linked to sex, in short, or policies that provide special treatment will never be cost-free. Implicit in the "equal treatment" stance is the conviction that equality in law promotes equality in fact.[26]

Feminists willing to consider "special treatment" in public policy argue that equality in law does not necessarily ensure substantive equality, or equality in fact; indeed, strict equality policies can deny difference, disregard inequality, and require women to conform to standards set by men. Equal employment opportunity, for instance, writes Jo Freeman in a recent essay, has usually meant that "women who are like men should be treated equally with men." Strict equality policies, moreover, tend to reward those with a greater share of power and resources and to increase disadvantage for those with less. For instance, gender-neutral policies (such as no-fault divorce) do not necessarily provide equitable results if the resources of the parties are unequal; even the gender-neutral family leave policy, it can be argued, favors those well-off enough to take advantage of it. Legal equality, in short, may be irrelevant if structural equality exists in the family or the labor market. According to the "special treatment" argument, to deny difference and insist on strict equality in all circumstances can increase disadvantage.[27]

The history of protective laws has given women cause to suspect both equal treatment and special treatment, since each has the potential to extract a price. We have not seen the last of this dilemma, since the exact nature of sexual difference, like the precise meaning of equality, is unfixed, uncertain, and likely to be the subject of further contention, in the courts and outside them. Meanwhile, feminist theorists strive to transcend the equal/different dichotomy, to revise standards based solely on men, and to promote legal strategies that improve women's lives. The recent legal death of the "dependent woman" has spurred extensive exploration of women's legal status and opened a new era of creative jurisprudence.[28]

Looking back across the decades at *Muller v. Oregon,* we are tempted to ask: What went wrong? Clearly, the path to modern labor standards was strewn with pitfalls and obstacles. Reformers faced powerful foes, a resistant labor movement, and the formidable doctrine of freedom of contract; these roadblocks narrowed their options and shaped their strategies. Clearly, too, in restrospect, the progressive campaign for protection was both effective and flawed. The "maternalism" of the women's reform network now seems like paternalism; the "entering wedge" rationale embraced contradictions, bound adherents to a defense of "difference," and in the long run backfired. Sociological jurisprudence, finally, had a conservative undertow; determining law by "social facts" runs the risk of embedding in law the remedies and convictions of bygone eras. The lesson of *Muller v. Oregon,* however, is not that sophisticated reformers, accomplished advocates, and Supreme Court justices can make mistakes (though that is true), but that public policies have tangled origins, complex histories, and unforeseen consequences.

NOTES

Introduction

[1] Louis D. Brandeis and Josephine Goldmark, *Women in Industry*, introduction by Leon Stein and Philip Taft (1908; reprint, New York: Arno Press, 1969), 47, 49; *Muller v. Oregon*, 208 U.S. 412 (1908).

[2] Thomas Alpheus Mason, "The Case of the Overworked Laundress," in John A. Garraty, ed., *Quarrels That Have Shaped the Constitution*, 2nd ed. (New York: Harper & Row, 1987), 193. The first edition appeared in 1964.

[3] Joan Hoff, *Law, Gender, and Injustice: A Legal History of U.S. Women* (New York: New York University Press, 1991), 200–1.

Chapter 1

[1] Leslie Woodcock Tentler, *Wage-Earning Women: Industrial Work and Family Life in the United States, 1900–1930* (New York: Oxford University Press, 1979), 14, 27.

[2] For maximum-hours laws affecting men, see Felix Frankfurter, assisted by Josephine Goldmark, *The Case for the Shorter Work Day* (New York: National Consumers' League, 1915), 1–10. Melvin I. Urofsky surveys the campaign for protection in *A March of Liberty* (New York: Knopf, 1988), vol. 2, ch. 24.

[3] Alice Hamilton, "Protection for Women Workers," *Forum* 72 (August 1924):160.

[4] Maud Swett, *Summary of Labor Laws in Force, 1909: Women's Work* (Madison, Wis.: American Association for Labor Legislation, 1909); Elizabeth Faulkner Baker, *Protective Labor Legislation* (New York: Columbia University Press, 1925), 59–71; Elizabeth Brandeis, "Labor Legislation and the Constitution," in John R. Commons, *History of Labor in the United States*, vol. 3 (New York: Macmillan, 1935), 457–70; Claudia Goldin, *Understanding the Gender Gap: An Economic History of American Women* (New York: Oxford University Press, 1990), 189. For analysis of protective laws for women workers, see Alice Kessler-Harris, *Out to Work: A History of Wage-Earning Women in the United States* (New York: Oxford University Press, 1982), ch. 7; and Ulla Wikander, Alice Kessler-Harris, and Jane Lewis, eds., *Protecting Women: Labor Legislation in Europe, the United States, and Australia, 1880–1920* (Urbana: University of Illinois Press, 1995).

[5] Judith A. Baer, *The Chains of Protection: The Judicial Response to Protective Labor Legislation* (Westport, Conn.: Greenwood, 1978), 17; Kessler-Harris, *Out to Work*, 184.

[6] Baker, *Protective Labor Legislation*, 57–59, 71–99, 144. For protective laws in Massachusetts, New York, and California, see Clara M. Beyer, *History of Labor Legislation for Women in Three States*, Bulletin 66, pt. 1, Women's Bureau, U.S. Department of Labor (Washington, D.C.: Government Printing Office, 1929).

[7] For progressive activities and mentality, see Arthur S. Link, *American Epoch* (New York: Knopf, 1955), ch. 4; Robert H. Wiebe, *The Search for Order, 1877–1920* (New York: Hill & Wang, 1967); and Robert M. Crunden, *Ministers of Reform: The Progressives' Achievements in American Civilization, 1889–1920* (New York: Basic Books, 1982).

[8] Theda Skocpol, *Protecting Soldiers and Mothers: The Political Origins of Social Policy in the United States* (Cambridge: Harvard University Press, 1992), 378–79. For "social workers," see Linda Gordon, *Pitied but Not Entitled: Single Mothers and the History of Welfare* (New York: Free Press, 1994), 73.

[9] Skocpol, *Protecting Soldiers and Mothers*, 396–404; Nancy Schrom Dye, *As Equals and Sisters: Feminism, the Labor Movement, and the Women's Trade Union League of New York* (Columbia: University of Missouri Press, 1980), ch. 7.

[10] Maud Nathan, *The Story of an Epoch-Making Movement* (New York: Doubleday, Page, 1926), xiii; Skocpol, *Protecting Soldiers and Mothers*, 368–69. William L. O'Neill provides insightful summaries of the NCL's role in *Feminism in America: A History*, 2nd rev. ed. (New Brunswick: Transaction, 1989), 95–98, 151–53.

[11] Annie Marion MacLean, *Wage-Earning Women* (New York, 1910), 177–78, cited in Susan Lehrer, *Origins of Protective Labor Legislation for Women, 1905–1925* (Albany: State University of New York Press, 1987), 37. For the reformers' crusade against industrial homework, see Eileen Boris, *Home to Work: Motherhood and the Politics of Industrial Homework in the United States* (New York: Cambridge University Press, 1994), ch. 3. For mothers' pensions, see Linda Gordon, *Pitied but Not Entitled*, ch. 3.

[12] Kathryn Kish Sklar, "Hull House in the 1890s: A Community of Women Reformers," *Signs* 10 (Summer 1985): 675; Florence Kelley, *Some Ethical Gains in Legislation* (New York: Macmillan, 1905), 133; Brandeis, "Labor Legislation," 462. Elizabeth Faulkner Baker uses the term "entering wedge" in *Protective Labor Legislation*, 438.

[13] Chris Cook and John Stevenson, *The Longman Handbook of Modern British History, 1714–1980* (London and New York: Longman, 1983), 107–8. For protective policies in England, see John Trevor Ward, *The Factory Movement, 1830–1855* (London: Macmillan, 1962); Derek Fraser, *The Evolution of the British Welfare State* (London: Macmillan, 1973); Pat Thane, *Foundations of the Welfare State* (London and New York: Longman, 1982); Vivien Hart, *Bound by Our Constitution: Women Workers and the Minimum Wage* (Princeton: Princeton University Press, 1994), chs. 2 and 3; and Wikander, Kessler-Harris, and Lewis, *Protecting Women*, ch. 3.

[14] Kathryn Kish Sklar, "The Historical Foundations of Women's Power in the Creation of the American Welfare State, 1830–1930," in Seth Koven and Sonya Michel, eds., *Mothers of a New World: Maternalist Politics and the Origins of Welfare States* (New York: Routledge, 1993), 49; Skocpol, *Protecting Soldiers and Mothers*, 398.

[15] *American Federationist* 21 (July 1914): 544, cited in Lehrer, *Origins*, 152; Harold C. Livesay, *Samuel Gompers and Organized Labor in America* (Boston: Little, Brown, 1978), 132–35; James Weinstein, *The Corporate Ideal in the Liberal State, 1900–1918* (Boston: Beacon Press, 1968), 43–44, 48. For the labor movement's goals in the 1880s and 1890s, see William E. Forbath, *Law and the Shaping of the American Labor Movement* (Cambridge: Harvard University Press, 1991), ch. 2. On AFL attitudes toward women workers, see Kessler-Harris, *Out to Work*, 151–55, 202–5; and "Where Are the Organized Women Workers?" *Feminist Studies* 3 (Fall 1975): 92–105.

[16] Lehrer, *Origins*, ch. 8; Sklar, "Hull House," 676. For the activities of the National Association of Manufacturers, see Robert H. Wiebe, *Businessmen and Reform: A Study of the Progressive Movement* (Cambridge: Harvard University Press, 1962), 25–32 and *passim*.

[17] Melvin I. Urofsky, *A Mind of One Piece: Brandeis and American Reform* (New York: Charles Scribner's Sons, 1971), 24–26; Lehrer, *Origins*, 59. For Brewer's speech, see David J. Brewer, "The Nation's Safeguard," *Proceedings of the New York State Bar Association, Sixteenth Annual Meeting, 1893* (New York: Stumpf & Steurer, 1893), 37–47; and Arnold M. Paul, *Conservative Crisis and the Rule of Law: Attitudes of Bar and Bench, 1887–1895* (Ithaca: Cornell University Press, 1960), 83–84.

[18] Melvin I. Urofsky, "State Courts and Protective Legislation during the Progressive Era: A Reevaluation," *Journal of American History* 72 (June 1985): 65–66; *Ritchie v. People*, 155 Ill. 98 (1895).

[19] *Slaughterhouse Cases*, 16 Wall. 36 (1873); Paul, *Conservative Crisis*, 6–7.

[20] *In re Jacobs*, 98 N.Y. 98 (1885); *Godcharles v. Wigeman*, 113 Pa. St. 431 (1886); *Millet v. People*, 117 Ill. 194 (1886); *Allgeyer v. Louisiana*, 165 U.S. 578 (1897).

[21] Josephine Goldmark, *Fatigue and Efficiency* (New York: Charities Publication Committee, 1912), 244; G. Edward White, *Oliver Wendell Holmes: Law and the Inner Self* (New York: Oxford University Press, 1993), 326.

[22] Urofsky, "State Courts," 67.

[23] Howard Gillman, *The Constitution Besieged: The Rise and Demise of Lochner Era Police Powers Jurisprudence* (Durham: Duke University Press, 1993), 7, 15.

[24] *Commonwealth v. Hamilton Manufacturing Co.*, 120 Mass. 383 (1876).

[25] *Ritchie v. People*, 155 Ill. 98 (1895).

[26] Josephine Goldmark, *Impatient Crusader: Florence Kelley's Life Story* (Urbana: University of Illinois Press, 1953), 144.

[27] *In re Bradwell,* 55 Ill. 535 (1869); *Bradwell v. Illinois,* 83 U.S. (16 Wall.) 130 (1873); Sklar, "Hull House," 658–77, discusses the origins and impact of the 1893 law; Frances E. Olsen, "From False Paternalism to False Equality: Judicial Assaults on Feminist Community, Illinois, 1869–1895," *Michigan Law Review* 84 (June 1986): 1518–41, compares the *Bradwell* and *Ritchie* cases.

[28] The Judiciary Act of 1789, which remained in effect until 1914, permitted appeals to the U.S. Supreme Court only when the state's highest court had upheld the *denial* of a right arising under the U.S. Constitution or federal law.

[29] *Holden v. Hardy,* 169 U.S. 366 (1898); Frankfurter and Goldmark, *Case for the Shorter Workday,* 1–10. The Utah law upheld in *Holden v. Hardy* was a provision in the state constitution; see Owen M. Fiss, *Troubled Beginnings of the Modern State, 1888–1910* (New York: Macmillan, 1993), 172.

[30] *Commonwealth v. Beatty,* 15 Pa. Sup. 5 (1900); Baker, *Protective Labor Legislation,* 61–62.

[31] *State v. Buchanan,* 29 Wash. 602 (1902); *Wenham v. State,* 65 Neb. 394 (1902); *Low v. Rees Printing Co.,* 41 Neb. 127 (1894); Baker, *Protective Labor Legislation,* 62–63; Baer, *Chains of Protection,* 54–55.

[32] *Lochner v. New York,* 198 U.S. 45 (1905).

[33] Sidney G. Tarrow presents the background of the 1896 law in "Lochner versus New York: A Political Analysis," *Labor History* 5 (Fall 1964): 277–312. For conflicting interpretations of *Lochner,* see Gillman, *Constitution Besieged,* 1–18. For an analysis of its significance, see Cass R. Sunstein, "Lochner's Legacy," *Columbia Law Review* 87 (1987): 873–919.

[34] *Landmark Briefs and Arguments of the Supreme Court of the United States,* ed. Philip B. Kurland and Gerhard Casper, vol. 14 (Arlington, Va.: University Publications of America, 1975), 726–30, 674–76, 706–14. Briefs on both sides in *Ritchie v. People* (1895) also presented "social science" data; see Nancy Erickson, "*Muller v. Oregon* Reconsidered: The Origins of a Sex-Based Doctrine of Liberty of Contract," *Labor History* 30 (Spring 1989): 241.

[35] *People v. Williams,* 189 N.Y. 131 (1907).

Chapter 2

[1] Ronald K. L. Collins and Jennifer Friesen, "Looking Back on *Muller v. Oregon,*" *American Bar Association Journal* 69 (March 1983): 294–96.

[2] Ibid., 295–96. One legal distinction between the sexes in Oregon in 1905 and 1906 was that women lacked the vote. Oregon rejected woman suffrage five times by referenda between 1884 and 1910. Finally, in 1912, the state enfranchised women.

[3] Dorothy Rose Blumberg, "'Dear Mr. Engels': Unpublished Letters, 1884–1894, of Florence Kelley to Friedrich Engels," *Labor History* 5 (Spring 1964):109. For Kelley's early career, see Blumberg, *Florence Kelley: The Making of a Social Pioneer* (New York: A. M. Kelley, 1966); Kathryn Kish Sklar, "Hull House in the 1890s: A Community of Women Reformers," *Signs* 10 (Summer 1985): 658–77; and Sklar, *Florence Kelley and the Nation's Work: The Rise of Women's Political Culture, 1830–1900* (New Haven: Yale University Press, 1995).

[4] Florence Kelley, *Some Ethical Gains in Legislation* (New York: Macmillan, 1905), 144, 147; Josephine Goldmark, *Impatient Crusader: Florence Kelley's Life Story* (Urbana: University of Illinois Press, 1953), 57–59; Sklar, *Florence Kelley,* 256–57.

[5] Goldmark, *Impatient Crusader,* 51–53; Maud Nathan, *The Story of an Epoch-Making Movement* (New York: Doubleday, Page, 1926), 59.

[6] Goldmark, *Impatient Crusader,* 57–59; George Martin, *Madame Secretary: Frances Perkins* (Boston: Houghton Mifflin, 1976), 52.

[7] Susan Ware, *Partner and I: Molly Dewson, Feminism, and New Deal Politics* (New Haven: Yale University Press, 1987), 94; "Josephine Goldmark," *Notable American Women* (Cambridge: Harvard University Press, 1971), 2:60–61.

[8] Clement E. Vose, "The National Consumers' League and the Brandeis Brief," *Midwest Journal of Political Science* 1 (November 1957): 268, 270, 272; Theda Skocpol, *Protecting Soldiers and Mothers: The Political Origins of Social Policy in the United States* (Cambridge: Harvard University Press, 1992), 382–96; Kathryn Kish Sklar, "The Historical Foundations of Women's Power in the Creation of the American Welfare State, 1830–1930," in Seth Koven and Sonya Michel, eds., *Mothers of a New World* (New York: Routledge, 1993), 75.

[9] Kelley, *Some Ethical Gains,* 168, 107–9, 126, 142, 112.

[10] Ibid., 128, 163–68, 144, 135.

[11] Ibid., 155.

[12] Goldmark, *Impatient Crusader,* 143, 154; Felix Frankfurter, *Reminiscences* (New York: Reynal, 1960), 95.

[13] Goldmark, *Impatient Crusader,* 143.

[14] Melvin I. Urofsky, *A Mind of One Piece: Brandeis and American Reform* (New York: Charles Scribner's Sons, 1971), 25–42. See also Thomas K. McGraw, *Prophets of Regulation* (Cambridge: Harvard University Press, 1984), 82–87.

[15] Marion E. Doro, "The Brandeis Brief," *Vanderbilt Law Review* 11 (1958): 786; William W. Fisher III, Morton J. Horwitz, Thomas A. Reed, eds., *American Legal Realism* (New York: Oxford University Press, 1993), xii; Frankfurter, *Reminiscences, 95.* Sociological jurisprudence, defined at length by Harvard Law School dean Roscoe Pound, was the Progressive-era antecedent of legal realism, which reached full stride in the 1920s and 1930s, notably at law schools like Columbia and Yale. For the links and distinctions between the two modes of legal thought, see Laura Kalman, *Legal Realism at Yale, 1927–1960* (Chapel Hill: University of North Carolina Press, 1986), ch. 2; Morton J. Horwitz, *The Transformation of American Law, 1870–1960: The Crisis of Legal Orthodoxy* (New York: Oxford University Press, 1992), 169–70; and G. Edward White, "From Sociological Jurisprudence to Realism: Jurisprudence and Social Change in Early Twentieth-Century America," *Virginia Law Review* 58 (September 1972): 999–1028.

[16] Urofsky, *Mind of One Piece,* 34–35; Louis D. Brandeis, "The Opportunity in the Law," *American Law Review* 39 (July–August 1905): 555, 559.

[17] Brandeis, "The Living Law," *Illinois Law Review* 10 (February 1916): 463, 469–70.

[18] Ibid., 467; Doro, "Brandeis Brief," 788; Goldmark, *Impatient Crusader,* 155.

[19] Barbara Allen Babcock et al., *Sex Discrimination and the Law* (Boston: Little, Brown, 1975), 28–29; Deborah L. Rhode, *Justice and Gender* (Cambridge: Harvard University Press, 1989), 40.

[20] Ann Corinne Hill, "Protection of Women Workers and the Courts: A Legal Case History," *Feminist Studies* 5 (Summer 1979): 252; Philippa Strum, *Louis D. Brandeis: Justice for the People* (Cambridge: Harvard University Press, 1984), 119–20.

[21] Goldmark, *Impatient Crusader,* 155.

[22] Louis D. Brandeis and Josephine Goldmark, *Women in Industry,* introduction by Leon Stein and Philip Taft (New York: Arno Press, 1969), 9–10.

[23] Ibid., 18, 24, 35, 51, 55.

[24] Ibid., 57, 58, 59, 77, 82, 103; Clementina Black, "Some Current Objections to Factory Legislation for Women," *The Case for the Factory Acts,* ed. Beatrice Webb (London: Grant Richards, 1901), 209, 211. For Beatrice Webb, her defense of the factory laws, her brand of Fabian socialism, and her role in British women's politics, see Deborah Epstein Nord, *The Apprenticeship of Beatrice Webb* (Amherst: University of Massachusetts Press, 1985), 116–17, 150–52, 272.

[25] Brandeis and Goldmark, *Women in Industry,* 104–12. For contemporary accounts of commercial laundry work, see Josephine Goldmark, *Fatigue and Efficiency: A Study in Industry* (New York: Charities Publication Committee, 1912), 489–99, an updated version of the Brandeis brief section on laundries; Caroline J. Gleason, *Report of the Industrial Welfare Commission in the State of Oregon on the Power Laundries in Portland* (Salem, Ore.: State Printing Department, 1914); and Elizabeth Butler, *Women and the Trades:*

Pittsburgh, 1907–1908 (New York: Charities Publication Committee, 1909), 161–91; see also Patricia E. Malcolmson, *English Laundresses: A Social History, 1850–1930* (Urbana: University of Illinois Press, 1986).

[26] Brandeis and Goldmark, *Women in Industry,* 113.

[27] "Brief for the State of Oregon," *Landmark Briefs and Arguments of the Supreme Court of the United States,* ed. Philip B. Kurland and Gerhard Casper (Arlington, Va.: University Publications of America, 1975), 16:37–61; Nancy S. Erickson, "Historical Background of 'Protective' Labor Legislation: *Muller v. Oregon,*" in D. Kelly Weisberg, ed., *Women and the Law* (Cambridge: Schenkman, 1982), 2:160.

[28] Judith A. Baer, *The Chains of Protection* (Westport, Conn.: Greenwood, 1978), 57–61; Erickson, "Historical Background," 159–60. Critiques of the brief include Babcock et al., *Sex Discrimination,* 29–30; Rhode, *Justice and Gender,* 40–42; Joan Hoff, *Law, Gender, and Injustice* (New York: New York University Press, 1991), 196–203; Susan Lehrer, *Origins of Protective Labor Legislation for Women, 1905–1925* (Albany: State University of New York Press, 1987), 54–56; Lise Vogel, *Mothers on the Job* (New Brunswick: Rutgers University Press, 1993), 16–21. The "hodgepodge" label is from Owen M. Fiss, *Troubled Beginnings of the Modern State, 1888–1910* (New York: Macmillan, 1993), 175.

[29] David P. Bryden, "Brandeis's Facts," *Constitutional Commentary* 1 (Summer 1984): 294–95; Dean Acheson, *Morning and Noon* (Boston: Houghton Mifflin, 1965), 53.

[30] Bryden, "Brandeis's Facts," 292; Baer, *Chains of Protection,* 80.

[31] "Brief for Plaintiff in Error," *Landmark Briefs,* 16:4–35.

[32] Ibid., 9, 17, 19, 22, 23, 27, 34–35.

[33] Leonard Baker, *Brandeis and Frankfurter: A Dual Biography* (New York: Harper & Row, 1984), 5; Bryden, "Brandeis's Facts," 292.

[34] *Muller v. Oregon,* 208 U.S. 412 (1908); Brandeis and Goldmark, *Women in Industry,* 4–5. The unusual reference to the Brandeis brief at the start of the decision is open to interpretation; it may have been a form of praise or, conversely, a "distancing technique" that pushed the brief aside; see Fiss, *Troubled Beginnings,* 176.

[35] Brandeis, "Living Law," 470; Strum, *Brandeis,* 122.

[36] *Loewe v. Lawler,* 208 U.S. 274 (1908); *Adair v. United States,* 208 U.S. 161 (1908); Howard Gillman, *The Constitution Besieged: The Rise and Demise of Lochner Era Police Powers Jurisprudence* (Durham: Duke University Press, 1993), 139.

[37] Felix Frankfurter, "Hours of Labor and Realism in Constitutional Law," *Harvard Law Review* 29 (February 1916): 365; Vogel, *Mothers on the Job,* 22–23.

[38] *New York Times,* February 26, 1908, and *Women's Journal,* March 7, 1908, 38, 40, cited in Erickson, "Historical Background," 167, 169. Erickson's article describes the reception of the *Muller* decision in 1908.

[39] *Woman's Journal,* March 21, 1908, 48, cited in Erickson, "Historical Background," 171–72; Vogel, *Mothers on the Job,* 26.

[40] Baer, *Chains of Protection,* 123; Rhode, *Justice and Gender,* 40; Erickson, "Historical Background," 163; Erickson, "*Muller v. Oregon* Reconsidered: The Origins of a Sex-Based Doctrine of Liberty of Contract," *Labor History* 30 (Spring 1989): 249.

[41] Baer, *Chains of Protection,* 123; Kessler-Harris, *Out to Work,* 181; Vogel, *Mothers on the Job,* 24; Frances E. Olsen, "The Family and the Market: A Study of Ideology and Legal Reform," *Harvard Law Review* 96 (May 1983): 1557; Lehrer, *Origins of Protective Labor Legislation,* 206, 227, 236.

[42] *American Industries* 14 (May 1914): 15, cited in Lehrer, *Origins of Protective Labor Legislation,* 206; Olsen, "Family and Market," 1556; Jennifer Friesen and Ronald K. L. Collins, "Looking Back on *Muller v. Oregon,*" *American Bar Association Journal* 69 (April 1983): 472.

Chapter 3

[1] Josephine Goldmark, *Impatient Crusader: Florence Kelley's Life Story* (Urbana: University of Illinois Press, 1953), 139; Clement E. Vose, "The National Consumers' League and the Brandeis Brief," *Midwest Journal of Political Science* 1 (November 1957): 287.

[2] Goldmark, *Impatient Crusader,* 158–64; Elizabeth Brandeis, "Labor Legislation," in John R. Commons et al., eds., *History of Labor in the United States,* vol. 3 (New York: Macmillan, 1935), 459, 474; *Ritchie v. Wayman,* 244 Ill. 509 (1910).

[3] Philippa Strum, *Louis D. Brandeis: Justice for the People* (Cambridge: Harvard University Press, 1984), 123; Felix Frankfurter, "Hours of Labor and Realism in Constitutional Law," *Harvard Law Review* 29 (February 1916): 356.

[4] Judith A. Baer, *The Chains of Protection* (Westport, Conn.: Greenwood, 1978), 79–85; Louis D. Brandeis and Josephine Goldmark, *The People of the State of New York, Respondent, against Charles Schweinler Press* (New York: National Consumers' League, 1914), 176.

[5] *People v. Charles Schweinler Press,* 214 N.Y. 395 (1915); Josephine Goldmark, *Fatigue and Efficiency: A Study in Industry* (New York: Charities Publication Committee, 1912), 260. Night work laws, Alice Kessler-Harris points out, were a device to facilitate enforcement of maximum-hours laws, which "would be stymied if women worked split shifts or if they took a second job." For the significance of the night work issue, see Kessler-Harris, "The Paradox of Motherhood: Night Work Restrictions in the United States," in Ulla Wikander, Alice Kessler-Harris, and Jane Lewis, eds., *Protecting Women: Labor Legislation in Europe, the United States, and Australia, 1880–1920* (Urbana: University of Illinois Press, 1995), ch. 12.

[6] *Women's Journal* 39 (April 25, 1908): 68, cited in Nancy Erickson, "Historical Background of 'Protective' Labor Legislation: *Muller v. Oregon,*" in D. Kelley Weisberg, ed., *Women and the Law: A Social Historical Perspective,* vol. 2 (Cambridge: Schenkman, 1982), 194; Strum, *Brandeis,* 128.

[7] Goldmark, *Fatigue and Efficiency,* pt. 1, 281; Susan Lehrer, *Origins of Protective Labor Legislation for Women, 1905–1925* (Albany: State University of New York Press, 1987), 34–35; Martha Banta, *Taylored Lives: Narrative Productions in the Age of Taylor, Veblen, and Ford* (Chicago: University of Chicago Press, 1993), 128–29, 143–47.

[8] Goldmark, *Fatigue and Efficiency,* pt. 1, 130, 279, 254–55, 283.

[9] Frankfurter, "Hours of Labor," 367, 370.

[10] Jennifer Friesen and Ronald K. L. Collins, "Looking Back on *Muller v. Oregon,*" *American Bar Association Journal* 69 (April 1983): 473; Felix Frankfurter, *Reminiscences* (New York: Reynal, 1960), 97.

[11] Felix Frankfurter, assisted by Josephine Goldmark, *The Case for the Shorter Work Day* (New York: National Consumers' League, 1916), 360–61, 404, 417–18, 428, 532.

[12] Ibid., iii.

[13] Frankfurter, *Reminiscences,* 103; *Bunting v. Oregon,* 243 U.S. 426 (1917).

[14] Brandeis, "Labor Legislation," 558–59; Elizabeth Brandeis, "Protective Legislation," in Milton Derber and Edwin Young, eds., *Labor and the New Deal* (Madison: University of Wisconsin Press, 1957), 197.

[15] Emily Josephine Hutchinson, *Women's Wages: A Study of the Wages of Industrial Women and Measures Suggested to Increase Them* (New York: Longman Green, 1919), 75; Brandeis, "Labor Legislation," 502–7; Theda Skocpol, *Protecting Soldiers and Mothers: The Political Origins of Social Policy in the United States* (Cambridge: Harvard University Press, 1992), 404–5.

[16] Rev. Edwin V. O'Hara, *Welfare Legislation for Women and Minors* (Portland: Consumers' League of Oregon, 1912); Caroline J. Gleason, *Report of the Social Survey Committee of the Consumers' League of Oregon* (Portland: Consumers' League of Oregon, 1913), 20–21.

[17] Skocpol, *Protecting Soldiers and Mothers,* 407; Friesen and Collins, "Looking Back," 473.

[18] *American Labor Legislation Review* 3 (February 1913): 98; Skocpol, *Protecting Soldiers and Mothers,* 413.

[19] R. G. Brown, "Oregon Minimum Wage Cases," *Minnesota Law Review* 1 (June 1917): 486; Howard Gillman, *The Constitution Besieged: The Rise and Demise of Lochner Era Police Powers Jurisprudence* (Durham: Duke University Press, 1993), 163.

[20] *Stettler v. O'Hara*, 69 Ore. 519 (1914); *Simpson v. O'Hara*, 70 Ore. 261 (1914); Friesen and Collins, "Looking Back," 474.

[21] Felix Frankfurter, assisted by Josephine Goldmark, *Oregon Minimum Wage Cases* (New York: National Consumers' League, 1916), 556, 581, 663, 694.

[22] Frankfurter and Goldmark, *Oregon Minimum Wage Cases*, 99; David P. Bryden, "Brandeis's Facts," *Constitutional Commentary* 1 (Summer 1984): 305–11.

[23] *Stettler v. O'Hara*, 243 U.S. 629 (1917).

[24] Skocpol, *Protecting Soldiers and Mothers*, 415, 417; Bryden, "Brandeis's Facts," 303; Brandeis, "Labor Legislation," 503.

[25] Brandeis, "Labor Legislation," 680; Lise Vogel, *Mothers on the Job* (New Brunswick: Rutgers University Press, 1993), 17; Eileen Boris, *Home to Work: Motherhood and the Politics of Industrial Homework in the United States* (New York: Cambridge University Press, 1994), 158.

[26] Alice Kessler-Harris, *Out to Work: A History of Wage-Earning Women in the United States* (New York: Oxford University Press, 1982), 193–94. For streetcar conductors, see Maureen Weiner Greenwald, *Women, War, and Work: The Impact of World War I on Women Workers in the United States* (Westport, Conn.: Greenwood, 1980), ch. 4.

[27] Nancy F. Cott, *The Grounding of Modern Feminism* (New Haven: Yale University Press, 1987), 124. For the reorganization of the National Woman's Party, see Christine Lunardini, *From Equal Suffrage to Equal Rights: Alice Paul and the National Woman's Party, 1910–1928* (New York: New York University Press, 1986), ch. 9.

[28] Joan G. Zimmerman, "The Jurisprudence of Equality: The Women's Minimum Wage, the First Equal Rights Amendment, and *Adkins v. Children's Hospital*, 1905–1923," *Journal of American History* 78 (June 1991): 203.

[29] Elizabeth Faulkner Baker, *Protective Labor Legislation* (New York: Columbia University Press, 1925), 84–88. For a discussion of the minimum-wage battle and the *Adkins* case, see Vivien Hart, *Bound by Our Constitution: Women, Workers, and the Minimum Wage* (Princeton: Princeton University Press, 1994), ch. 6.

[30] Florence Kelley, "The Right to Differ," *Survey* 49 (December 15, 1922): 375–76; *Adkins v. Children's Hospital*, 284 Fed. Rep. 613 (1922).

[31] James T. Patterson, "Mary W. Dewson and the American Minimum Wage Movement," *Labor History* 5 (Spring 1964): 136–42; Susan Ware, *Partner and I: Molly Dewson, Feminism, and New Deal Politics* (New Haven: Yale University Press, 1987), 97–99.

[32] Felix Frankfurter, with the assistance of Mary W. Dewson, *District of Columbia Minimum Wage Cases, Brief for Appellants*, vol. 2 (New York: Steinberg Press, n.d.), 872, 1023, 1053; Sybil Lipschultz, "Social Feminism and Legal Discourse, 1908–1923," *Yale Journal of Law and Feminism* 2 (Fall 1989): 154.

[33] Zimmerman, "Jurisprudence of Equality," 209, 221.

[34] "Oral Argument of Wade H. Ellis," *Landmark Briefs and Arguments of the Supreme Court of the United States,* ed. Philip B. Kurland and Gerhard Casper, vol. 21 (Arlington, Va.: University Publications of America, 1975), 623, 630, 636–37, 656–57.

[35] *Adkins v. Children's Hospital*, 261 U.S. 525 (1923); Friesen and Collins, "Looking Back," 476; Zimmerman, "Jurisprudence of Equality," 213–14, 221; Bryden, "Brandeis's Facts," 312. For a defense of the *Adkins* decision, see Hadley Arkes, *The Return of George Sutherland: Restoring a Jurisprudence of Natural Rights* (Princeton: Princeton University Press, 1994), 71–82.

[36] Zimmerman, "Jurisprudence of Equality," 222–23.

[37] Ibid., 225; Lipschultz, "Social Feminism," 151.

[38] Baer, *Chains of Protection*, 97; *Radice v. New York*, 264 U.S. 292 (1924).

[39] National Consumers' League, *The Supreme Court and Minimum Wage Legislation,* introduction by Roscoe Pound (New York: New Republic, 1925), 91, 114, 214; T. R. Powell, "The Judiciality of Minimum Wage Legislation," *Harvard Law Review* 37 (1925): 545–73.

[40] Lipschultz, "Social Feminism," 131–33; Zimmerman, "Jurisprudence of Equality," 193, 209, 224–25. For differences between lawyers and reformers, see Hart, *Bound by Our Constitution*, 108–11, 220.

Chapter 4

[1] Nancy F. Cott, *The Grounding of Modern Feminism* (New Haven: Yale University Press, 1987), 128; Susan D. Becker, *The Origin of the Equal Rights Amendment: American Feminism between the Wars* (Westport, Conn.: Greenwood, 1981), 143; William H. Chafe, *The Paradox of Change: American Women in the Twentieth Century* (New York: Oxford University Press, 1991), 55; William L. O'Neill, *Feminism in America: A History* (New Brunswick, N.J.: Transaction, 1989), 281, 285–86.

[2] Clara Mortensen Beyer, "What Is Equality?" *Nation* 116 (January 31, 1923); "Chivalry and the Labor Laws," *Nation* 128 (December 12, 1928): 648, cited in Becker, *Origin of the Equal Rights Amendment,* 142. For a discussion of the 1920s controversy, see Martha Minow, *Making All the Difference: Inclusion, Exclusion, and American Law* (Ithaca: Cornell University Press, 1990), 257–66.

[3] J. Stanley Lemons, *The Woman Citizen: Social Feminism in the 1920s* (Urbana: University of Illinois Press, 1973), 143–44, 146; Chafe, *Paradox of Change,* 91; Elizabeth Brandeis, "Labor Legislation," in John R. Commons et al., eds., *History of Labor in the United States,* vol. 3 (New York: Macmillan, 1935), 518–19.

[4] *The Effect of Labor Legislation on the Employment of Women,* Bulletin No. 65, Women's Bureau, U.S. Department of Labor (Washington, D.C.: Government Printing Office, 1928), 45–46; Alice Kessler-Harris, *Out to Work: A History of Wage-Earning Women* (New York: Oxford University Press, 1982), 210–11; Barbara Allen Babcock et al., *Sex Discrimination and the Law* (Boston: Little, Brown, 1975), 251–52.

[5] Elizabeth Faulkner Baker, "At the Crossroads in the Legal Protection of Women in Industry," *Annals of the American Academy of Political and Social Science* 143 (May 1929): 265–79; Elizabeth Faulkner Baker, *Protective Labor Legislation* (New York: Columbia University Press, 1925), 331, 336, 425–26. Baker (1885–1973), a graduate of the University of California in 1914, received a Ph.D. from Columbia in 1925 and taught economics at Barnard from 1919 to 1952. Her study of protective laws, a doctoral dissertation, remains a valuable source. Recent assessments of the impact of maximum-hours laws include Kessler-Harris, *Out to Work,* ch. 7; Claudia Goldin, *Understanding the Gender Gap* (New York: Oxford University Press, 1990), 195–98; and Elisabeth Landes, "The Effect of Some Maximum-Hours Laws on the Employment of Women in 1920," *Journal of Political Economy* 88 (June 1980), 476–94.

[6] Brandeis, "Labor Legislation," 458–60. For a summary of protective laws affecting women workers through 1928, excluding minimum-wage laws, see Florence P. Smith, *Chronological Development of Labor Legislation for Women in the United States,* Bulletin No. 66, pt. 2, Women's Bureau, U.S. Department of Labor (Washington, D.C.: Government Printing Office, 1929).

[7] Susan Ware, *Beyond Suffrage: Women in the New Deal* (Cambridge: Harvard University Press, 1981), 39, 77.

[8] Elizabeth Brandeis, "Protective Legislation," in Milton Derber and Edwin Young, eds., *Labor and the New Deal* (Madison: University of Wisconsin Press, 1957), 230; Frances Perkins, *The Roosevelt I Knew* (New York: Viking, 1946), 265–66. New Deal policies are discussed in Vivien Hart, *Bound by Our Constitution: Women, Workers, and the Minimum Wage* (Princeton: Princeton University Press, 1994), ch. 8; Eileen Boris, *Home to Work: Motherhood and the Politics of Industrial Homework in the United States* (New York: Cambridge University Press, 1994), chs. 7, 8; Linda Gordon, *Pitied but Not Entitled: Single Mothers and the History of Welfare, 1890–1935* (New York: Free Press, 1994), chs. 7, 8.

[9] Chafe, *Paradox of Change,* 91–92; William E. Leuchtenberg, *The Supreme Court Reborn: The Constitutional Revolution in the Age of Roosevelt* (New York: Oxford University Press, 1995), ch. 5. The president's judicial reorganization bill died in committee and Congress approved a modified measure, the Judicial Reform Act, without the court-packing provision.

[10] *West Coast Hotel Co. v. Parrish,* 300 U.S. 397 (1937); Leuchtenberg, *Supreme Court*

Reborn, ch. 6; Ronnie Steinberg, *Wages and Hours: Labor and Reform in the Twentieth Century* (New Brunswick: Rutgers University Press, 1982), 207.

[11] *United States v. Darby,* 300 U.S. 100 (1941); Alice Kessler-Harris, "Law and a Living: The Gendered Content of 'Free Labor,' " in Noralee Frankel and Nancy S. Dye, eds., *Gender, Class, Race, and Reform in the Progressive Era* (Lexington: University of Kentucky Press, 1991), 105.

[12] Hart, *Bound by Our Constitution,* 167–70; Babcock et al., *Sex Discrimination,* 272.

[13] *Goesaert v. Cleary,* 355 U.S. 464 (1948); Susan M. Hartmann, *The Home Front and Beyond: American Women in the 1940s* (Boston: Twayne, 1982), 131–33.

[14] Cynthia Harrison, *On Account of Sex: The Politics of Women's Issues, 1945–1968* (Berkeley: University of California Press, 1988), 127, 151–54. Murray approved sexual classification if laws protected "maternal and family functions" but argued that the principle of *Muller* had been extended to institutionalize a virtual "separate but equal" doctrine.

[15] Ibid., ch. 6.

[16] Brandeis, "Protective Legislation," 233; Babcock et al., *Sex Discrimination,* 261; Deborah L. Rhode, *Justice and Gender: Sex Discrimination and the Law* (Cambridge: Harvard University Press, 1989), 46; Leo Kanowitz, *Women and the Law* (Albuquerque: University of New Mexico Press, 1969), 154; *Hoyt v. Florida,* 368 U.S. 57 (1961).

[17] Carl M. Brauer, "Women Activists, Southern Conservatives, and the Prohibition of Sex Discrimination in Title VII of the 1964 Civil Rights Act," *Journal of Southern History* 49 (1983), 37–65; Michael Evan Gold, "A Tale of Two Amendments: The Reasons Congress Added Sex to Title VII and Their Implication for the Issue of Comparable Worth," *Duquesne Law Review* 19 (Spring 1981), 453–77; Ann Corinne Hill, "Protection of Women Workers and the Courts: A Legal Case History," *Feminist Studies* 5 (Summer 1979): 261–62.

[18] Babcock et al., *Sex Discrimination,* 262, 263, 266; Alice Cook, "Women and American Trade Unionism," *Annals of the American Academy of Political and Social Science* 375 (January 1968): 127. For the pivotal role of the UAW, see Nancy Gabin, *Feminism in the Labor Movement: Women and the United Auto Workers, 1935–1975* (Ithaca: Cornell University Press, 1990), ch. 5, and "Time Out of Mind: The UAW's Response to Female Labor Laws and Mandatory Overtime in the 1960s," in Ava Baron, ed., *Work Engendered: Toward a New History of American Labor* (Ithaca: Cornell University Press, 1991), 351–74.

[19] *Rosenfeld v. Southern Pacific Company,* 292 F. Supp. 1219 (C.D. Cal. 1968) and 444 F. 2nd 1219 (9th Cir., 1971); *Weeks v. Southern Bell,* 408 F. 2nd 228 (9th Cir., 1969); *Phillips v. Martin Marietta,* 416 F. 2nd 1257 (5th Cir., 1969) and 400 U.S. 452 (1971); Babcock et al., *Sex Discrimination,* 267; Hill, "Protection," 262–63; Judith A. Baer, *The Chains of Protection* (Westport, Conn.: Greenwood, 1978), 164–67; Rosalind Rosenberg, *Divided Lives: American Women in the Twentieth Century* (New York: Hill and Wang, 1992), 213–18.

[20] Babcock et al., *Sex Discrimination,* 267, 270–71; Rosenberg, *Divided Lives,* 215–16; *Reed v. Reed,* 404 U.S. 71 (1971); *Frontiero v. Richardson* 411 U.S. 677 (1973).

[21] *Mendelkoch v. Industrial Welfare Commission,* 442 F. 2nd 1119 (9th Cir., 1971); *Sail'er Inn v. Kirby,* 5 Cal. 3rd 1, 485 P. 2nd 529 (1971).

[22] Lise Vogel, "Debating Difference: Feminism, Pregnancy, and the Workplace," *Feminist Studies* 16 (Spring 1990): 9–32.

[23] *California Federal Savings and Loan v. Guerra,* 479 U.S. 222 (1987); Lise Vogel, *Mothers on the Job: Maternity Policy in the U.S. Workplace* (New Brunswick: Rutgers University Press, 1993), 153–56.

[24] *UAW v. Johnson Controls,* 499 U.S. 197 (1991). Cynthia R. Daniels discusses the *Johnson Controls* case in *At Woman's Expense: State Power and the Politics of Fetal Rights* (Cambridge: Harvard University Press, 1993), ch. 3. See also Mary Becker, "From *Muller v. Oregon* to Fetal Vulnerability Policies," *University of Chicago Law Review* 53 (Fall 1986): 1219–66.

[25] James T. Kloppenberg, *Uncertain Victory: Social Democracy and Progressivism in*

European and American Thought, 1870–1920 (New York: Oxford University Press, 1986), 10; Nancy F. Cott, *Grounding of Modern Feminism,* ch. 1.

[26] For an excellent discussion of the "equal treatment" versus "special treatment" debate, see Vogel, *Mothers on the Job,* ch. 9.

[27] Vogel, *Mothers on the Job,* 130; Jo Freeman, "Women and Public Policy: An Overview," in Ellen Boneparth, ed., *Women, Power, and Policy* (New York: Pergamon, 1982), 63. See also Frances E. Olsen, "From False Paternalism to False Equality," *Michigan Law Review* 84 (June 1986): 1518–41.

[28] See, for instance, Rhode, *Justice and Gender;* Joan Hoff, *Law, Gender, and Justice* (New York: New York University Press, 1991); Katherine T. Bartlett and Roseanne Kennedy, eds., *Feminist Legal Theory: Readings in Law and Gender* (Boulder, Colo.: Westview Press, 1991); Marianne Hirsch and Evelyn Fox Keller, eds., *Conflicts in Feminism* (New York: Routledge, 1990); Patricia Smith, ed., *Feminist Jurisprudence* (New York: Oxford University Press, 1993); Frances E. Olsen, "The Family and the Market: A Study of Ideology and Legal Reform," *Harvard Law Review* 96 (May 1983): 1497–1538; and Elizabeth Kiss, "Alchemy or Fool's Gold? Assessing Feminist Doubts about Rights," *Dissent* 42 (Summer 1995): 342–47.

Florence Kelley in 1899, when she became the general secretary of the National
Consumers' League. Former Hull House resident and Illinois factory inspector,
longtime socialist and tireless campaigner, Kelley steered the NCL to the fore-
front of the battle for protective labor laws. She remained at its helm until her
death in 1932.

Josephine Goldmark of New York began her reform career in 1903 as an aide to Florence Kelley at the National Consumers' League. As head of the NCL's committee on legislation, she led the team of researchers that amassed data for the Brandeis brief and coauthored the brief with her brother-in-law, Louis D. Brandeis.

Admired for his winning strategies and courtroom triumphs, Boston lawyer
Louis D. Brandeis took on cases in the public interest, including *Muller v.
Oregon* and subsequent efforts for the NCL. Above, Brandeis in 1916, when the
Senate confirmed his controversial nomination to the U.S. Supreme Court.

The Lochner bakeshop, a small nonunion operation in Utica, New York, entered history when its owner, Joseph Lochner, challenged the section of a New York law that limited employment in bakeries to ten hours a day and sixty a week. In *Lochner v. New York* (1905), the U.S. Supreme Court declared New York's law unconstitutional. Above, the Lochner bakeshop around 1905.

Portland laundry owner Curt Muller challenged an Oregon law of 1903 that curbed women's hours of work in factories and laundries. After two defeats in state courts, he brought his appeal to the U.S. Supreme Court in *Muller v. Oregon* (1908) and lost again. Above, Muller (with his arms folded) in front of one of his laundries.

The U.S. Supreme Court that unanimously upheld Oregon's ten-hour law in *Muller v. Oregon.* From left to right, Justice Edward D. White, William R. Day, John M. Harlan, Joseph McKenna, Melville W. Fuller (chief justice), Oliver Wendell Holmes Jr., David J. Brewer (writer of the *Muller* opinion), William H. Moody, and Rufus W. Peckham.

Above: Alice Paul, head of the National Woman's Party, toasts the victory of woman suffrage in August 1920. Paul had led the militant wing of the woman suffrage movement since 1916. In the 1920s the NWP campaigned for an equal rights amendment, first proposed to Congress in 1923, which threatened protective laws for women workers. *Left:* Massachusetts suffragist, social worker, and minimum-wage advocate, Mary W. Dewson prepared the lengthy brief that NCL lawyer Felix Frankfurter used to defend the District of Columbia's minimum-wage law for women workers in *Adkins v. Children's Hospital* (1923). This portrait was taken in 1917, two years before Dewson became Florence Kelley's assistant at the NCL.

The Documents

1

Ritchie v. People (1895)

Illinois's maximum-hours law of 1893, the first protective law with teeth, launched the progressive campaign for labor reform. Promoted by Florence Kelley, a coalition of women reformers, and representatives of the labor community, this pioneer statute mandated an eight-hour day for women and teenagers, and banned child labor, in factories. It also provided for a team of factory inspectors to enforce the law and monitor its impact. Hostile to the new statute, Chicago employers joined forces in a manufacturers association to support a challenge in the state courts.

In 1895, the Illinois Supreme Court upset the section of the law concerning women workers. Justice Benjamin Magruder's opinion in Ritchie v. People, *the first decision against a maximum-hours law, was as innovative as the 1893 statute: It set forth the constitutional issues that would dominate court battles over protective laws for the next thirty years. First, Magruder showed that "freedom of contract" and "class legislation" were viable arguments against protective laws. Second, he forged a link between freedom of contract and equal rights for women. The due process clause of the Fourteenth Amendment, he contended, applied to women as well as to men.*

Did Magruder present a convincing argument for sexual equality? Or did he posit a "false" or "fictitious" equality—that is, did he insist on equality in law when it did not exist in fact?

Mr. Justice Magruder delivered the opinion of the Court. . . .

The present prosecution, as is conceded by counsel on both sides, is for an alleged violation of section 5 of said Act [to regulate the manufacture of clothing]. That section is as follows: "No female shall be employed in any factory or workshop more than eight hours in any one day or forty-eight hours in any one week." . . .

Does the provision in question restrict the right to contract? The words, "no female shall be employed," import action on the part of two persons. There must be a person who does the act of employing, and a person who consents to the act of being employed. . . . The prohibition of the statute is, therefore, twofold, first, that no manufacturer, or proprietor

155 Ill. 106 (1895).

of a factory or workshop, shall employ any female therein more than eight hours in one day, and, second, that no female shall consent to be so employed. It thus prohibits employer and employee from uniting their minds, or agreeing, upon any longer service during one day than eight hours. In other words, they are prohibited, the one from contracting to employ, and the other from contracting to be employed, otherwise than as directed. . . .

Is the restriction thus imposed an infringement upon the constitutional rights of the manufacturer and the employee? Section 2 of article 2 of the constitution of Illinois provides, that "no person shall be deprived of life, liberty, or property, without due process of law." . . . The privilege of contracting is both a liberty and property right. . . . Liberty includes the right to acquire property, and that means and includes the right to make and enforce contracts. . . . The right to use, buy, and sell property and contract in respect thereto is protected by the constitution. Labor is property, and the laborer has the same right to sell his labor, and to contract with reference thereto, as has any other property owner. In this country the legislature has no power to prevent persons who are *sui juris*[1] from making their own contracts, nor can it interfere with the freedom of contract between the workman and the employer.

This right to contract, which is thus included in the fundamental rights of liberty and property, cannot be taken away "without due process of law." . . . The legislature has no right to deprive one class of persons of privileges allowed to other persons under like conditions.

We are not unmindful, that the right to contract may be subject to limitations growing out of the duties which the individual owes to society, to the public, or to the government. . . . But the power of the legislature to thus limit the right to contract must rest upon some reasonable basis, and cannot be arbitrarily exercised. . . .

Applying these principles to the consideration of section 5, we are led irresistibly to the conclusion, that it is an unconstitutional and void enactment. . . . If it be construed as applying only to manufacturers of clothing, wearing apparel and articles of a similar nature, we can see no reasonable ground for prohibiting such manufacturers and their employees from contracting for more than eight hours of work in one day, while other manufacturers and their employees are not forbidden to so contract. If the Act be construed as applying to manufacturers of all kinds of products, there is no good reason why the prohibition should be directed against manufacturers and their employees, and not against merchants,

[1] Literally, "of one's own right," that is, persons with full legal rights.

or builders, or contractors, or carriers, or farmers, or persons engaged in other branches of industry, and their employees therein. Women, employed by manufacturers, are forbidden by section 5 to make contracts to labor longer than eight hours in a day, while women employed as saleswomen in stores, or as domestic servants, or as bookkeepers, or stenographers, or typewriters, or in laundries, or other occupations not embraced under the head of manufacturing, are at liberty to contract for as many hours of labor in a day as they choose. The manner, in which the section thus discriminates against one class of employers and employees and in favor of all others, places it in opposition to the constitutional guaranties hereinbefore discussed, and so renders it invalid. . . .

But it is claimed on behalf of defendant in error, that this section can be sustained as an exercise of the police power of the State. The police power of the State is that power which enables it to promote the health, comfort, safety, and welfare of society. It is very broad and far reaching, but is not without its limitations. Legislative acts passed in pursuance of it must not be in conflict with the constitution, and must have some relation to the ends sought to be accomplished; that is to say, to the comfort, welfare or safety of society. Where the ostensible object of an enactment is to secure the public comfort, welfare, or safety, it must appear to be adapted to that end; it cannot invade the rights of person and property under the guise of a mere police regulation, when it is not such in fact. . . .

There is nothing in the title of the Act of 1893 to indicate that it is a sanitary measure. . . .

It is not the nature of the things done, but the sex of the persons doing them, which is made the basis of the claim that the Act is a measure for the promotion of the public health. It is sought to sustain the Act as an exercise of the police power upon the alleged ground, that it is designed to protect woman on account of her sex and physique. It will not be denied, that woman is entitled to the same rights, under the constitution, to make contracts with reference to her labor as are secured thereby to men. The first section of the fourteenth amendment to the constitution of the United States provides: "No State shall make or enforce any law which shall abridge the privileges or immunities of citizens of the United States, nor shall any State deprive *any person* of life, liberty, or property without due process of law, nor deny to any person within its jurisdiction the equal protection of the law." It has been held that a woman is both a "citizen" and a "person" within the meaning of this section. . . .

As a citizen, woman has the right to acquire and possess property of every kind. As a "person," she has the right to claim the benefit of the constitutional provision that she shall not be deprived of life, liberty, or property without due process of law. Involved in these rights thus guaranteed to her is the right to make and enforce contracts. The law accords to her, as to every other citizen, the natural right to gain a livelihood by intelligence, honesty, and industry in the arts, the sciences, the professions, or other vocations. Before the law, her right to a choice of vocations cannot be said to be denied or abridged on account of sex. . . .

The tendency of legislation in this State has been to recognize the rights of woman in the particulars here specified. The Act of 1867, as above quoted, by the use of the words, "he or she," plainly declares that no woman shall be prevented by anything therein contained from working as many hours overtime or extra hours as she may agree; and thereby recognizes her right to contract for more than eight hours of work in one day. An Act approved March 22, 1872, entitled "An Act to secure freedom in the selection of an occupation," etc., provides that "no person shall be precluded or debarred from any occupation, profession or employment (except military) on account of sex." . . . The Married Woman's Act of 1874 authorizes a married woman to sue and be sued without joining her husband, and provides that contracts may be made and liabilities incurred by her and enforced against her to the same extent and in the same manner as if she were unmarried, and that she may receive, use and possess her own earnings, and sue for the same in her own name, free from the interference of her husband, or his creditors. . . .

. . . As a general thing, it is the province of the legislature to determine what regulations are necessary to protect the public health and secure the public safety and welfare. But inasmuch as sex is no bar, under the constitution and the law, to the endowment of woman with the fundamental and inalienable rights of liberty and property which include the right to make her own contracts, the mere fact of sex will not justify the legislature in putting forth the police power of the State for the purpose of limiting her exercise of those rights, unless the courts are able to see, that there is some fair, just, and reasonable connection between such limitation and the public health, safety, or welfare proposed to be secured by it. . . .

Our conclusion is, that section 5 of the Act of 1893, and the first clause of section 10 thereof, are void and unconstitutional for the reasons here stated. . . .

The judgment of the Criminal Court of Cook County is reversed, and the cause is remanded to that Court with directions to dismiss the prosecution. *Reversed and remanded.*

2

Holden v. Hardy (1898)

A Utah law of 1896 prohibited the employment of men in mines, smelters, or ore refineries for more than eight hours a day. Two years later, the U.S. Supreme Court upheld the law by a 7–2 vote. In the majority opinion, Justice Henry B. Brown conceded the right of freedom of contract under the due process clause but asserted that it was "subject to certain limitations which the state may lawfully impose in the exercise of its police powers." In this case, limitation was justified because mining was a hazardous and unhealthful job. Moreover, labor and management did not "stand upon an equality" in bargaining power; therefore, the legislature was justified to "interpose its authority." With this salient statement, the Supreme Court identified a major flaw in the "legal fiction" of freedom of contract.

A triumph for the newborn movement to protect industrial workers, Holden v. Hardy extended the police power to cover shorter workdays for men in dangerous occupations. In the following section of the decision, Justice Brown justifies the use of the police power. Which of his contentions seem useful to reformers as precedents for the future defense of protective laws?

Mr. Justice Brown delivered the opinion of the Court.

... This right of contract, however, is itself subject to certain limitations which the State may lawfully impose in the exercise of its police powers. While this power is inherent in all governments, it has doubtless been greatly expanded in its application during the past century, owing to an enormous increase in the number of occupations which are dangerous, or so far detrimental to the health of employees as to demand special precautions for their well-being and protection, or the safety of adjacent property. While this court has held ... that the police power cannot be put forward as an excuse for oppressive and unjust legislation, it may be lawfully resorted to for the purpose of preserving the public health, safety, or morals, or the abatement of public nuisances, and a large discretion "is necessarily vested in the legislature to determine not only what the

---

169 U.S. 366 (1898).

interests of the public require, but what measures are necessary for the protection of such interests." . . .

While the business of mining coal and manufacturing iron began in Pennsylvania as early as 1716, and in Virginia, North Carolina, and Massachusetts even earlier than this, both mining and manufacturing were carried on in such a limited way and by such primitive methods that no special laws were considered necessary, prior to the adoption of the Constitution, for the protection of the operatives; but, in the vast proportions which these industries have since assumed, it has been found that they can no longer be carried on with due regard to the safety and health of those engaged in them, without special protection against the dangers necessarily incident to these employments. In consequence of this, laws have been enacted in most of the States designed to meet these exigencies and to secure the safety of persons peculiarly exposed to these dangers. Within this general category are ordinances providing for fire escapes for hotels, theaters, factories, and other large buildings, a municipal inspection of boilers, and appliances designed to secure passengers upon railways and steamboats against the dangers necessarily incident to these methods of transportation. In States where manufacturing is carried on to a large extent, provision is made for the protection of dangerous machinery against accidental contact, for the cleanliness and ventilation of working rooms, for the guarding of well holes, stairways, elevator shafts, and for the employment of sanitary appliances. In others, where mining is the principal industry, special provision is made for the shoring up of dangerous walls, for ventilation shafts, bore holes, escapement shafts, means of signaling the surface, for the supply of fresh air and the elimination, as far as possible, of dangerous gases, for safe means of hoisting and lowering cages, for a limitation upon the number of persons permitted to enter a cage, that cages shall be covered, and that there shall be fences and gates around the top of shafts, besides other similar precautions. . . .

But if it be within the power of a legislature to adopt such means for the protection of the lives of its citizens, it is difficult to see why precautions may not also be adopted for the protection of their health and morals. It is as much for the interest of the State that the public health should be preserved as that life should be made secure. . . .

Upon the principles above stated, we think the act in question may be sustained as a valid exercise of the police power of the State. The enactment does not profess to limit the hours of all workmen, but merely those who are employed in underground mines, or in the smelting, reduction, or refining of ores or metals. These employments, when too long pursued, the legislature has judged to be detrimental to the health of the employees, and, so long as there are reasonable grounds for believing that this is so, its decision upon this subject cannot be reviewed by the Federal courts. . . .

The legislature has also recognized the fact, which the experience of legislators in many states has corroborated, that the proprietors of these establishments and their operatives do not stand upon an equality, and that their interests are, to a certain extent, conflicting. The former naturally desire to obtain as much labor as possible from their employees, while the latter are often induced by the fear of discharge to conform to regulations which their judgment, fairly exercised, would pronounce to be detrimental to their health or strength. In other words, the proprietors lay down the rules, and the laborers are practically constrained to obey them. In such cases self-interest is often an unsafe guide, and the legislature may properly interpose its authority. . . .

We are of opinion that the act in question was a valid exercise of the police power of the State, and the judgments of the Supreme Court of Utah are, therefore, *Affirmed.*

Mr. Justice Brewer and Mr. Justice Peckham dissented.

3

Lochner v. New York (1905)

At issue in the Lochner *case was a section of a New York law of 1896, sustained by the state courts, that limited bakers to a ten-hour day and sixty-hour week. Other sections of the law, which were uncontested, provided health regulations for bakeries in areas such as drainage and ventilation. New York's attorney general, Julius M. Mayer, contended that the disputed section of the law was a valid exercise of the police power because long hours were detrimental to bakers' health. In a 5–4 decision, the Supreme Court rejected Mayer's claim. Although freedom of contract could be limited, said the majority opinion by Justice Rufus W. Peckham, there were also limits to the exercise of the police power, which in this instance was unreasonable. The New York law involved "neither the safety, the morals, nor the welfare of the public"; bakers were not "wards of*

198 U.S. 45 (1905).

*the state" or unequal "in intelligence and capacity to men in other trades";
hours limitations on "grown and intelligent men" were "mere meddlesome
interferences with the rights of the individual"; other sections of the law in
question sufficed to protect the health of bakers; and, finally, were bakers'
rights of freedom of contract curtailed, there would be no limit to legislative regulation of all occupations.*

The majority opinion in Lochner v. New York *set the stage for the*
Muller *case by pointing to defects in New York's argument. According to
the majority opinion, the state had not done enough to prove the "reasonableness" of the law. "There must be more than the mere fact of the
possible existence of some small amount of unhealthiness to warrant legislative interference with liberty," Justice Peckham declared. "There must be
some fair ground, reasonable in and of itself, to say that there is a material danger to the public health or the employees, if the hours of labor are
not curtailed." In dissenting opinions, to which reformers would frequently
refer, Justices John Marshall Harlan and Oliver Wendell Holmes attacked
the majority decision. Justice Harlan presented "health" evidence that had
been cited by the New York Court of Appeals to support the reasonableness
of the law. Justice Holmes accused the majority opinion of substituting the
Court's views for that of the legislature and of voicing a theory of laissez-
faire that was not written into the Constitution.*

*If called on to defend the maximum-hours provision of the New York
law in 1905, what arguments would you have presented? If asked to write
a fourth opinion in this case, how would you either amplify or dissent
from the majority opinion?*

Mr. Justice Peckham delivered the opinion of the Court. . . .

The statute necessarily interferes with the right of contract between
the employer and employees, concerning the number of hours in which
the latter may labor in the bakery of the employer. The general right to
make a contract in relation to his business is part of the liberty of the
individual protected by the Fourteenth Amendment of the Federal Constitution. *Allgeyer v. Louisiana.* . . . Under that provision no State can
deprive any person of life, liberty, or property without due process of law.
. . . There are, however, certain powers, existing in the sovereignty of each
State in the Union, somewhat vaguely termed police powers [which]
relate to the safety, health, morals, and general welfare of the public. . . .

It must of course be conceded that there is a limit to the valid exercise
of the police power by the State. . . . In every case that comes before this
court, therefore, where legislation of this character is concerned . . . the

question necessarily arises: Is this a fair, reasonable, and appropriate exercise of the police power of the State, or is it an unreasonable, unnecessary, and arbitrary interference with the right of the individual to his personal liberty or to enter into those contracts in relation to labor which may seem to him appropriate or necessary for the support of himself and his family? . . .

The question whether this act is valid as a labor law, pure and simple, may be dismissed in a few words. There is no reasonable ground for interfering with the liberty of person or the right of free contract, by determining the hours of labor, in the occupation of a baker. There is no contention that bakers as a class are not equal in intelligence and capacity to men in other trades or manual occupations, or that they are not able to assert their rights and care for themselves without the protecting arm of the State. . . . They are in no sense wards of the State. . . . [A] law like the one before us involves neither the safety, the morals, nor the welfare of the public. . . . The law must be upheld, if at all, as a law pertaining to the health of the individual engaged in the occupation of a baker. It does not affect any other portion of the public. . . . Clean and wholesome bread does not depend upon whether the baker works but ten hours per day or only sixty hours a week. The limitation of the hours of labor does not come within the police power on that ground.

. . . The mere assertion that the subject relates though but in a remote degree to the public health does not necessarily render the enactment valid. The act must have a more direct relation, as a means to an end, and the end itself must be appropriate and legitimate. . . .

. . . This case has caused much diversity of opinion in the state courts . . . [T]he Court of Appeals has upheld the act as . . . a health law. One of the judges of the Court of Appeals, in upholding the law, stated that . . . the regulation in question could not be sustained unless they were able to say, from common knowledge, that working in a bakery and candy factory was an unhealthy employment. The judge held that, while the evidence was not uniform, it still led him to the conclusion that the occupation of a baker or confectioner was unhealthy and tended to result in diseases of the respiratory organs. Three of the judges dissented from that view, and they thought the occupation of a baker was not to such an extent unhealthy as to warrant the interference of the legislature with the liberty of the individual.

We think the limit of the police power has been reached and passed in this case. There is, in our judgment, no reasonable foundation for holding this to be necessary or appropriate as a health law to safeguard the public health or the health of the individuals who are following the trade of a baker.

. . . To the common understanding the trade of a baker has never been regarded as an unhealthy one. Very likely physicians would not recommend the exercise of that or of any other trade as a remedy for ill health. . . . There must be more than the mere fact of the possible existence of some small amount of unhealthiness to warrant legislative interference with liberty. It is unfortunately true that labor, even in any department, may possibly carry with it the seeds of unhealthiness. But are we all, on that account, at the mercy of legislative majorities? . . . No trade, no occupation, no mode of earning one's living, could escape this all-pervading power, and the acts of the legislature in limiting the hours of labor in all employments would be valid, although such limitation might seriously cripple the ability of the laborer to support himself and his family. . . .

It is also urged, pursuing the same line of argument, that it is to the interest of the State that its population should be strong and robust, and therefore any legislation which may be said to tend to make people healthy must be valid as health laws, enacted under the police power. If this be a valid argument and a justification for this kind of legislation, it follows that the protection of the Federal Constitution from undue interference with liberty of person and freedom of contract is visionary. . . . Scarcely any law but might find shelter under such assumptions. . . . Not only the hours of employees, but the hours of employers, could be regulated, and doctors, lawyers, scientists, all professional men, as well as athletes and artisans, could be forbidden to fatigue their brains and bodies in prolonged hours of exercise, lest the fighting strength of the State be impaired. We mention these extreme cases because the contention is extreme. . . . [W]e think that such a law as this, although passed in the assumed exercise of the police power, and as relating to the public health, or the health of the employees named, is not within that power, and is invalid. . . . Statutes of the nature of that under review, limiting the hours in which grown and intelligent men may labor to earn their living, are mere meddlesome interferences with the rights of the individual. . . .

Justice Harlan, with whom Justice White and Justice Day concurred, dissenting.

While this court has not attempted to mark the precise boundaries of what is called the police power of the State, the existence of the power has been uniformly recognized, both by the Federal and state courts.

All the cases agree that this power extends at least to the protection of the lives, the health, and the safety of the public against the injurious exercise by any citizen of his own rights. . . .

It is plain that this statute was enacted in order to protect the physical well-being of those who work in bakery and confectionery establishments. It may be that the statute had its origin, in part, in the belief that employers and employees in such establishments were not upon an equal footing, and that the necessities of the latter often compelled them to submit to such exactions as unduly taxed their strength.

Be this as it may, the statute must be taken as expressing the belief of the people of New York that, as a general rule, and in the case of the average man, labor in excess of sixty hours during a week in such establishments may endanger the health of those who thus labor. . . . I submit that this court will transcend its functions if it assumes to annul the statute of New York. It must be remembered that this statute does not apply to all kinds of business. It applies only to work in bakery and confectionery establishments, in which, as all know, the air constantly breathed by workmen is not as pure and healthful as that to be found in some other establishments or out of doors.

Professor Hirt in his treatise on the "Diseases of the Workers" has said: "The labor of the bakers is among the hardest and most laborious imaginable, because it has to be performed under conditions injurious to the health of those engaged in it. It is hard, very hard work, not only because it requires a great deal of physical exertion in an overheated workshop and during unreasonably long hours, but more so because of the erratic demands of the public, compelling the baker to perform the greater part of his work at night, thus depriving him of an opportunity to enjoy the necessary rest and sleep, a fact which is highly injurious to his health." Another writer says: "The constant inhaling of flour dust causes inflammation of the lungs and of the bronchial tubes. The eyes also suffer through this dust, which is responsible for the many cases of running eyes among the bakers. The long hours of toil to which all bakers are subjected produce rheumatism, cramps, and swollen legs. The intense heat in the workshops induces the workers to resort to cooling drinks, which together with their habit of exposing the greater part of their bodies to the change in the atmosphere, is another source of a number of diseases of various organs. Nearly all bakers are pale-faced and of more delicate health than the workers of other crafts, which is chiefly due to their hard work and their irregular and unnatural mode of living, whereby the power of resistance against disease is greatly diminished. The average age of a baker is below that of other workmen; they seldom live over their fiftieth year, most of them dying between the ages of forty and fifty.

During periods of epidemic diseases the bakers are generally the first to succumb to the disease. . . ."

A decision that the New York statute is void under the Fourteenth Amendment will, in my opinion, involve consequences of a far-reaching and mischievous character; for such a decision would seriously cripple the inherent power of the States to care for the lives, health, and well-being of their citizens. Those are matters which can be best controlled by the States. . . .

The judgment in my opinion should be affirmed.

Mr. Justice Holmes dissenting.

. . . This case is decided upon an economic theory which a large part of the country does not entertain. If it were a question whether I agreed with that theory, I should desire to study it further and long before making up my mind. But I do not conceive that to be my duty, because I strongly believe that my agreement or disagreement has nothing to do with the right of a majority to embody their opinions in law. It is settled by various decisions of this court that state constitutions and state laws may regulate life in many ways which we as legislators might think as injudicious or if you like as tyrannical as this, and which equally with this interfere with the liberty to contract. Sunday laws and usury laws are ancient examples. A more modern one is the prohibition of lotteries. The liberty of the citizen to do as he likes so long as he does not interfere with the liberty of others to do the same, which has been a shibboleth for some well-known writers, is interfered with by school laws, by the Post Office, by every state or municipal institution which takes his money for purposes thought desirable, whether he likes it or not. The Fourteenth Amendment does not enact Mr. Herbert Spencer's Social Statics.[1] . . . [A] constitution is not intended to embody a particular economic theory, whether of paternalism and the organic relation of the citizen to the State or of laissez faire. It is made for people of fundamentally differing views, and the accident of our finding certain opinions natural and familiar or novel and even shocking ought not to conclude our judgment upon the question whether statutes embodying them conflict with the Constitution of the United States. . . .

General propositions do not decide concrete cases. The decision will depend on a judgment or intuition more subtle than any articulate major premise. But I think that the proposition just stated, if it is accepted, will carry us far toward the end. Every opinion tends to become a law. I think that the word liberty in the Fourteenth Amendment is perverted when it

[1] English philosopher Herbert Spencer described society as a jungle in which only the strongest and most fit survive. His books, including *Social Statics* (1851), won attention in the United States in the 1870s and 1880s.

is held to prevent the natural outcome of a dominant opinion, unless it can be said that a rational and fair man necessarily would admit that the statute proposed would infringe fundamental principles as they have been understood by the traditions of our people and our law. It does not need research to show that no such sweeping condemnation can be passed on the statute before us. A reasonable man might think it a proper measure on the score of health. . . .

4

"The Right to Leisure"

Florence Kelley, 1905

In Some Ethical Gains in Legislation, *published just as the Supreme Court announced the* Lochner *decision, Florence Kelley posited a "right to leisure" to which all workers were entitled. Why? First, according to Kelley, because they deserved to share in the gains of increased productivity, and second, because all parts of society were interdependent; what injured the workforce damaged not only workers but society at large. The "right to leisure," of course, did not exist. The Constitution mentioned no such right. It was rather a vision, a goal, a demand, and a rubric for the shortened workday. But by adopting the language of "rights," Kelley pursued an important strategy for promoting* new *rights.*

In the following passages, Kelley sets forth some of the dangers of overlong hours of work—which, she contends, blight childhood, stupefy minds, preclude self-improvement, induce premature old age, cause urban congestion, and abet the spread of tuberculosis and vice. Her plea for the shorter workday applies to both men and women, although each group seems affected by different hazards.

In what ways does Kelley's argument differ from or resemble those of the Brandeis *brief (pp. 109–33)? How does a "rights" argument differ from an argument for "protection"?*

The effort to establish the right to leisure was a distinctive movement of the nineteenth century, accompanying the development of machinery. It assumed Protean forms, among others that of Sunday rest, the Saturday

Florence Kelley, *Some Ethical Gains in Legislation* (New York, 1905), 105–11.

half-holiday, Decoration Day, Labor Day, Lincoln's Birthday, Washington's Birthday, St. Patrick's Day, Good Friday, and Easter. The early closing of the stores, wherever accomplished, is one result of this effort. The prohibition of the work of women and minors at night was an important aspect of the movement, and the effort on behalf of child labor legislation is largely directed towards securing fourteen free years for school and wholesome growth before children enter upon the life of steady work. In its most virile form, the effort to establish the right to leisure was known as the ten hours movement, and later as the eight hours movement.

America having produced no great philanthropic leader devoted to securing leisure for the young and defenseless workers, . . . the task of establishing their right went by default to the trade unions, to whom is due the credit for all child labor legislation prior to the year 1889. Now, however, the effort has become national in its scope, enlisting the most diverse advocates. . . .

The struggle for the shorter working day is commonly described as the effort of the laborer to give as little exertion as possible in return for the pay which he receives and many workingmen passively accept this statement of the animus of their movement. It is, however, susceptible of interpretation as the effort of wage-earning people to obtain, in the form of leisure, a part of their share of the universal gain arising from the increased productivity of every occupation, and due to the incessant improvement of machinery. . . .

Assured daily leisure is an essential element of healthy living. Without it childhood is blighted, perverted, deformed; manhood becomes ignoble and unworthy of citizenship in the Republic. Self-help and self-education among the wage-earners are as dependent upon daily leisure as upon daily work. Excessive fatigue precludes the possibility of well-conducted meetings of classes, lodges, cooperative societies, and all other forms of organized effort for self-improvement. . . .

As machinery becomes increasingly automatic, and the work of the machine-tender reduces itself more completely to watching intently the wholly monotonous performance of the one part confided to his care, leisure becomes indispensable for him in order to counteract the deadening effect upon his mind exercised by his daily work. Instead of educating the worker, the breadwinning task of today too often stupefies and deforms the mind; and leisure is required to undo the damage wrought in the working-hours, if the worker is to remain fit for citizenship in the Republic. Without regular, organized leisure, there can be no sustained intelligence in the voting constituency. . . .

Daily assured leisure serves a purpose of the highest social value by enabling the wage-earner to husband that resource of nervous energy which is required to continue active working-life after the passing of youth. In the garment-trades, men are old at forty and women are superannuated at thirty, largely by reason of the alternations of overwork and enforced idleness, and the absence of that regularly recurring sufficient period of rest between the close of one day's work and the beginning of the next, which alone permits body and mind to bear years of continuous work without wearing out. Premature old age is induced by overwork as effectively as by dissipation; and old age in the wage-earning class means dependence, if not pauperism. To assure a regular period of fifteen hours between one day's work and the next for young women and girls engaged in manufacturing and commerce would undoubtedly do as much to prolong their years of self-support and diminish their period of enforced dependence upon others as any measure avowedly in the interest of hygiene and public well-being which could be enacted.

The philanthropic world is all astir on behalf of the crusade against tuberculosis. Funds are readily forthcoming for the foundation of sanatoria for the use of working people, especially for young girls and children. But tuberculosis is promoted by overwork as much as by any other single cause. To shorten the hours of daily labor, to afford daily leisure for rest and recreation to young employees during the years of life in which the susceptibility to infection is greatest, years which coincide with the term of employment of girls and women in largest numbers, is quite as clearly a life saving service as to build and maintain sanatoria. . . .

Vice flourishes wherever self-support for honest working-women is unusually difficult. . . . To establish effective restrictions upon the hours of labor in the needle-trades would equalize the burden borne by these workers, spreading work over more days and weeks, granting more daily leisure, and thus making righteous living easier for tens of thousands of young working people whose traditions are entirely honorable, but who are now subjected to a pressure to which all too many victims succumb.

It may be fairly claimed, then, that the establishment of regular daily leisure contributes to the health, intelligence, morality, lengthened trade life, freer choice of home surroundings, thrift, self-help, and family life of working people. Granted that not all workers make equally valuable use of free time, just as members of the leisure class vary in the uses to which they apply their leisure, it remains true that, without free time, these benefits are impossible. To be deprived of leisure is to be deprived of those things which make life worth living.

5

"The Opportunity in the Law"

Louis D. Brandeis, 1905

While Florence Kelley turned the NCL into a formidable pressure group, Louis D. Brandeis pursued his exceptionally successful law career in Boston. On May 4, 1905, Brandeis addressed the young men of the Harvard Ethical Society on future careers in the law. His remarks provided a précis of the progressive outlook. "We hear much of the 'corporate lawyer' and too little of 'the people's lawyer,'" Brandeis told the students. The lawyer, he urged, should assume "a position of independence between the wealthy and the people" and "stand . . . ready to protect also the interests of the people." At the end of his speech, excerpted here, Brandeis voiced a barrage of progressive ideas: an antagonism to corporate power ("industrial absolutism"), a concern about inequality of wealth, an interest in the "labor question," and a preference for "evolution" over "revolution."

When their paths converged in the Muller *case in 1908, Florence Kelley, formulator of "rights," and Louis D. Brandeis, exemplary professional, had much in common, but their approaches to reform also embodied differences. On the basis of the short selections from their comments in 1905, in what ways were their concerns as reformers similar or dissimilar?*

Here, consequently, is the great opportunity of the bar. The next generation must witness a continuing and ever-increasing contest between those who have and those who have not. The industrial world is in a state of ferment. The ferment is in the main peaceful, and, to a considerable extent, silent; but there is felt today very widely the inconsistency in this condition of political democracy and industrial absolutism. The people are beginning to doubt whether in the long run democracy and absolutism can coexist in the same community; beginning to doubt whether there is a justification for the great inequalities in the distribution of wealth, for the rapid creation of fortunes, more mysterious than the deeds of Aladdin's lamp. The people have begun to think; and they show evidences on all sides of a tendency to act. Those of you who have not

---

Louis D. Brandeis, "The Opportunity in the Law," *American Law Review* 39 (July–August 1905): 562–63.

had an opportunity of talking much with laboring men can hardly form a conception of the amount of thinking that they are doing. With many it is the all-absorbing occupation, the only thing that occupies their minds. Many of these men otherwise uneducated talk about the relation of employer and employee far more intelligently than most of the best educated men in the community. The labor question involves for them the whole of life and they must in the course of a comparatively short time realize the power which lies in them. Many of their leaders are men of signal ability, men who can hold their own in discussion or action with the ablest and best educated men in the community. The labor movement must necessarily progress; the people's thought will take shape in action, and it lies with us, with you to whom in part the future belongs, to say on what lines the action is to be expressed; whether it is to be expressed wisely and temperately, or wildly and intemperately; whether it is to be expressed on lines of evolution or on lines of revolution. Nothing can better fit you for taking part in the solution of these problems, than the study and preeminently the practice of law. Those of you who feel drawn to that profession may rest assured that you will find in it an opportunity for usefulness which is probably unequaled. There is a call upon the legal profession to do a great work for this country.

6

"The Dangers of Long Hours"
From the Brandeis Brief, 1908

A collaborative effort by Louis Brandeis and Josephine Goldmark, the 113-page Brandeis brief was an innovative tactic to persuade the Supreme Court of the "reasonableness" of Oregon's ten-hour law and of the law's "direct relation" to public health, safety, and welfare. By immersing the Court in "the facts of common knowledge," Brandeis intended to educate the justices about industrial conditions; divert them from legal abstractions; and cut through the insulation of precedents on which courts relied — precedents that protected property more than people. The brief illustrates the Brandeis mode of attack: It reveals the extent of a problem,

---

Louis D. Brandeis and Josephine Goldmark, *Women in Industry,* introduction by Leo Stein and Philip Taft (1908; reprint, New York: Arno Press, 1969), 9–10, 18–55.

explains why the law at issue is needed, shows how the law would remedy the problem, and, finally, anticipates and dispels potential objections to the law.

In his terse legal argument, Brandeis shifts the burden of proof to his opponents. The long first section of the brief, "The Dangers of Long Hours" (slightly abridged here), is an argument supported by nonlegal sources: the opinions and observations of experts. The sources, primarily English, range back over the nineteenth century but are concentrated in the years since 1890. Records of British medical commissions and factory commissions and reports from states with bureaus of labor statistics are prominent. The experts cited are primarily doctors and factory inspectors. Occasionally, the voices of workers emerge; more often, experts cite other experts. Parts of the brief discuss the impact of overwork without reference to sex. The crucial sections, however, are those that draw a connection between women's health and society at large: "Specific Evil Effects on Childbirth and Female Functions" (pp. 121–26) and "Bad Effect of Long Hours on General Welfare" (pp. 128–33).

(1) Is the argument of the Brandeis brief convincing? Why or why not? (2) Could Brandeis have used the Muller *case to challenge the* Lochner *decision? If so, what sort of "facts" should he have presented? (3) NCL lawyer Felix Frankfurter in 1916 praised the Brandeis brief for shifting the Supreme Court's focus from individuals to the "community." More recent commentators, however, disagree. The brief, they charge, gives precedence to the welfare of society at large over the welfare of women workers. Who is right? Does the argument of the brief rest mainly on injuries of overwork to women workers or to society? Are the interests of women and society at large in fact identical or distinct?*

ARGUMENT

The legal rules applicable to this case are few and are well established, namely:

First: The right to purchase or to sell labor is a part of the "liberty" protected by the Fourteenth Amendment of the Federal Constitution.

Lochner v. New York, 198 U.S. 45, 53.

Second: This right to "liberty" is, however, subject to such reasonable restraint of action as the State may impose in the exercise of the police power for the protection of health, safety, morals, and the general welfare.

Lochner v. New York, 198 U.S. 45, 53, 67.

Third: The mere assertion that a statute restricting "liberty" relates, though in a remote degree, to the public health, safety, or welfare does not render it valid. The act must have a "real or substantial relation to the protection of the public health and the public safety."

Jacobson v. Mass, 197 U.S. 11, 31.

It must have "a more direct relation, as a means to an end, and the end itself must be appropriate and legitimate."

Lochner v. New York, 198 U.S. 45, 56, 57, 61.

Fourth: Such a law will not be sustained if the Court can see that it has no real or substantial relation to public health, safety, or welfare, or that it is "an unreasonable, unnecessary, and arbitrary interference with the right of the individual to his personal liberty or to enter into those contracts in relation to labor which may seem to him appropriate or necessary for the support of himself and his family."

But "If the end which the Legislature seeks to accomplish be one to which its power extends, and if the means employed to that end, although not the wisest or best, are yet not plainly and palpably unauthorized by law, then the Court cannot interfere. In other words, when the validity of a statute is questioned, the burden of proof, so to speak, is upon those" who assail it.

Lochner v. New York, 198 U.S. 45–68.

Fifth: The validity of the Oregon statute must therefore be sustained unless the Court can find that there is no "fair ground, reasonable in and of itself, to say that there is material danger to the public health (or safety), or to the health (or safety) of the employees (or to the general welfare), if the hours of labor are not curtailed."

Lochner v. New York, 198 U.S. 45, 61.

The Oregon statute was obviously enacted for the purpose of protecting the public health, safety, and welfare. Indeed it declares:

"Section 5. Inasmuch as the female employees in the various establishments are not protected from overwork, an emergency is hereby declared to exist, and this act shall be in full force and effect from and after its approval by the Governor."

The facts of common knowledge of which the Court may take judicial notice —

See *Holden v. Hardy,* 169 U.S. 366.
  Jacobson v. Mass, 197 U.S. 11.
  Lochner v. New York, 198 U.S. 481.

establish, we submit, conclusively, that there is reasonable ground for holding that to permit women in Oregon to work in a "mechanical establishment, or factory, or laundry" more than ten hours in one day is dangerous to the public health, safety, morals, or welfare.

These facts of common knowledge will be considered under the following heads:

Part I. Legislation (foreign and American) restricting the hours of labor for women.

Part II. The world's experience upon which the legislation limiting the hours of labor for women is based. . . .

PART SECOND: THE WORLD'S EXPERIENCE UPON WHICH THE LEGISLATION LIMITING THE HOURS OF LABOR FOR WOMEN IS BASED

I. The Dangers of Long Hours

A. CAUSES

(1) Physical differences between men and women.   The dangers of long hours for women arise from their special physical organization taken in connection with the strain incident to factory and similar work.

Long hours of labor are dangerous for women primarily because of their special physical organization. In structure and function women are differentiated from men. Besides these anatomical and physiological differences, physicians are agreed that women are fundamentally weaker than men in all that makes for endurance: in muscular strength, in nervous energy, in the powers of persistent attention and application. Overwork, therefore, which strains endurance to the utmost, is more disastrous to the health of women than of men, and entails upon them more lasting injury.

Report of Select Committee on Shops Early Closing Bill, BRITISH HOUSE OF COMMONS, 1895.

Dr. Percy Kidd, physician in Brompton and London Hospitals:

The most common effect I have noticed of the long hours is general deterioration of health; very general symptoms which we medically attribute to overaction, and debility of the nervous system; that includes a great deal more than what is called nervous disease, such as indigestion, constipation, a general slackness, and a great many other indefinite symptoms.

Are those symptoms more marked in women than in men?

I think they are much more marked in women. I should say one sees a great many more women of this class than men; but I have seen precisely the same symptoms in men, I should not say in the same proportion, because one has not been able to make anything like a statistical inquiry. There are other symptoms, but I mention those as being the most common. Another symptom especially among women is anemia, bloodlessness or pallor, that I have no doubt is connected with long hours indoors. (Page 215.)

Report of Committee on Early Closing of Shops Bill, BRITISH HOUSE OF LORDS, 1901.

Sir W. MacComac, President of the Royal College of Surgeons:

Would you draw a distinction between the evil resulting to women and the evil resulting to men?

You see men have undoubtedly a greater degree of physical capacity than women have. Men are capable of greater effort in various ways than women. If a like amount of physical toil and effort be imposed upon women, they suffer to a larger degree. (Page 219.)

Report of the Maine Bureau of Industrial and Labor Statistics, 1888.

Let me quote from Dr. Ely Van der Warker (1875):

Woman is badly constructed for the purposes of standing eight or ten hours upon her feet. I do not intend to bring into evidence the peculiar position and nature of the organs contained in the pelvis, but to call attention to the peculiar construction of the knee and the shallowness of the pelvis, and the delicate nature of the foot as part of a sustaining column. The knee joint of woman is a sexual characteristic. Viewed in front and extended, the joint in but a slight degree interrupts the gradual taper of the thigh into the leg. Viewed in a semi-flexed position, the joint forms a smooth ovate spheroid. The reason of this lies in the smallness of the patella in front, and the narrowness of the articular surfaces of the tibia and femur, and which in man form the lateral prominences, and thus is much more perfect as a sustaining column than that of a woman. . . .

Report of the Massachusetts Bureau of Labor Statistics, 1875.

A "lady operator," many years in the business, informed us: "I have had hundreds of lady compositors in my employ, and they all exhibited, in a marked manner, both in the way they performed their work and in its results, the difference in physical ability between themselves and men. They cannot endure the prolonged close attention and confinement which is a great part of typesetting. I have few girls with me more than two or three years at a time; they must have vacations, and they break down in health rapidly. I know no reason why a girl could not set as much type as a man, if she were as strong to endure the demand on mind and body." (Page 96.) . . .

Hygiene of Occupations. BY DR. THEODORE WEYL. JENA, 1894.

The investigations of Schuler and Burkhardt embracing 18,000 members of Swiss insurance against sickness (about 25 percent of the Swiss factory workers and fifteen industries), show that factory work, even in a short period, produces very unfavorable effects upon the development of the body of young men. It is even more conspicuous in the case of women. Thus of 1000 men in the manufacture of embroidery, 302 were sick to 332 women. In bleaching and dyeing, 279 men, 316 women; also in cotton spinning and weaving, the morbidity of women was much greater than of men.

Similarly the number of working days lost through illness was more among women than among men, being 6.47 among women to 6.25 among men. . . .

A second form of physical inferiority of women is their lessened refractoriness to external injurious conditions. All statistics dealing with the relative morbidity of men and women employed in factories justify the deduction that the greater number of days lost from work by women indicate that disease makes greater inroads upon them, and that in general industrial labor is more injurious to women than to men. (Page 86.) . . .

Man and Woman. HAVELOCK ELLIS.

In strength as well as in rapidity and precision of movement women are inferior to men. This is not a conclusion that has ever been contested. It is in harmony with all the practical experience of life. It is perhaps also in harmony with the results of those investigators . . . who have found that, as in the blood of women, so also in their muscles, there is more water than in those of men. To a very great extent it is a certainty, a matter of difference in exercise and environment. It is probably, also, partly a matter of organic constitution. (Page 155.)

The motor superiority of men, and to some extent of males generally, is, it can scarcely be doubted, a deep-lying fact. It is related to what is most fundamental in men and in women, and to their whole psychic organization. (Page 156.)

There appears to be a general agreement that women are more docile and amenable to discipline; that they can do light work equally well; that they are steadier in some respects; but that, on the other hand, they are often absent on account of slight indisposition, and they break down sooner under strain. (Page 183.)

History of Factory Legislation. HUTCHINS AND HARRISON. 1903.

Women are "not only much less free agents than men," but they are physically incapable of bearing a continuance of work for the same length of time as men, and a deterioration of their health is attended with far more injurious consequences to society. (Page 84.) . . .

Hygiene of Occupation in Reference Handbook of the Medical Sciences. GEORGE M. PRICE, M.D., MEDICAL SANITARY INSPECTOR, HEALTH DEPARTMENT OF THE CITY OF NEW YORK. VOL. VI.

In many industries . . . female labor is very largely employed; and the effect of work on them is very detrimental to health. The injurious influences of female labor are due to the following factors: (1) The comparative physical weakness of the female organism; (2) The greater predisposition to harmful and poisonous elements in the trades; (3) The periodical semi-pathological state of health of women; (4) The effect of labor on the reproductive organs; and (5) The effects on the offspring. As the muscular organism of woman is less developed than that of man, it is evident that those industrial occupations which require intense, constant, and prolonged muscular efforts must become highly detrimental to their health. This is shown in the general debility, anemia, chlorosis, and lack of tone in most women who are compelled to work in factories and in shops for long periods. . . .

. . . The female organism, especially when young, offers very little resistance to the inroads of disease and to the various dangerous elements of certain trades. . . .

It has been estimated that out of every one hundred days women are in a semi-pathological state of health for from fourteen to sixteen days. The natural congestion of the pelvic organs during menstruation is augmented and favored by work on sewing machines and other industrial occupations necessitating the constant use of the lower part of the body. Work during these periods tends to induce chronic congestion of the uterus and appendages, and dysmenorrhea and flexion of the uterus are well known affections of working girls. (Page 321.)

(2) The new strain in manufacture.   Such being their physical endowment, women are affected to a far greater degree than men by the growing strain of modern industry. Machinery is increasingly speeded up, the number of machines tended by individual workers grows larger, pro-

cesses become more and more complex as more operations are performed simultaneously. All these changes involve correspondingly greater physical strain upon the worker.

Reports of Medical Commissioners on the Health of Factory Operatives, Parliamentary Papers, 1833, VOL. XXI.

The first and most influential of all disadvantages of factory work is the indispensable, undeviating necessity of forcing both their mental and bodily exertions to keep exact pace with the motions of machinery propelled by unceasing, unvarying power. (Page 72.)

FACTORY AND WORKSHOP ACT COMMISSION, 1875. *British Sessional Papers,* 1876.

We have already referred more than once to the unremitting and monotonous character of all labor at a machine driven by steam. If the day's work of a housemaid or even of a charwoman be closely looked at and compared with that of an ordinary mill hand in a card room or spinning room, it will be seen that the former, though occasionally making greater muscular efforts than are ever exacted from the latter, is yet continually changing both her occupation and her posture, and has very frequent intervals of rest. Work at a machine has inevitably a treadmill character about it; each step may be easy, but it must be performed at the exact moment under pain of consequences. . . .

Report of the Maine Bureau of Industrial and Labor Statistics, 1892.

The constant nervous tension from continued exertion in a modern factory or workshop, for a period of ten hours, is a severe strain upon the physical system. Work is not done in the old, slow way, and, in nearly all industries, by the present methods, from two to four times the quantity of product is turned out in the ten hours. How much faster is the operative compelled to work, and how much greater is the strain, to accomplish this amount of work, in comparison with the old twelve-hour method. (Page 11.)

The Effect of Machinery on Wages. LONDON, 1892.

The power of machinery is from one point of view too great and continuous — machines breathing fire and smoke, those slaves of iron and steel . . . can go on night and day at high pressure. Hence results the tendency of machinery to add enormously to the toil of the laborers by increasing the day's labor both in length and intensity. . . .

Report of the United States Industrial Commission, 1900.

Mrs. Robertson tells me that when she was a girl, to run one or two looms was as much as any woman would have tried. Now, in some instances, there are women running nine looms, and the looms have more than doubled or trebled their speed. This means more work and harder work. (Page 63.)

Report of the United States Industrial Commission, 1901.
It is brought out that in nearly all occupations an increasing strain and intensity of labor is required by modern methods of production. . . . The introduction of machinery and the division of labor have made it possible to increase greatly the speed of the individual workman. . . .

Dangerous Trades. BY THOMAS OLIVER, M.A., M.D., F.R.C.P., MEDICAL EXPERT ON THE WHITE LEAD, DANGEROUS TRADES, POTTERY, AND LUCIFER MATCH COMMITTEES OF THE HOME OFFICE. LONDON, 1902.
The introduction of steam has revolutionized industry. . . . Machinery acts with unerring uniformity. At times so simple is its mechanism that a child can almost guide it, yet how exacting are its demands. While machinery has in some senses lightened the burden of human toil, it has not diminished fatigue in man. All through the hours of work in a factory the hum of the wheels never ceases. . . .

The Working Hours of Female Factory Hands. FROM THE REPORTS OF FACTORY INSPECTORS, COLLATED IN THE IMPERIAL HOME OFFICE. BERLIN, 1905.
From Frankfurt am Oder it is reported that the insurance records for two textile mills show steady deterioration in the health of the women employed eleven hours a day. One reason for this is believed to be the speeding up of the machinery. Vigorous weavers stated repeatedly that the old slow looms exhausted them less in twelve and thirteen hours than the swift new looms in eleven hours. . . .

B. BAD EFFECT OF LONG HOURS ON HEALTH

The fatigue which follows long hours of labor becomes chronic and results in general deterioration of health. Often ignored, since it does not result in immediate disease, this weakness and anemia undermines the whole system; it destroys the nervous energy most necessary for steady work, and effectually predisposes to other illness. The long hours of standing, which are required in many industries, are universally denounced by physicians as the cause of pelvic disorders.

(1) General injuries from long hours

Reports of Medical Commissioners on the Health of Factory Operatives. DAVID BARRY. *British Sessional Papers,* 1833, VOL. XXI.

Evidence of Francis Sharp, at Leeds, member of College of Surgeons in London, student of medical profession for fourteen years, house surgeon of Leeds Infirmary for four years:

"The nervous energy of the body I consider to be weakened by the very long hours, and a foundation laid for many diseases. . . . Were it not for the individuals who join the mills from the country, the factory people would soon be deteriorated." (Pages 12, 13).

"Females whose work obliges them to stand constantly, are more subject to varicose veins of the lower extremities and to a larger and more dangerous extent than ever I have witnessed even in foot-soldiers." (Page 73.)

Massachusetts Legislative Documents. HOUSE, 1866, No. 98.

(Specific) cases are not necessary to show the injurious effect of constant labor at long hours. . . . There may be serious evils from constant and exhausting labor, that do not show themselves in any positive, clearly defined disease: while nevertheless the vital forces of the whole man, physical and mental, are very greatly impaired. (Page 35.)

Dr. Jarvis, physician of Dorchester, says:

"Every man has a certain amount of constitutional force. This is his vital capital which must not be diminished. Out of this comes daily a certain and definite amount of available force, which he may expend in labor of muscle or brain, without drawing on his vital capital. He may and he should work every day and expend so much force and no more, that he shall awake the next morning and every succeeding morning until he shall be threescore and ten, and find in himself the same amount of available force, the same power, and do his ordinary day's work, and again lie down at night with his . . . constitutional force unimpaired."

Judging by this standard, there can be no doubt of the serious injury often resulting from overwork, even when no palpable evidence appears. (Page 36.)

Dr. Ordway, practicing physician many years (in Lawrence), has no hesitation in saying that mill work, long continued, is injurious to bodily and mental health, and materially shortens life, especially of women. (Page 63.)

Reports of Commissioners on the Hours of Labor. Massachusetts Legislative Documents. HOUSE, 1867, No. 44.

Women are held under the present customs and ideas to at least five hours each half day of continuous work, often in the most tedious, minute, and monotonous employ. It is assumed . . . that they have no lower limbs to ache with swollen or ruptured veins, no delicacy of nerve, or versatility of mind, to revolt from such severity of application. (Page 66.)

MASSACHUSETTS BUREAU OF STATISTICS OF LABOR. *Domestic Labor and Woman's Work,* 1872.

In the cotton mills at Fitchburg the women and children are pale, crooked, and sickly looking. The women appear dispirited, and the children without the bloom of childhood in their cheeks, or the elasticity that belongs to that age. Hours, 60 to 67¾ a week. (Page 94.)

Report of the British Chief Inspector of Factories and Workshops, 1873, VOL. XIX.

The house surgeon of a large hospital has stated that every year he had a large number of cases of pulmonary disease in girls, the origin of which he could distinctly trace to long and late hours in overcrowded and unhealthy workrooms. (Page 43.)

FACTORY AND WORKSHOPS ACT COMMISSION, 1875. MISS A. E. TODD. *Great Britain Sessional Papers,* 1876, VOL. XXIX, APPENDIX D.

I would say that factory work is often, but not always, injurious to those engaged in it; country girls especially suffer from the close air and confinement; many of them fall into consumption or bad health of some kind. I have known many deaths from this cause in this class. I have also found much derangement of the liver, stomach, and digestive organs, owing, I think, partially to the rapidity with which they are obliged to eat their meals. (Page 164.)

Report of the Maine Bureau of Industrial and Labor Statistics, 1888.

Many saleswomen are so worn out, when their week's work is ended, that a good part of their Sundays is spent in bed, recuperating for the next week's demands. And one by one girls drop out and die, often from sheer overwork. This I know from observation and personal acquaintance. (Page 142.)

Report of Select Committee on Shops Early Closing Bill, BRITISH HOUSE OF COMMONS, 1895.

Miss MacDonald, M.B., now attached to the Hospital for Women in Euston Road:

Dr. Kidd told us just now that in his experience at Brompton Hospital there was a good deal of general deterioration of health among women?

That is exactly what I should say, anemia and general nervous debility.

And would not standing so long very much affect women, if they were married, afterwards?

It is not good for women to stand . . . at all really.

If it is not good for them to stand at all, still less will it be good for them to stand thirteen hours a day?
I think it is shocking. . . .

Report of British Chief Inspectors of Factories and Workshops, 1901.

Ten and a half hours sitting bent over stitching, requiring very careful attention, with two intervals so short that only a hasty meal can be eaten, that there is no time for exercise, even were the workers permitted to go out, and that, day after day, might well try the strongest constitutions and ruin the best digestions and nerves. That its effect on the health is injurious is constantly brought before one, and anemic and heavy-eyed workers who suffer from neuralgia who form too large a proportion of the whole number, make one feel very strongly that some reform is needed. (Page 176.) . . .

Journal of Royal Sanitary Institute, Vol. XXV. M. G. BONDFIELD. LONDON, 1904.

Sir William MacCormac, giving evidence before the Lords' Committee on The Early Closing of Shops, said, "There is no doubt, I think in my mind, that such long hours must contribute to the incidence of disease; that it must lower the general vitality of persons so engaged, and render them more liable than they otherwise would be to attacks of different forms of disease. . . . It must have an influence on their offspring, undoubtedly. . . .

From the Reports of Factory Inspectors. COLLATED IN THE IMPERIAL HOME OFFICE, BERLIN, 1905. THE WORKING HOURS OF FEMALE FACTORY HANDS.

Report for Bremen: The reduction for the working hours for women will be of great value to the entire working population, and more especially to workingmen's families. It is of great hygienic importance on account of the more delicate physical organization of woman, and will contribute much toward the better care of children and the maintenance of a regular family life. . . .

The inspector for Erfurt reports that when a working girl marries, unless she is very strong she gradually fails in health and is frequently unfitted for giving birth to healthy children or to nurse those who are born. (Page 111.) . . .

From Reports by the District Inspectors (of France) upon the Question of Night Work (PARIS, 1900). BY M. LEGARD, INSPECTEUR DIVISIONNAIRE DE LA 10^e CIRCONSCRIPTION À MARSEILLE.

During an investigation made by the inspector (lady) of work in the dressmaking establishments of the city of Marseilles, several workingwomen complained that after a certain number of evenings of overtime, they did not recover their sleep, dispelled by fatigue. . . .

Everything which affects the hygiene of sleep constitutes a danger, because the equilibrium of the nervous system is jeopardized. (Page 71.) . . .

AGE AND SEX IN OCCUPATIONS. *Twentieth Century Practice of Medicine,* 1895, VOL. III. BY DR. JAMES H. LLOYD.

Woman may suffer in health in various ways that do not affect materially her mortality — neurasthenia, the bane of overworked and underfed women, does not leave a definite trace on the mortality tables.

Again, woman's ill health and drudgery in a factory may affect her progeny in a way that the statistician cannot estimate. (Page 326) . . .

Journal of the American Medical Association, MAY 19, 1906. FATIGUE. BY DR. FREDERICK S. LEE, PROF. PHYSIOLOGY, COLUMBIA UNIVERSITY, N.Y.

There are probably few physiologic functions that are not affected unfavorably by the prolonged and excessive activity of the muscular and the nervous systems. In such a condition the normal action of the tissues may easily give place to pathologic action.

Fatigue undoubtedly diminishes the resistance of the tissues to bacteria, and also predisposes the individual to attacks from diseases other than bacterial. . . . Only the assimilation and detoxication that normally come with rest, and best, rest with sleep, are capable of adequate restoring power.

The Hygiene, Diseases, and Mortality of Occupations. 1892. J. T. AR-LIDGE, M.D., F.R.C.P., LATE MELROY LECTURER AT ROYAL COLLEGE.

Excessive exertion may operate either over a long period and pro-duce its ill results slowly, or be sudden and severe. . . . When such people are seized by some definite lesion, attention is so completely attracted to it that the antecedent overtoil laying the foundation for the malady is apt to be overlooked. (Page 16.) . . .

(2) Specific evil effects on childbirth and female functions. The evil effect of overwork before as well as after marriage upon childbirth is marked and disastrous.

Report of Select Committee on Shops Early Closing Bill. BRITISH HOUSE OF COMMONS, 1895.

Testimony of Dr. W. Chapman Grigg (formerly outpatient physician for the diseases of women at Westminster Hospital, and senior physician to the Queen Charlotte Lying-in Hospital and the Victoria Hospital for Children).

Would you please tell us in a general way your experience as to the effects of these prolonged hours on health?

It has a very grave effect upon the generative organs of women, entailing a great deal of suffering and also injuring a very large body of them permanently, setting up inflammation in the pelvis in connection with those organs. . . .

I have had a great many sad cases come before me of women who were permanent invalids in consequence.

If the matter could be gone into carefully, I think the committee would be perfectly surprised to find what a large number of these women are rendered sterile in consequence of these prolonged hours.

I believe that is one of the greatest evils attached to these prolonged hours. I have seen many cases in families where certain members who have pursued the calling of shop-girl assistants have been sterile, while other members of the family have borne children. I know of one case where four members of a family who were shop-girls were sterile, and two other girls in the family, not shop-girls, have borne children; and I have known other cases in which this has occurred. . . . I have patients come to me from all parts of London. It appears to be a most common condition.

When these women have children, do you find that the children themselves suffer from the woman having been affected by these very long hours?

I have seen many cases where I have attributed the mischief arising in childbed to this inflammatory mischief in the mother, which, after delivery, has set up fresh mischief, and I have seen serious consequences resulting. (Page 219.)

Report to the Local Governing Board on Proposed Changes in Hours and Ages of Employment in Textile Factories. BY J. H. BRIDGES, M.D., AND T. HOLMES. *British Parliamentary Papers.* 1873. VOL. LV.

Experience afforded by residence in the worsted manufacturing town of Bradford, and extensive practice among its population during periods of from one to thirty-five years:

A. Amongst the *women* of factory operatives, much more than among the general population, derangements of the digestive organs are common, e.g., pyrosis, sickness, constipation, vertigo, and headache, generated by neglect of the calls of nature through the early hours of work, the short intervals at meals, the eating and drinking of easily prepared foods, as bread, tea, and coffee, and the neglect of meat and fresh cooked vegetables. Other deranged states of a still worse character are present, e.g., leucorrhea and too frequent and profuse menstruation. Cases also of displacement, flexions, and versions of the uterus, arising from the constant standing and the increased heat of and confinement in the mill. . . . Edema and varicose veins of the legs are common amongst female mill-workers of middle age.

Q. Has the labor any tendency to increase the rate of infant mortality?

A. Yes. The evils occurring in women as detailed in answer to question 2 indirectly affect the more perfect growth of the child in utero, and dispose it when born more easily to become diseased.

Signed on behalf of the Bradford Medico Chirurgical Society, at a meeting held February 4, 1873. . . . (Page 39.)

Report of the British Chief Inspector of Factories and Workshops, 1873. DR. R. H. LEACH, CERTIFYING SURGEON FOR OVER THIRTY YEARS.

Shorten their hours of labor, for I believe that scores of infants are annually lost under the present system. As things now stand, a mother leaves her infant (say of two months old) at 6 A.M., often asleep in bed, at 8 she nurses it, then until 12:30 the child is bottle fed, or stuffed with indigestible food. On her return at noon, overheated and exhausted, her milk is unfit for the child's nourishment, and this state of things is again repeated until 6 P.M.; the consequence is, that the child suffers from spasmodic diarrhea, often complicated with convulsions and ending in death.

Report of Massachusetts Bureau of Labor Statistics, 1875.

It seems to be the back that gives out. Girls cannot work more than eight hours, and keep it up; they know it, and they rarely will, — and even this seems to "pull them down," so that it is extremely rare that a girl continues more than a few years at the business.

Mr. B ——, foreman of a large printing establishment, says: "Girls must sit at the 'case.'[1] I never knew but one woman, and she a strong, vigorous Irishwoman, of unusual height, who could stand at the case like a man. Female compositors, as a rule, are sickly, suffering much from backache, headache, weak limbs, and general 'female weakness.'"

Miss ———, for several years in charge of the female department of one of the largest offices in the country, testified: "One year is as long as one can work in a busy office without a good vacation. The confined position, constipation, heat, and dizzy headache, I think, are the most noticeable troubles of 'lady operators' who are 'grown up.' The hours are too long for such strained employment. From 8 A.M. to 6 P.M., with only an hour for dinner, makes too long a day for the kind of work." (Pages 90–92.)

Miss J ——, a lady compositor, says: "We cannot stand at the 'case.' It increases back and head ache, and weakness of limbs, as

---

[1] The tray or compartment in which metal type was stored.

well as a dragging weight about the hips. I have been at this work five years, but have been frequently obliged to give up for vacations from peculiar troubles and general debility. I began to menstruate when fourteen; I am now twenty-two. I was well until I had set type for a year, when I began to be troubled with difficult periods, and have been more or less ever since. When I go away I get better, but, as often as I return to my work, I am troubled again. Have wholly lost color, and am not nearly as fleshy and heavy as when I began work. I have now a good deal of pain in my chest, and some cough, which increases, if I work harder than usual. I am well acquainted with many other lady compositors who suffer as I do."

Miss S——, a lady long in charge of the "composing room" (female department) of a large printing establishment testifies: "I was myself a compositor, and have had scores of girls under me and with me, many of whom I have known intimately. I have no hesitation in saying that I think I never knew a dozen lady compositors who were 'well.' Their principal troubles are those belonging to the sex, and great pain in back, limbs, and head."

Report of the Massachusetts Bureau of Statistics of Labor, 1884.

We secured the personal history of these 1032 of the whole 20,000 working girls of Boston, a number amply sufficient for the scientific purposes of the investigation. (Page 5.)

Long hours, and being obliged to stand all day, are very generally advanced as the principal reasons for any lack or loss of health occasioned by the work of the girls. . . . There appears, as far as my observation goes, quite a predisposition to pelvic disease among the female factory operatives. . . . The necessity for instrumental delivery has very much increased within a few years, owing to the females working in the mills while they are pregnant and in consequence of deformed pelvis. Other uterine diseases are produced, and, in other cases, aggravated in consequence of the same. (Page 69.)

Report of the California Bureau of Labor Statistics, 1887–1888.

Dr. F. B. Kane of San Francisco says: "Very many times my attention has been drawn professionally to the injury caused by the long hours of standing required of the saleswomen in this city, the one position most calculated to cause the manifold diseases peculiar to their sex, and direfully does Nature punish the disobedience of her laws." . . .

Report of the New Jersey Bureau of Statistics of Labor and Industries, 1902.

The weak, physical condition of the operatives, especially the females, is very noticeable. . . .

The long hours of labor, frequently ten or twelve, and the foul air of the workroom is most marked in its effects upon the female operatives. In addition to throat and lung diseases, which are almost equally prevalent among both sexes, the sufferings of the female operatives from causes peculiar to the sex is very greatly aggravated by the conditions under which they work.

A physician of high standing whose practice is largely among the operatives of these mills is authority for the statement that a large majority of female mill workers are sufferers from some one or more of the organic complaints brought on or intensified by the conditions under which they work. If no such disease existed before entering the mill, it was almost sure to develop soon after beginning work; if it did exist before, it was aggravated to a degree that made them easy victims of consumption [tuberculosis]....

La Réglémentation Légale du Travail des Femmes et des Enfants dans l'Industrie Italienne. Lionel Baudoin.

. . . Women employed in the manufacture of tobacco and of matches are subject to gastric, intestinal troubles, and affections of the respiratory tract, necrosis of the jaw, and are liable to miscarriage. Women employed in sorting rags used in the manufacture of paper are liable to smallpox or carbuncle. Tuberculosis spreads with alarming rapidity, especially among cotton and wool weavers. Those whom tuberculosis spares drag along with anemia, the most common malady of the women factory workers, especially the textile workers, who are subject to long hours of labor....

Infant Mortality: A Social Problem. Geo. Newman, M.D., London, 1906.

Physical fatigue, particularly if accompanied by a strain and stress, are likely to exert a decided effect in the production of premature birth, particularly if these conditions are accompanied by long hours of work and poor or insufficient nourishment. (Page 80.) . . .

The direct injuries to women and girls employed in factories and workshops are: . . . Injury through fatigue and strain, long hours and insufficient periods of rest for food, . . . and . . . Too short a period of rest at the time of childbirth.

Over and over again, in the official reports of factory inspectors or medical officers of health, does one meet with evidences of these injuries. Where the conditions resulting in these evils, coupled with the absence of the mother from home, are present, the infant mortality is high; where they are not present, it is usually low. (Page 131.) . . .

In a general way it may be said that it is the employment of women from girlhood all through married life and through the period of child-bearing, the continual stress and strain of the work and hours, and general conditions prevailing in women's labor, that is exerting its baneful influence on the individual and on the home. (Page 134.)

C. BAD EFFECT OF LONG HOURS ON SAFETY

Accidents to working women occur most frequently at the close of the day, or after a long period of uninterrupted work. The coincidence of casualties and fatigue due to long hours is thus made manifest.

British Parliamentary Debates. THIRD SERIES. 1844. VOL. LXXIII. LORD ASHLEY'S SPEECH.

"Those honorable gentlemen who have been in the habit of perusing the melancholy details of mill accidents should know that a large proportion of those accidents — particularly those which may be denominated the minor class, such as loss of fingers and the like — occur in the last hours of the evening, when the people become so tired that they absolutely get reckless of the danger. I state this on the authority of several practical spinners. Hence arise many serious evils to the working classes, none greater than the early prostration of their strength." (Page 1082.)

Report of the German Imperial Factory Inspectors, 1895.

The ten-hour day, with the exceptions necessary for certain trades, is a measure which can be introduced without great difficulty, and which would prevent many dangers threatening the health of workers. Many accidents are no doubt due to the relaxed vigilance and lessening of bodily strength following excessive hours of work. (Page 369.)

Report of the British Chief Inspector of Factories and Workshops, 1900.

One can only feel surprise that accidents are not more numerous (in laundries), when one realizes that the slightest carelessness or inattention may result in the fingers or hand being drawn between the hot cylinders, and when one considers how easily such inattention may arise in the case of the overtired young workers. (Page 383.)

Report of the British Chief Inspector of Factories and Workshops, 1903.

The comparative immunity from accidents in the laundries in the West Riding of Yorkshire may be possibly due in some measure to the moderate hours of employment.

The incidents of accidents according to time of day is somewhat surprising, the most dangerous hours apparently being 11 A.M. to 12 noon and 4 to 6 P.M. . . . Probably 11 A.M. to 12 noon is more generally than any other time the last tiring hour of a day['s] five hours' spell; 4–6 P.M. covers the time when most generally the transition is from daylight to artificial light. (Page 210.) . . .

D. BAD EFFECT OF LONG HOURS ON MORALS

The effect of overwork on morals is closely related to the injury to health. Laxity of moral fiber follows physical debility. When the working day is so long that no time whatever is left for a minimum of leisure or home life, relief from the strain of work is sought in alcoholic stimulants and other excesses.

Massachusetts Legislative Document. HOUSE, 1866, No. 98.

Overwork is the fruitful source of innumerable evils. Ten and eleven hours daily of hard labor are more than the human system can bear, save in a few exceptional cases. . . . It cripples the body, ruins health, shortens life. It stunts the mind, gives no time for culture, no opportunity for reading, study, or mental improvement. It leaves the system jaded and worn, with no ability to study. . . . It tends to dissipation in various forms. The exhausted system craves stimulants. This opens the door to other indulgences, from which flow not only the degeneracy of individuals, but the degeneracy of the race. (Page 24.)

Relations between Labor and Capital. U.S. SENATE COMMITTEE, 1883. VOL. I. TESTIMONY OF ROBERT HOWARD, MULE SPINNER IN FALL RIVER COTTON MILLS.

I have noticed that the hard, slavish overwork is driving those girls into the saloons, after they leave the mills evenings. . . good, respectable girls, but they come out so tired and so thirsty and so exhausted . . . from working along steadily from hour to hour and breathing the noxious effluvia from the grease and other ingredients used in the mill.

Wherever you go . . . near the abodes of people who are overworked, you will always find the sign of the rum shop.

Drinking is most prevalent among working people where the hours of labor are long, (Page 647.)

The Case for the Factory Acts. EDITED BY MRS. SIDNEY WEBB. LONDON, 1901.

If working long and irregular hours, accepting a bare subsistence wage and enduring insanitary conditions tended to increase women's physical strength and industrial skill — if these conditions of unregulated industry even left unimpaired the woman's natural stock of strength and skill — we might regard factory legislation as irrelevant. But as a matter of fact a whole century of evidence proves exactly the contrary. To leave women's labor unregulated by law means inevitably to leave it exposed to terribly deteriorating influences. The woman's lack of skill and lack of strength is made worse by lack of regulation. And there is still a further deterioration. Anyone who has read the evidence . . . will have been struck by the invariable coincidence of a low standard of regularity, sobriety, and morality, with the conditions to which women, under free competition, are exposed. (Page 209.)

Dangerous Trades. THOMAS OLIVER, M.D. LONDON, 1902.

It is frequently asserted that laundry women as a class are intemperate and rougher than most industrial workers. That they are peculiarly irregular in their habits it is impossible to deny; and the long hours, the discomfort, and exhaustion due to constant standing in wet and heat, discourage the entrance into the trade of a better class of workers is certain. . . . The prevalence of the drink habit among many of them, of which so much is said, is not difficult to account for: the heat of an atmosphere often laden with particles of soda, ammonia, and other chemicals has a remarkably thirst-inducing effect; the work is for the most part exhausting, even apart from the conditions, and the pernicious habit of quenching the thirst, and stimulating an overtired physical condition, with beer. (Page 672.)

Report of the British Chief Inspector of Factories and Workshops, 1902.

The result is disastrous, even from the point of view of this industry itself, which if properly organized would be capable of offering really desirable employment to skilled workers instead of being, as it too often is, the last resort of the idle and intemperate. . . . I would add that too often the very intemperance is created by the conditions of employment, by the excessive overstrain of endurance. (Page 174.)

Report of the British Association for the Advancement of Science: The Economic Effect of Legislation Regulating Women's Labor, 1902.

On the morals of the workers there has been a marked effect [by the Factory Acts]. "Saint Monday"[2] is now a thing of the past, and just as irregularity conduces to drunkenness and irregular living, and the rush of overtime at the end of the week, with nothing to do in the early parts, induced an irregular and careless mode of life, so the comparative steadiness of the present methods have tended to raise the standard of morality and sobriety. (Page 287.)

E. BAD EFFECT OF LONG HOURS ON GENERAL WELFARE

The experience of manufacturing countries has illustrated the evil effect of overwork upon the general welfare. Deterioration of any large portion of the population inevitably lowers the entire community physically, mentally, and morally. When the health of women has been injured by

[2] A worker's absence on Monday for the purpose of relaxation; a prolongation of the Sunday "day off."

long hours, not only is the working efficiency of the community impaired, but the deterioration is handed down to succeeding generations. Infant mortality rises, while the children of married working women, who survive, are injured by inevitable neglect. The overwork of future mothers thus directly attacks the welfare of the nation.

(1) The state's need of protecting woman

Report of the Massachusetts State Board of Health, 1873. EDWARD JARVIS, M.D.

All additions to the physical, moral, or intellectual power of individuals — in any individual — are, to that extent, additions to the energy and the productive force — the effectiveness of the State; and on the contrary, all deductions from these forces, whether of mind or body — every sickness, and injury or disability, every impairment of energy — take so much from the mental force, the safe administration of the body politic. . . .

The State thus has an interest not only in the prosperity, but also in the health and strength and effective power of each one of its members. . . .

Report of the Massachusetts Bureau of Labor Statistics, 1871.

It is claimed that legislation on this subject is an interference between labor and capital. . . . But legislation has interfered with capital and labor both, in the demand for public safety and the public good. Now public safety and public good, the wealth of the commonwealth, centered, as such wealth is, in the well-being of its common people, demands that the State should interfere by special act in favor of . . . working women, and working children, by enacting a ten-hour law, to be enforced by a system of efficient inspection. (Page 567.) . . .

Proceedings of the French Senate. SESSION OF JULY 7, 1891. M. JULES SIMON.

It is impossible for me not to tell the Senate what I think of the position of women in industry, and that I may gain your favor, gentlemen, I ask permission to tell you that for at least forty years I have applied myself to this question. (Page 573.)

When I ask, when we ask, for a lessening of the daily toil of women, it is not only of the women that we think; it is not principally of the women, it is of the whole human race. It is of the father, it is of the child, it is of society, which we wish to reestablish on its foundation, from which we believe it has perhaps swerved a little. (Page 575.)

Report of the New York Bureau of Labor Statistics, 1900.

The family furnishes the really fundamental education of the growing generation — the education of character; and the family life thus really determines the quality of the rising generation as efficient or nonefficient wealth producers. If a reduction in the hours of labor does promote the growth of a purer and better family life, it will unquestionably result in the production of greater material wealth on the part of the generation trained under its influence; nothing else in fact will so effectively diminish the vast number of criminals, paupers, and idlers, who, in the present generation, consume the people's substance. When one or both parents are away from home for twelve or thirteen hours (the necessary period for those who work ten hours) a day, the children receive comparatively little attention. . . .

Hygiene of Occupations. DR. THEODORE WEYL. JENA, 1904.

Women bear the following generation whose health is essentially influenced by that of the mothers, and the State has a vital interest in securing for itself future generations capable of living and maintaining it. (Page 84.) . . .

LEGISLATIVE CONTROL OF WOMEN'S WORK. BY S. P. BRECKINRIDGE. *Journal of Political Economy.* VOL. XIV. 1906.

The assumption of control over the conditions under which industrial women are employed is one of the most significant features of recent legislative policy. In many of the advanced industrial communities the State not only undertakes to prescribe a minimum of decency, safety, and healthfulness, below which its wage earners may not be asked to go, but takes cognizance in several ways of sex differences and sex relationships. . . . In the third place, the State sometimes takes cognizance of the peculiarly close relationship which exists between the health of its women citizens and the physical vigor of future generations. . . . It has been declared a matter of public concern that no group of its women workers should be allowed to unfit themselves by excessive hours of work, by standing, or other physical strain, for the burden of motherhood which each of them should be able to assume. (Page 107.)

The object of such control is the protection of the physical well-being of the community by setting a limit to the exploitation of the improvident, unworkmanlike, unorganized women who are yet the mothers, actual or prospective, of the coming generation. (Pages 108, 109.)

Physical and Medical Aspects of Labor and Industry. BY J. L. HOFFMAN. *Annals of American Academy of Political and Social Science.* VOL. XXVII. MAY 1906.

Again, in longevity, an increase of vitality, a decrease in disease liability, are all economic elements of the greatest possible economic importance. They lie at the root of the true labor problem, for they determine in the long run the real and enduring progress, prosperity, and well-being of the masses. . . .

. . . The interests of the nation, of wage earners as a class, and of society as a whole, transcend the narrow and selfish interests of short-sighted employers of labor, who, disregarding the teachings of medical and other sciences, manage industry and permit the existence of conditions contrary to a sound industrial economy and a rational humanitarianism.

Labor Laws for Women in Germany. DR. ALICE SALOMON. PUBLISHED BY THE WOMEN'S INDUSTRIAL COUNCIL. LONDON, 1907.

A study of the laws relating to female labor reveals that it has been the special aim of the legislators to protect and preserve the health of the women in their character as wives and as the mothers of future generations. On the one hand, the regulations are intended to prevent injury to health through overlong hours, or the resumption of work too soon after confinement [childbirth], often the cause of serious illness which may render the patient incapable of bearing healthy offspring. . . . But if work in the factory be a necessity for women — even for married ones — it is all the more desirable that protective legislation should be so extended and worked out in such detail as to ensure the fullest attainment of its object, viz.: protection for the health of the female working population, as well as for the family and the home. (Page 5.)

Report of the Maine Bureau of Labor Statistics, 1892.

Employers should realize that long hours at a severe tension are a cause of irritation among their employees, and they become ripe for almost any trouble, and trifles are often sufficient to precipitate violent strikes. The real cause of many of these strikes is overwork. (Page 11.)

(2) The effect of women's overwork on future generations

Report of the Massachusetts Bureau of Labor Statistics, 1871.

14. Progressive physical deterioration produced by family labor in factories. It is well known that like begets like, and if the parents are feeble in constitution, the children must also inevitably be feeble. Hence, among that class of people, you find many puny, sickly, partly developed children; every generation growing more and more so.

15. Connection between continuous factory labor and premature old age. It is a fact, patent to everyone, that premature old age is fully developed, in consequence of long hours of labor and close confinement. Very few live to be old that work in a factory. (Page 504.)

Proceedings of the French Senate, JULY 9, 1891. *Arguments for a Ten-Hour Day for Women.*

The woman wage earner, gentlemen, does not always live at the mill gates; she is therefore obliged to make a half or three-quarters' hour journey before she arrives; consequently she will leave home at half-past five in the morning, only to return at half-past eight or nine o'clock in the evening. Is that living? Under such circumstances can a woman truly care for her children and her home? (Page 581.)

Report of the Maryland Bureau of Industrial Statistics, 1896.

Once inside the walls of the factory a weary day's work of ten hours' duration is begun, with an intermission for lunch at noon. . . .

When the day's work is at last over, the wearied crowd trooping from their place of employment hasten in all directions to their homes, which in many instances are in the extreme suburbs of the city. Once home, they swallow a hasty supper and soon retire to a needed and deserved rest, with no pleasant anticipations for the morrow.

What lives are these for future wives and mothers? Future generations will answer. (Page 52.)

Report of the United States Industrial Commission, 1901.

Factory life brings incidentally new and depressing effects, which those whose experience has been wholly agricultural do not appreciate. But the experience of States which have pushed their way from agricultural to manufacturing industries, and have found that their delay in protecting their factory employees has weakened the physical and moral strength of the new generation of working people, would seem to be an experience which the citizens of new manufacturing States should hope to avoid. (Page 788.) . . .

The Case for the Factory Acts. EDITED BY MRS. SIDNEY WEBB.

It may be enough for the individual employer if his workpeople remain alive during the period for which he hires them. But for the continued efficiency of the nation's industry, it is indispensable that its citizens should not merely continue to exist for a few months or years, but should be well brought up as children, and maintained for their full normal life unimpaired in health, strength, and character.

. . . Industries yielding only a bare minimum of momentary subsistence are therefore not really self-supporting. In deteriorating the physique, intelligence, and character of their operatives, they are drawing on the capital stock of the nation. And even if the using up is not actually so rapid as to prevent the "sweated" workers from producing a new generation to replace them, the trade is none the less parasitic. In persistently deteriorating the stock it employs, it is subtly draining away the vital energy of the community. It is taking from these workers, week by week, more than its wages can restore to them. A whole community might conceivably thus become parasitic on itself, or, rather, upon its future. (Page 20.) . . .

Infant Mortality. A Social Problem. GEORGE NEWMAN, M.D. LONDON, 1906.

A nation grows out of its children, and if its children die in infancy, it means that the sources of a nation's population are being sapped, and further that the conditions that kill such a large proportion of infants injure many of those which survive. Last year, 1905, there was a loss to the nation of 120,000 dead infants, in England and Wales alone, a figure which is almost exactly one quarter of all the deaths in England and Wales in that year. (Page 2.)

And this enormous sacrifice of human life is being repeated year by year and is not growing less. (Page 7.)

Nor is England alone. . . . The birth rate is declining in civilized nations with few exceptions; and the same may be said of the death rate. But the infant mortality rate, as a rule, is stationary or even increasing.

There are two features, however, which appear to be common to the high infant mortality districts, namely, a high density of population and a considerable degree of manufacturing industry. (Page 26.)

7

"Women Are Both Persons and Citizens"
The Brief for Curt Muller, 1907

The brief for Curt Muller, submitted by his lawyers, William D. Fenton and Henry H. Gilfry, at the end of 1907, argued that the Oregon ten-hour law of 1903 impeded freedom of contract, that it was illegitimate class legislation rather than a reasonable health and welfare measure, and that it denied women their constitutional rights. "[W]omen's rights are as sacred under the Fourteenth Amendment as are men's," the brief declared. "The classification is based wholly upon her sex . . . and without regard to any question of morals or danger to the public health." To make the case for Muller, his lawyers offered rhetorical questions, comparisons, and analogies, all of

Landmark Briefs and Arguments of the Supreme Court of the United States, ed. Philip B. Kurland and Gerhard Casper, vol. 16 (Arlington, Va.: University Publications of America, 1975), 8, 13–32.

which suggested that the statute was arbitrary, unreasonable, and unconstitutional. In conclusion, they declared the Oregon law an ominous precedent because the state might curtail women's opportunities in limitless ways.

A traditional brief, the brief for Muller was an argument bolstered by precedents—the opinions of judges in previous cases. Muller's lawyers cited supportive decisions, such as Ritchie *and* Lochner, *to make their case, as well as unsupportive decisions, such as* Wenham v. State, *in order to dispute them. They also cited two conservative legal authorities: Thomas M. Cooley, whose* Treatise on Constitutional Limitations *(1868) advised against meddling with the economic system, and Christopher G. Tiedeman, whose* Treatise on the Limitations of the Police Power *(1886) recommended extreme limitations. William Fenton had never attended law school. A graduate of Christian College in Monmouth, Oregon, he read law for a year in Salem, Oregon, and was admitted to the state bar in 1875. Active in the Democratic Party, Fenton served as a member of the Oregon House of Representatives in 1876, ran for Congress in 1882, and was a Democratic presidential elector in 1884. He remained the general counsel to the Southern Pacific Railroad in Oregon until 1917.*

In what ways does the brief for Muller anticipate contemporary arguments against sex discrimination? In what ways are any of its contentions now invalid?

CONTENTIONS OF PLAINTIFF IN ERROR

The plaintiff in error contends that the statute pursuant to which the information was filed is unconstitutional, and that a violation thereof does not constitute a crime, for the following reasons, to wit:

(1) Because the statute attempts to prevent persons, *sui juris,*[1] from making their own contracts, and thus violates the provisions of the Fourteenth Amendment, as follows:

"No state shall make or enforce any law which shall abridge the privileges or immunities of citizens of the United States; nor shall any state deprive any person of life, liberty, or property without due process of law, nor deny to any person within its jurisdiction the equal protection of the laws."

(2) Because the statute does not apply equally to all persons similarly situated, and is class legislation.

(3) The statute is not a valid exercise of the police power. The kinds

---

[1] In their own right.

of work proscribed are not unlawful, nor are they declared to be immoral or dangerous to the public health; nor can such a law be sustained on the ground that it is designed to protect women on account of their sex. There is no necessary or reasonable connection between the limitation prescribed by the Act and the public health, safety, or welfare. . . .

ARGUMENT

. . . The limitation is that no female shall be employed more than ten hours during any one day, although the hours of work may be so arranged as to permit the employment at any time during the twenty-four hours of any one day. The limitation applies to *all women,* without regard to age or marriage. It may be well to note that in the State of Oregon women have been completely emancipated from the disabilities of the common law. . . .

Women, whether married or single, who are of adult age, have all the rights enjoyed by men, other than the right to vote or hold office, and in the States of Colorado, Idaho, and Wyoming there is no difference.

It is not denied that women are both persons and citizens within the meaning of the Federal and State Constitutions. In *Minor v. Happersett,*[2] . . . Chief Justice Waite said:

There is no doubt that women may be citizens. They are persons and by the Fourteenth Amendment "all persons born or naturalized in the United States and subject to the jurisdiction thereof" are expressly declared to be "citizens of the United States and of the state wherein they reside." . . .

In *Ritchie v. People,* . . . Mr. Justice Magruder said:

It will not be denied that woman is entitled to the same rights, under the Constitution, to make contracts with reference to her labor as are secured thereby to men. . . .

In *State v. Buchanan,* . . . where the Supreme Court of Washington sustains a similar statute as a legitimate exercise of the police power of the state, the Court quotes with approval the language used by Cooley in his *Constitutional Limitations,* 7th Ed., page 889, as follows:

[2] Virginia Minor, a member of the National Woman Suffrage Association, attempted to register and vote in 1872. She claimed that the Fourteenth Amendment conferred suffrage on women as a privilege of citizenship. The Supreme Court in 1875 conceded that Minor was a citizen but denied her claim to the vote.

The general rule undoubtedly is, that any person is at liberty to pursue any lawful calling, and to do so in his own way, not encroaching upon the rights of others. This general right cannot be taken away. . . . But here, as elsewhere, it is proper to recognize distinctions that exist in the nature of things, and under some circumstances to inhibit employments to some one class while leaving them open to others. Some employments, for example, may be admissible for males and improper for females, and regulations recognizing the impropriety and forbidding women engaging in them would be open to no reasonable objection.

The exception here noted, however, has relation to the employment of females in vocations that may be said to be immoral or that might have relation to the public morals, or possibly employments that might be considered peculiarly dangerous or hazardous, and known to be such, and service therein may be forbidden on the ground of conservation of the public health or public morals.

The employment of women may be forbidden entirely. This, however, is a very different thing from regulation of such employment in a perfectly moral and healthful vocation. Under the statute under review, the employment of women is expressly recognized as proper, and the business in which they are to be employed is not hazardous, dangerous, or immoral. The right to employ women is assumed, but in so far as the law restricts the hours of service it must be sustained if at all upon the ground that employment of women for a greater length of time than ten hours in any one day endangers the public health. There is no question of morals or general welfare involved. It is not a labor statute as such, and is not promulgated or sought to be sustained upon any economic theory of wages. It is purely and simply a limitation of the hours of service of an adult woman, whether married or single, in a healthful employment, and in a business not condemned as immoral or dangerous. It is not within the police power of the state to deprive her of the right to dispose of her labor in such an employment at pleasure, and for such length of time and under such conditions as she may desire. Upon what theory can the state become her guardian and interfere with her freedom of contract and the right of her employer to contract with her freely and voluntarily, as if she were a man? This is the question for decision. It is to be observed also, that this law forbids a woman, whether married or single, from doing what would be perfectly lawful and proper for her brother or husband to contract to do in the same service. The classification is based wholly upon her sex, and without regard to her safety or the safety of those with whom she is working, and without regard to any question of morals or danger to the public health.

To put the case concretely; suppose the plaintiff in error at a given time should employ a man and woman in his laundry, and each to work eleven hours during each twenty-four hours. In the one case the employment would subject him to prosecution for violation of this statute. In the other his contract of hiring would be valid, and he would not be liable to prosecution. These two persons have equal rights before the law in every respect, excepting that the one may not be able to exercise the elective franchise, or hold office. In all other respects they are equal before the law. Upon what ground can the classification be justified? Why may not the employer freely and properly contract for the same services for the same length of time in the same employment, without regard to the sex of the employee? It is true that the statute applies to all women, and therefore the Supreme Court of the State of Oregon held that it was not class legislation. But if the statute had forbidden employment for more than ten hours, of all persons of white color, the statute would have had application to all of that class, and yet no one would contend that the classification was reasonable or one that could be sustained. The statute might have forbidden employment for more than ten hours of all persons forty years of age, and yet the classification would have been arbitrary, unreasonable, and invalid, and yet it would apply to all persons of the forbidden class. And so, in the exercise of the police power the statute must have some sort of relation to subjects properly within the police power of the state. . . .

It will be noticed that this statute does not limit the restriction to married women, but the limitation applies to all women. It is not conceded that if the statute had limited the restriction to the employment of married women that it would have been valid, for in principle there is no reason why a married woman completely emancipated under local law so that she has all of her civil rights and who may contract and be contracted with as a *feme sole*,[3] should not have the right to contract freely for her services in a healthful and moral employment. Nor is there any reason in principle or in the nature of her relation as a member of the household why the legislature should exercise a sort of paternalism over her in respect to the hours of service she may perform in a given employment, which it would not exercise in respect to a contract of service made by her husband. Why should women employed in a laundry be placed under

[3] The *feme sole,* or single woman, had common-law rights that the *feme covert,* or married woman, lacked, such as the right to contract. During the nineteenth century, the states extended the rights of wives through married women's property acts.

disability to contract freely with reference to their employment, when women in all other useful vocations may contract freely as to the hours of service? If this is a valid exercise of the police power of the state, why may not the legislature in its discretion limit the hours of service of stenographers employed in offices? Why may not the protecting arm of the legislature deny women in all other useful employments the right to contract for continuous services beyond a period of ten hours daily, and if the legislature may make the act of employment of an adult woman in a healthful business unlawful if she is employed more than ten hours, why may not the same legislative authority forbid her employment for a longer term than six hours on any given day? What magic is there in the limitation of precisely ten hours, and no more? What relation has this limit to her if it does not apply with like force and effect to her adult brother, who works at the same desk, either as bookkeeper or at the mangle, or at the irons? Is there only the difference of sex, and upon what basis does the legislative authority declare that under the police power of the state the woman cannot do the same work for the same length of time that her adult brother can and may properly do?

It is respectfully submitted that the classification is unreasonable, arbitrary, and a denial of her constitutional right and of the right of her employer to contract with her with the same freedom and obligation as he may with her brother, in the same kind of employment.

In *Re Jacobs,* . . . Mr. Justice Earl, speaking for the Court, said:

> Generally it is for the legislature to determine what laws and regulations are needed to protect the public health and secure the public comfort and safety, and while its measures are calculated, intended, convenient, and appropriate to accomplish these ends, the exercise of its discretion is not subject to review by the Courts. But they must have some relation to these ends. Under the mere guise of police regulations, personal rights and private property cannot be arbitrarily invaded and the determination of the legislature is not final or conclusive. . . .

In *Wenham v. State,* . . . where the Court sustains a similar statute to that under consideration, the Court says:

> It may be well contended that plaintiff's business is property, and that the ability of the women who may be employed by him to labor, is also property. It is the means by which they earn their living, and perhaps contribute to the help of indigent ones who may be dependent upon them in whole or in part, for support. It would seem at first

blush as though a law having the effect to interfere with the business of the one, or shorten the hours of labor of the other, would be repugnant to these constitutional provisions.

Notwithstanding this concession, which seems to be well founded in principle, the Court holds that all property is held subject to rules regulating the common good and the general welfare of the people, and that therefore it was within the police power of the state to limit the hours of service of women.

This reasoning would lead to ultimate state socialism. It is in this case also stated that:

> Women and children have always, to a certain extent, been wards of the state. Women in recent years have been partly emancipated from their common-law disabilities. They may own property, real and personal, in their own right, and may engage in business on their own account. But they have no voice in the enactment of the laws by which they are governed, and can take no part in municipal affairs. They are unable, by reason of their physical limitations, to endure the same hours of exhaustive labor as may be endured by adult males. Certain kinds of work which may be performed by men without injury to their health, would wreck the constitutions and destroy the health of women, and render them incapable of bearing their share of the burdens of the family and the home. The state must be accorded the right to guard and protect women, as a class, against such a condition; and the law in question, to that extent, conserves the public health and welfare.

This reasoning assumes the very question in dispute. The woman employed by the plaintiff in error in the case at bar may have been a widow, and had the care of a family of dependent children; she may have been and no doubt was perfectly willing to contract with plantiff in error for the services forbidden. The statute proposes to and does interfere with this right. Her property right is sacrificed for the public good under the pretense of the police power exercised in an attempt to conserve the public health and welfare. In such situation the Court must see from the law itself that the restriction which deprives her of her property and of her liberty is one that is exercised and imposed to preserve the public health. In what way does the restriction in her case tend to preserve the public health? Suppose that the woman employed was an adult, single woman, and that the work in the laundry was peculiarly suitable to her sex. Can the Court say that her contract to work ten and a half hours in that service tends to impair the public health, and that in the distant and remote future the possible children which she may bear will need the protection of this statute? Can it be assumed that the employment would be any more injurious to her or to any woman in good health than to a man of equal age?

In *Comm v. Beatty, . . .* the Court says:

> The whole argument in this case is based on the injury done to the adult females, whose right to labor as long as they please is alleged to be violated. . . . Adult females are a class as distinct as minors, separated by natural conditions from all other laborers, and are so constituted as to be unable to endure physical exertion and exposure to the extent and degree that is not harmful to adult males; and employments which under favorable conditions are not injurious, are rightly limited as to time by this statute, so as not to become harmful by prolonged engagements.

How can the Court say that employment in a laundry requires such physical exertion and exposure that would be harmful to females working longer than ten hours, when such employment would not be harmful to adult males? What conditions of employment exist in a laundry that endanger a healthy woman that do not apply alike to a healthy man?

The case last cited sustains the local statute, but it is respectfully submitted that the conclusions are based upon the assumption that injury to the health of females by reason of longer employment than ten hours was inherent in the *very act of service,* without regard to the *dangers or hazards* of such service.

In I Tiedeman, *State and Federal Control of Persons and Property,* pages 335, 337, the author says:

> Minors are the wards of the Nation, and even the control of them by their parents is subject to the unlimited supervisory control of the State. The position of women is different. While women, married and single, have always been under restrictions as to the kinds of employment in which they might engage, and are still generally denied any voice in the government of the country, single women have always had an unrestricted liberty of contract, and the contractual power of married women was taken away from them on the ground of public policy, in order to unify the material interests as well as the personal relations of husband and wife. With the gradual breaking down of these restrictions upon the right of married women to contract, there seems to be no escape from the conclusion that the constitutional guaranty of the liberty of contract applies to women, married or single, as well as to men. . . .

We freely concede the principle declared by Mr. Justice Brown, speaking for the Court, in *Holden v. Hardy,* . . . where he says:

> This right of contract, however, is itself subject to certain limitations which the state may lawfully impose in the exercise of its police powers. While this power is inherent in all governments, it has doubtless been greatly expanded in its application during the past century, owing to an enormous increase in the number of occupations which are dangerous, or so far detrimental to the health of employees as to demand special precautions for their well being and protection, or to the safety of adjacent property.

This principle was illustrated and sustained in that case, but it will be observed that the limitation of eight hours applied to workmen in a dangerous and unhealthy employment. . . .

But conceding that it is now settled in accordance with the rule laid down in *Holden v. Hardy,* . . . that where the employment is peculiarly dangerous to the health of the employees, and many citizens are thereby endangered, the legislature may, under the police power of the state, limit the hours of service, it does not follow that the hours of service of all employees in all employments, may be limited. If any limitation is sought to be imposed, it must rest upon the inherent dangers of the particular service, independent of the nationality, race, or sex of the employees. The employment must be such as to justify supervision, regulation, and police control. The employees of adult age, whether men or women, in the same service, are alike entitled to equal protection and freedom of contract. It is difficult to imagine any employment that may be dangerous to women employees that would not be equally dangerous to men. The health of men is no less entitled to protection than that of women. For reasons of chivalry, we may regret that all women may not be sheltered in happy homes, free from the exacting demands upon them in pursuit of a living, but their right to pursue any honorable vocation, any business not forbidden as immoral, or contrary to public policy, is just as sacred and just as inviolate as the same right enjoyed by men. In many vocations women far excel, in proficiency, ability, and efficiency, the most proficient men. Some callings are peculiarly adapted to the temperament, training, and skill of women. What would be thought of a law which attempted to forbid women working as nurses, beyond ten hours of any day in the hospitals of the country, or in the homes of the people, and at the same time imposed no restrictions upon the hours of service of men employed in the same service? Why limit the hours of service of women employees in the great mercantile establishments of the country, and assume that this may be done, to protect the public health, or that of the employee, when a like statute would be held beyond the police powers of the state if made applicable to men, standing behind the same counter, or keeping books at the same desk? Why is the power of the state effective to drive all women from the thousands of offices of the country, after ten hours' continuous service, and the state, under the same police power, is powerless to send any man from the same employment, whether he works ten or fifteen hours? The women may earn the same wages, their services may be equally effective, and as much desired, and they may demand the right of private contract and may deserve this right, equally with their male associates, but the barrier of sex forbids their employment and makes the contract of hiring, as to the one a crime, as to the other an obligation protected as property under a constitution which guarantees to both equal protection. It is, as it seems to us, a fundamental error to assume that difference in sex justifies the distinction.

The argument based on sex ought not to prevail, because women's rights are as sacred under the Fourteenth Amendment as are men's. The Supreme Court of Illinois in *Ritchie v. People, supra,* in speaking of this point, at page 111 et seq., very forcefully says:

> It is not the nature of the things done, but the sex of the persons doing them, which is made the basis of the claim that the act is a measure for the promotion of the public health. . . .

Is there any difference between the case of a healthy, adult woman, contracting for service for more than ten hours in a laundry, and that of a man employed as a baker for more than ten hours a day? Certainly conditions are as favorable in a laundry as in a bakery. The character of labor is not such in the case of a laundry to justify the assumption that it is more dangerous than that of the work of a baker.

The statute, then, to be sustained, must rest upon the theory that the health of the employee is endangered by permitting her to work longer than ten hours in any particular service where the employment is not in and of itself dangerous to health, life, or limb, or obnoxious to public morals. If the legislature may limit and restrict the hours of service of a healthy, adult female in a laundry, or may do so in any other healthy employment, and if such restriction is valid, it must be because the employee, on account of sex, is necessarily under the protection and guardianship of a paternal government, anticipating that an extra hour of service may endanger the lives and health of possible children or the life and health of the possible mother. It proceeds upon the theory that the statute is an exercise of the police power for the preservation of the health of the women citizens who may be compelled to labor for a livelihood. . . .

The facts before the court in *Lochner v. New York*, . . . and the conclusion to which the Court there arrived, justify the contention that a statute which attempts to restrict the hours of service of all women, without relation to the dangers of the employment or the character of the service, is invalid. In that case a statute of the State of New York provided that no employees should be required or permitted to work in bakeries more than sixty hours in a week, or ten hours a day, and this statute was held to be invalid and not within the police power of the state, although it was there claimed and apparently conceded that the labor of the baker was not only laborious, but performed under conditions peculiarly injurious to his health. It is true that in that case it appeared that the employees were all men, but it is not perceived that a difference in sex would or could have made any difference in the decision. . . .

The three leading cases sustaining this character of legislation are: *Commonwealth v. Hamilton Mnfg. Co.*, . . . *State v. Buchanan*, . . . *Wenham v. State*. . . . And the leading case holding a contrary view is *Ritchie v. People*. . . .

It is respectfully submitted that the reasoning of the Supreme Court of Illinois is conclusive unless the Court is prepared to proceed upon the theory that women are the wards of the state; that by reason of sex they are inherently disqualified to follow any useful labor without the protecting guardianship of a paternal government. The case, therefore, is one of great importance. . . .

It is respectfully submitted that there is no necessary difference between the two employees on account of sex that would justify the classification or the discrimination. As said by the Court in the *Lochner* case,

It might be safely affirmed that almost all occupations more or less affect the health. There must be more than the mere fact of the possible existence of some small amount of unhealthiness to warrant legislative interference with liberty. It is unfortunately true that labor, even in any department, may possibly carry with it the seeds of unhealthiness. But are we all, on that account, at the mercy of legislative majorities? . . . No trade, no occupation, no mode of earning one's living, could escape this all-prevading power, and the acts of the legislature in limiting the hours of labor in all employments would be valid, although such limitation might seriously cripple the ability of the laborer to support himself and his family.

The question involved is far-reaching. If such legislation may be sustained and justified merely because the employee is a woman, and if such employment in a healthy vocation may be limited and restricted in her case, there is no limit beyond which the legislative power may not go. Women, in increasing numbers, are compelled to earn their living. They enter the various lines of employment hampered and handicapped by centuries of tutelage and the limitation and restriction of freedom of contract. Social customs narrow the field of her endeavor. Shall her hands be further tied by statute ostensibly framed in her interests, but intended perhaps to limit and restrict her employment, and whether intended so or not, enlarging the field and opportunity of her competitor among men? The extortions and demands of employers, if any such exist, should not be made the cover under which to destroy the freedom of individual contract and the right of individual action. It is respectfully submitted that the judgment of the Supreme Court of Oregon should be reversed.

Wm. D. Fenton,
Henry H. Gilfry,
Attorneys for Plaintiff in Error

8

Muller v. Oregon (1908)

Justice David J. Brewer's opinion in the landmark Muller *case accepted the premise of the Brandeis brief that the overwork of women injured public welfare, but it also went beyond that premise. First, Brewer conceded that the Court would accept "opinion" from nonjudicial sources, thus opening the door to "sociological jurisprudence." Second, following the argument of the Brandeis brief, he confirmed rather than repudiated the* Lochner *decision. Third, he contended that Oregon's maximum-hours law for women was a reasonable form of class legislation because women were different from men.*

To support the last contention, Brewer put forth a doctrine of female "exceptionalism," or immutable sexual difference. Here, in a crucial part of the opinion, he expounded social theory. Woman, said Brewer, was inherently and permanently dependent on man; she had innate psycholog-

ical differences from men that prevented her from asserting her rights; and "some legislation to protect her seems necessary to secure a real equality of right." Because woman was in a "class by herself," Brewer argued, laws "designed for her protection may be sustained," although similar laws for men could not.
Did Brewer indulge in "judicial overkill"? Was his portrait of the "dependent woman" a "legal fiction"? Does his opinion depend on the Brandeis brief or could he have issued the gist of the decision without the Brandeis brief? In what ways does Brewer's argument differ from recent arguments for affirmative action or comparable worth?

Mr. Justice Brewer delivered the opinion of the Court.

On February 19, 1903, the legislature of the State of Oregon passed an act (Session Laws, 1903, p. 148) the first section of which is in these words:

"Sec. 1. That no female (shall) be employed in any mechanical establishment, or factory, or laundry in this State more than ten hours during any one day. The hours of work may be so arranged as to permit the employment of females at any time so that they shall not work more than ten hours during the twenty-four hours of any one day."

Section 3 made a violation of the provisions of the prior sections a misdemeanor, subject to a fine of not less than $10 nor more than $25. On September 18, 1905, an information was filed in the Circuit Court of the State for the county of Multnomah, charging that the defendant "on the 4th day of September, A.D. 1905, in the county of Multnomah and State of Oregon, then and there being the owner of a laundry, known as the Grand Laundry, in the city of Portland, and the employer of females therein, did then and there unlawfully permit and suffer one Joe Haselbock, he, the said Joe Haselbock, then and there being an overseer, superintendent, and agent of said Curt Muller, in the said Grand Laundry, to require a female, to wit, one Mrs. E. Gotcher, to work more than ten hours in said Laundry on said 4th day of September, A.D. 1905, contrary to the statutes in such cases made and provided, and against the peace and dignity of the State of Oregon."

A trial resulted in a verdict against the defendant, who was sentenced to pay a fine of $10. The Supreme Court of the State affirmed the conviction . . . , whereupon the case was brought here on writ of error.

The single question is the constitutionality of the statute under which the defendant was convicted so far as it affects the work of a female in a laundry. That it does not conflict with any provisions of the State constitution is settled by the decision of the Supreme Court of the State. The contentions of the defendant, now plaintiff in error, are thus stated in his brief:

"(1) Because the statute attempts to prevent persons, *sui juris,*[1] from making their own contracts, and thus violates the provisions of the Fourteenth Amendment, as follows:

"'No State shall make or enforce any law which shall abridge the privileges or immunities of citizens of the United States; nor shall any State deprive any person of life, liberty, or property, without due process of law; nor deny to any person within its jurisdiction the equal protection of the laws.'

"(2) Because the statute does not apply equally to all persons similarly situated, and is class legislation.

"(3) The statute is not a valid exercise of the police power. The kinds of work proscribed are not unlawful, nor are they declared to be immoral or dangerous to the public health; nor can such a law be sustained on the ground that it is designed to protect women on account of their sex. There is no necessary or reasonable connection between the limitation prescribed by the act and the public health, safety, or welfare."

It is the law of Oregon that women, whether married or single, have equal contractual and personal rights with men. As said by Chief Justice Wolverton, in *First National Bank v. Leonard,* . . . after a review of the various statutes of the State upon the subject:

"We may therefore say with perfect confidence that, with these three sections upon the statute book, the wife can deal, not only with her separate property, acquired from whatever source, in the same manner as her husband can with property belonging to him, but that she may make contracts and incur liabilities, and the same may be enforced against her, the same as if she were a *feme sole.*[2] There is now no residuum of civil disability resting upon her which is not recognized as existing against the husband. The current runs steadily and strongly in the direction of the emancipation of the wife, and the policy, as disclosed by all recent legislation upon the subject in this State, is to place her upon the same footing as if she were a *feme sole,* not only with respect to her separate property, but as it affects her right to make binding contracts; and the most natural corollary to the situation is that the remedies for the enforcement of liabilities incurred are made co-extensive and co-equal with such enlarged conditions."

It thus appears that, putting to one side the elective franchise, in the matter of personal and contractual rights they stand on the same plane

[1] In their own right.
[2] Single woman.

as the other sex. Their rights in these respects can no more be infringed than the equal rights of their brothers. We held in *Lochner v. New York, . . .* that a law providing that no laborer shall be required or permitted to work in bakeries more than sixty hours in a week or ten hours in a day was not as to men a legitimate exercise of the police power of the State, but an unreasonable, unnecessary, and arbitrary interference with the right and liberty of the individual to contract in relation to his labor, and as such was in conflict with, and void under, the Federal Constitution. That decision is invoked by plaintiff in error as decisive of the question before us. But this assumes that the difference between the sexes does not justify a different rule respecting a restriction of the hours of labor.

In patent cases counsel are apt to open the argument with a discussion of the state of the art. It may not be amiss, in the present case, before examining the constitutional question, to notice the course of legislation as well as expressions of opinion from other than judicial sources. In the brief filed by Mr. Louis D. Brandeis, for the defendant in error, is a very copious collection of all these matters, an epitome of which is found in the margin.[3]

[3] The following legislation of the States impose restriction in some form or another upon the hours of labor that may be required of women: Massachusetts, 1874, Rev. Laws 1902, chap. 106, sec. 24; Rhode Island, 1885, Acts and Resolves 1902, chap. 994, p. 73; Louisiana, 1886, Rev. Laws 1904, vol. i, sec. 4, p. 989; Connecticut, 1887, Gen. Stat. revision 1902, sec. 4691; Maine, 1887, Rev. Stat. 1903, chap. 40, sec. 48; New Hampshire, 1887, Laws 1907, chap. 94, p. 95; Maryland, 1888, Pub. Gen. Laws 1903, art. 100, sec. 1; Virginia, 1890, Code 1904, tit. 51 a, chap. 178 a, sec. 3657b; Pennsylvania, 1897, Laws 1905, No. 226, p. 352; New York, 1899, Laws 1907, chap. 507, sec. 77, subdiv. 3, p. 1078; Nebraska, 1899, Comp. Stat. 1905, sec. 7955, p. 1986; Washington, Stat. 1901, chap. 68, sec. 1, p. 118; Colorado, Acts 1903, chap. 138, sec. 3, p. 310; New Jersey, 1892, Gen. Stat. 1895, p. 2350, secs. 66 and 67; Oklahoma, 1890, Rev. Stat. 1903, chap. 25, art. 58, sec. 729; North Dakota, 1877, Rev. Code 1905, sec. 9440; South Dakota, 1877, Rev. Code (Penal Code, sec. 764), p. 1185; Wisconsin, 1867, Code 1898, sec. 1728; South Carolina, Acts 1907, No. 233.

In foreign legislation Mr. Brandeis calls attention to these statutes: Great Britain, 1844, Law 1901, 1 Edw. VII, chap. 22; France, 1848, Act Nov. 2, 1892, and March 30, 1900; Switzerland, Canton of Glarus, 1848, Federal Law 1877, art. 2, sec. 1; Austria,1855, Acts 1897, art. 96 a, secs. 1 to 3; Holland, 1889, art. 5, sec. 1; Italy, June 19, 1902, art. 7; Germany, Laws 1891.

Then follow extracts from over ninety reports of committees, bureaus of statistics, commissioners of hygiene, inspectors of factories, both in this country and in Europe, to the effect that long hours of labor are dangerous for women, primarily because of their special physical organization. The matter is discussed in these reports in different aspects, but all agree as to the danger. It would of course take too much space to give these reports in detail. Following them are extracts from similar reports discussing the general benefits of short hours from an economic aspect of the question. In many of these reports individual instances are given tending to support the general conclusion. Perhaps the general scope and character of all these reports may be summed up in what an inspector for Hanover says: "The reasons for the reduction of the working day to ten hours — (a) the physical organization of woman, (b) her maternal functions, (c) the rearing and education of the children, (d) the maintenance of the home — are all so important and so far-reaching that the need for such reduction need hardly be discussed." [Justice Brewer's note]

While there have been but few decisions bearing directly upon the question, the following sustain the constitutionality of such legislation: *Commonwealth v. Hamilton Mfg. Co.,* . . . *Wenham v. State,* . . . *State v. Buchanan,* . . . *Commonwealth v. Beatty,* . . . against them in the case of *Ritchie v. People.* . . .

The legislation and opinions referred to in the margin may not be, technically speaking, authorities, and in them is little or no discussion of the constitutional question presented to us for determination, yet they are significant of a widespread belief that woman's physical structure, and the functions she performs in consequence thereof, justify special legislation restricting or qualifying the conditions under which she should be permitted to toil. Constitutional questions, it is true, are not settled by even a consensus of present public opinion, for it is the peculiar value of a written constitution that it places in unchanging form limitations upon legislative action, and thus gives a permanence and stability to popular government which otherwise would be lacking. At the same time, when a question of fact is debated and debatable, and the extent to which a special constitutional limitation goes is affected by the truth in respect to that fact, a widespread and long continued belief concerning it is worthy of consideration. We take judicial cognizance of all matters of general knowledge.

It is undoubtedly true, as more than once declared by this court, that the general right to contract in relation to one's business is part of the liberty of the individual, protected by the Fourteenth Amendment to the Federal Constitution; yet it is equally well settled that this liberty is not absolute and extending to all contracts, and that a State may, without conflicting with the provisions of the Fourteenth Amendment, restrict in many respects the individual's power of contract. Without stopping to discuss at length the extent to which a State may act in this respect, we refer to the following cases in which the question has been considered: *Allgeyer v. Louisiana,* . . . *Holden v. Hardy,* . . . *Lochner v. New York, supra.*

That woman's physical structure and the performance of maternal functions place her at a disadvantage in the struggle for subsistence is obvious. This is especially true when the burdens of motherhood are upon her. Even when they are not, by abundant testimony of the medical fraternity continuance for a long time on her feet at work, repeating this from day to day, tends to injurious effects upon the body, and as healthy mothers are essential to vigorous offspring, the physical well-being of woman becomes an object of public interest and care in order to preserve the strength and vigor of the race.

Still again, history discloses the fact that woman has always been dependent upon man. He established his control at the outset by superior physical strength, and this control in various forms, with diminishing intensity, has continued to the present. As minors, though not to the same extent, she has been looked upon in the courts as needing especial care that her rights may be preserved. Education was long denied her, and while now the doors of the schoolroom are opened and her opportunities for acquiring knowledge are great, yet even with that and the consequent increase of capacity for business affairs it is still true that in the struggle for subsistence she is not an equal competitor with her brother. Though limitations upon personal and contractual rights may be removed by legislation, there is that in her disposition and habits of life which will operate against a full assertion of those rights. She will still be where some legislation to protect her seems necessary to secure a real equality of right. Doubtless there are individual exceptions, and there are many respects in which she has an advantage over him; but looking at it from the viewpoint of the effort to maintain an independent position in life, she is not upon an equality. Differentiated by these matters from the other sex, she is properly placed in a class by herself, and legislation designed for her protection may be sustained, even when like legislation is not necessary for men and could not be sustained. It is impossible to close one's eyes to the fact that she still looks to her brother and depends upon him. Even though all restrictions on political, personal, and contractual rights were taken away, and she stood, so far as statutes are concerned, upon an absolutely equal plane with him, it would still be true that she is so constituted that she will rest upon and look to him for protection; that her physical structure and a proper discharge of her maternal functions — having in view not merely her own health, but the well-being of the race — justify legislation to protect her from the greed as well as the passion of man. The limitations which this statute places upon her contractual powers, upon her right to agree with her employer as to the time she shall labor, are not imposed solely for her benefit, but also largely for the benefit of all. Many words cannot make this plainer. The two sexes differ in structure of body, in the functions to be performed by each, in the amount of physical strength, in the capacity for long-continued labor, particularly when done standing, the influence of vigorous health upon the future well-being of the race, the self-reliance which enables one to assert full rights, and in the capacity to maintain the struggle for subsistence. This difference justifies a difference in legislation and upholds that which is designed to compensate for some of the burdens which rest upon her.

We have not referred in this discussion to the denial of the elective franchise in the State of Oregon, for while that may disclose a lack of political equality in all things with her brother, that is not of itself decisive. The reason runs deeper, and rests in the inherent difference between the two sexes, and in the different functions in life which they perform.

For these reasons, and without questioning in any respect the decision in *Lochner v. New York,* we are of the opinion that it cannot be adjudged that the act in question is in conflict with the Federal Constitution, so far as it respects the work of a female in a laundry, and the judgment of the Supreme Court of Oregon is

Affirmed.

9

Bunting v. Oregon (1917)

In Bunting v. Oregon, *the Supreme Court upheld an Oregon ten-hour law for all industrial workers, male and female. The law also provided for up to three hours of overtime if workers received one and one-half times their regular wages. The wage regulation absorbed the Court's attention. In the majority opinion, Justice Joseph McKenna dismissed the claim of employer Franklin Bunting's lawyers that the statute was a wage law and a price-fixing measure. The overtime clause, said the Court, was a penalty on employers, not a wage regulation. Only with this issue out of the way did the opinion turn to the major question: Was a maximum-hours law for men constitutional? Yes, said the Court, in the extract reprinted here, but with little comment. The law was a reasonable exercise of the police power, McKenna suggested (quoting the Oregon Supreme Court), because the ten-hour day was already "the custom" in Oregon industries.*

The Bunting *decision fulfilled a major, long-sought goal of reformers — the extension of protection to male workers in all industries. Moreover, it appeared to upset the* Lochner *decision, to which McKenna did not refer and which seemed to be silently overruled. But the assumption about* Lochner's *death was premature since the 1905 decision soon sprang to life again in* Adkins v. Children's Hospital *(1923).*

243 U.S. 426 (1917).

Compare the Bunting *and* Lochner *decisions. Could the* Bunting *opinion have set a stronger precedent and precluded the revival of* Lochner *in 1923?*

Mr. Justice McKenna delivered the opinion of the court.

The consonance of the Oregon law with the Fourteenth Amendment is the question in the case, and this depends upon whether it is a proper exercise of the police power of the state, as the supreme court of the state decided that it is.

That the police power extends to health regulations is not denied, but it is denied that the law has such purpose or justification. . . .

Section 1 of the law expresses the policy that impelled its enactment to be the interest of the state in the physical well-being of its citizens and that it is injurious to their health for them to work "in any mill, factory or manufacturing establishment" more than ten hours in any one day. . . .

There is a contention made that the law, even regarded as regulating hours of service, is not either necessary or useful "for preservation of the health of employees in mills, factories, and manufacturing establishments." The record contains no facts to support the contention, and against it is the judgment of the legislature and the supreme court, which said: "In view of the well-known fact that the custom in our industries does not sanction a longer service than ten hours per day, it cannot be held, as a matter of law, that the legislative requirement is unreasonable or arbitrary as to hours of labor. Statistics show that the average daily working time among workingmen in different countries, is, in Australia, 8 hours; in Britain, 9; in the United States, 9¾; in Denmark, 9¾; in Norway, 10; Sweden, France, and Switzerland, 10½; Germany, 10¼; Belgium, Italy, and Austria, 11; and in Russia, 12 hours.["]

Further discussion we deem unnecessary.

Judgment affirmed.

The Chief Justice, Mr. Justice Van Devanter, and Mr. Justice McReynolds, dissent [without written opinion].

10

A Living Wage in Oregon

Caroline J. Gleason, 1913

To promote minimum-wage legislation in the states, reformers produced detailed studies of women workers' wages and living expenses. In Oregon, a Social Survey Committee performed this task for the state Consumers' League in 1913. The director of investigation, Caroline J. Gleason, was a recent graduate of the University of Minnesota and had studied at the University of Chicago's School of Civics and Philanthropy. She had just completed a three-month investigation of women's workplaces in eastern cities and another study about the housing of "women adrift" (wage earners who lived apart from their families or employers).

Gleason employed the latest social science techniques. To gather data, her team of field workers first distributed questionnaires to Portland workingwomen about their wages and expenses; they approached employees in factories, stores, and offices at lunchtime, at closing time, and in their homes. Second, they solicited from employers both wage data and views about the feasibility of the minimum wage. Third, the researchers themselves became workers in twelve factories to corroborate the information provided by employers and employees. Finally, to assess the cost of living, they visited boardinghouses, checked clothing prices at department stores, and organized subcommittees in fourteen Oregon towns to collect further information. Overall, they amassed data about 8,736 workers, most of them in Portland. The report concluded that $10 a week was "the least on which the average girl can support herself decently." Women workers in Oregon, however, except stenographers, earned less. Whether she lived at home or not, "the average girl in every occupation, except office work, receives wages which are inadequate to her support, and consequently would face the end of the year in debt if she does not receive support from her family or some outside source," the report asserted. "This shows the extent to which industries employing women are parasitic in character."

Minimum-wage researchers carried out similar surveys in other states. Much of the data they collected subsequently appeared in the NCL's Stettler *brief and* Adkins *brief. The tables reprinted here, which present the Oregon survey's findings, suggest the nature of minimum-wage re-*

Caroline J. Gleason, *Report of the Social Survey Committee of the Consumers' League of Oregon* (Portland: Consumers' League of Oregon, 1913), 19–23.

search. The questionnaire distributed to workers soliciting data on wages and living expenses and table 3, on the cost of living, are especially interesting parts of the Oregon report.

Do Gleason's statistics present a persuasive argument for the minimum wage for women workers in Oregon? Is her evidence more or less convincing than the "facts" in the Brandeis brief?

The Questionnaire

MINIMUM WAGE INVESTIGATION

1. WHAT kind of ESTABLISHMENT are you working in? ....
2. WHAT is your work ....
3. WAGES—Week .... or Month ....
4. HOURS employed—Day........ or Week ....
5. LIVING at home? (Yes or No) ....
6. VACATION with pay? ....
7. HOW long with firm? ....
8. FIRST wage here? ....

COST OF LIVING

1. HOUSE or room rent, per year ....
2. FOOD, per year ....
3. CLOTHING, per year ....
4. CARFARE, per year ....
5. LAUNDRY, per year ....
6. DOCTOR bills, per year ....
7. CHURCH dues, per year ....
8. LODGE dues, per year ....
9. EDUCATION, per year (books, newspapers, etc.) ....
10. RECREATION, including vacation, per year ....

NOTE—On reverse side of card, give all other items of expense that you deem proper, or information concerning working conditions.

Table 1

Occupational distribution of 7,603 women workers in Portland employed in 39 occupations investigated in regard to wages, hours, conditions of work, and cost and standards of living.

Bag factories	137	Cleaning and dyeing	57
Broom and basket	43	Department stores	2,281
Can factories	65	Druggists (wholesale)	102
Canning factories	100	Dry goods (wholesale)	125
Chewing gum factories	80	Electric co.	314
Cigar box factories	3	Five and ten cent stores	120
Clothing factories	218	Grocers (wholesale)	73
Candy factories	212	Hairdressing	15
Cordage factories	16	Laundries	259
Creameries	17	Offices (general)	800
Curled hair factories	2	Printing and stationery	213
Flour mills	8	Stenographers	985
Furriers	9	Publishing	20
Mattress factories	12	Restaurants and hotels	363
Meat packers	12	Telephone	570
Paper box factories	63		
Packing	106	Total	6,297
Prune canneries	35	Factories	1,306
Pickle factories	16		
Shoe factories	2	Total	7,603
Soap factories	2		
Tobacco factories	10		
Tent and awning factories	39		
Mohair and woolen mills	99		
Factory Total	1,306		

Table 2
Average annual wage and expense of 509 women wage earners in Portland, classified by occupation and as to living at home or adrift.

NO.	AVERAGE ANNUAL WAGE	EXPENSE	DEFICIT	SAVING
Laundry				
9 At home	$423.00	$474.45	$ 51.45	
27 Adrift	464.00	475.05	11.05	
Factory				
82 At home	416.92	426.98	10.06	
18 Adrift	395.00	438.83	43.83	
Office				
57 At home	542.14	599.50	57.36	
31 Adrift	692.90	617.07		$ 75.83
Department Stores				
81 At home	459.50	605.36	145.86	
35 Adrift	480.57	572.42	91.85	
Miscellaneous				
99 At home	440.24	539.29	99.05	
70 Adrift	458.71	526.68	67.97	

Table 3
Average amount spent annually by 101 women wage earners in miscellaneous occupations in Oregon (outside Portland). Information obtained from Ashland, Baker, Eugene, Forest Grove, LaGrande, Medford, Oregon City, Pendleton, Salem, and Vale.

Room and Board	$278.62
Clothing	137.50
Laundry	16.00
Carfare	21.00
Doctor and Dentist	18.00
Church and lodge	12.52
Reading	6.54
Recreation	20.50
Total	$510.68

$9.82 a week; $42.55 a month.

Table 4

Summary of weekly wages of women employees in Portland.

OCCUPATION	NUMBER UNDER $10	NUMBER OVER $10	TOTAL	PERCENT UNDER $10	PERCENT OVER $10
Department stores	1,211	867	2,078	58.2	41.7
Factories	319	108	427	74.7	25.3
Hotels and restaurants	105	108	213	49.2	50.8
Laundries	130	10	140	92.6	7.4
Office help (not including stenographers)	59	67	126	46.4	53.6
Stenographers	19	66	85	22.4	77.5
Printing trades	32	25	57	56.1	43.8
Telephone operators	26	26	52	50.	50.
Miscellaneous	19	20	39	48.7	51.3
Total	1,920	1,297	3,217	59.6	40.4

Additional report of 53 factories representing 21 industries; 1,306 women employed; lowest wage reported, $3 a week; median wage, $8.20 a week.
Total number of wage schedules of women employees in Portland received and classified: 4,523.

Table 5

Wage information for 1,133 women wage earners in Oregon (outside of Portland). (Wage information was received from the following towns and cities: Albany, Ashland, Astoria, Baker, Cottage Grove, Dallas, Enterprise, Eugene, Forest Grove, Hood River, Grants Pass, LaGrande, McMinnville, Medford, Oregon City, Pendleton, Roseburg, Salem, Springfield, Stockton, The Dalles, Union, and Vale.)

NO. OF EMPLOYEES	INDUSTRY	AVERAGE MONTHLY WAGE
88	Canneries	$35.00
6	Condensed milk	38.00
280	Woolen mills	37.50
18	Hotels and restaurants	31.65
518	Laundries	39.50
45	Office help	35.50
140	Retail stores	39.21
16	Stenographers	50.00
22	Telephone operators	33.07

11

Adkins v. Children's Hospital (1923)

In Stettler v. O'Hara *(1917), a divided Supreme Court had let Oregon's minimum-wage law stand, though without a written opinion. This was not an auspicious precedent. The more conservative Court of the 1920s used the due process clause at a quickened pace to invalidate state laws, especially "social legislation." The federal minimum-wage law of 1918 for the District of Columbia was an early target. In 1923, after unexpected delays and a reversal in a lower federal court, the Supreme Court resuscitated the* Lochner *decision, presumed dead since* Bunting v. Oregon *(1917), and by a 5–4 vote declared the D.C. law unconstitutional. Ignoring the massive data in the brief submitted by Felix Frankfurter and Mary W. Dewson, the Court held the minimum-wage law in violation of the due process clause of the Fifth Amendment.*

In the majority opinion, Justice George Sutherland contended that the Nineteenth Amendment, ratified in 1920, which enfranchised women, had destroyed "the ancient inequality of the sexes, otherwise than physical," and, with it, the constitutional basis for class legislation for women. Sutherland's opinion drew on the link between sexual equality and freedom of contract that had emerged in the Ritchie *case of 1895, in William Fenton's brief for Curt Muller, and, most recently, in the oral argument of Wade H. Ellis, who represented Willie Lyons and Children's Hospital. But Sutherland did not discard the* Muller *decision. On the contrary, he distinguished* Muller, *which involved hours of work, from the issue at stake in* Adkins, *the minimum wage. Maximum-hours laws for women workers were acceptable, but the minimum wage, which struck at the "heart of the contract," was not. The "entering wedge" strategy, which had worked in the* Muller *and* Bunting *cases, now collapsed.*

The Adkins *decision evoked impassioned criticism in law journals. Disparaging Sutherland's logic, critics praised the dissenting opinions of Chief Justice William H. Taft and Justice Oliver Wendell Holmes. The dissenters attacked the majority opinion for reviving the* Lochner *precedent and for drawing a distinction between hours regulations and wage regulations.*

One interesting part of this case is that both Sutherland and the dissenters accept the Muller *decision. In what ways, however, do their interpreta-*

---

261 U.S. 525 (1923).

tions of Muller *differ? What are Sutherland's objections to the minimum wage? Do the dissenters respond to his objections?*

Mr. Justice Sutherland delivered the opinion of the Court.

The question presented for determination by these appeals is the constitutionality of the Act of September 19, 1918, providing for the fixing of minimum wages for women and children in the District of Columbia. . . .

The appellee in the first case is a corporation maintaining a hospital for children in the District. It employs a large number of women in various capacities, with whom it had agreed upon rates of wages and compensation satisfactory to such employees, but which in some instances were less than the minimum wage fixed by an order of the board made in pursuance of the act. The women with whom appellee had so contracted were all of full age and under no legal disability. . . .

In the second case the appellee, a woman twenty-one years of age, was employed by the Congress Hall Hotel Company as an elevator operator, at a salary of $35 per month and two meals a day. She alleges that the work was light and healthful, the hours short, with surroundings clean and moral, and that she was anxious to continue it for the compensation she was receiving, and that she did not earn more. Her services were satisfactory to the Hotel Company, and it would have been glad to retain her, but was obliged to dispense with her services by reason of the order of the board and on account of the penalties prescribed by the act. The wages received by this appellee were the best she was able to obtain for any work she was capable of performing, and the enforcement of the order, she alleges, deprived her of such employment and wages. She further averred that she could not secure any other position at which she could make a living, with as good physical and moral surroundings, and earn as good wages, and that she was desirous of continuing and would continue the employment, but for the order of the board. An injunction was prayed as in the other case. . . .

The statute now under consideration is attacked upon the ground that it authorizes an unconstitutional interference with the freedom of contract included within the guaranties of the due process clause of the Fifth Amendment. . . .

There is, of course, no such thing as absolute freedom of contract. It is subject to a great variety of restraints. But freedom of contract is, nevertheless, the general rule and restraint the exception, and the exercise of legislative authority to abridge it can be justified only by the existence of exceptional circumstances. Whether these circumstances exist in the present case constitutes the question to be answered. It will be helpful to this end to review some of the decisions where the interference has been upheld. . . .

Statutes fixing hours of labor. . . . In some instances the statute limited the hours of labor for men in certain occupations, and in others it was confined in its application to women. No statute has thus far been brought to the attention of this court which by its terms applied to all occupations. In *Holden v. Hardy,* . . . the court considered an act of the Utah Legislature, restricting the hours of labor in mines and smelters. This statute was sustained as a legitimate exercise of the police power, on the ground that the Legislature had determined that these particular employments, when too long pursued, were injurious to the health of the employees, and that, as there were reasonable grounds for supporting this determination on the part of the Legislature, its decision in that respect was beyond the reviewing power of the federal courts.

That this constituted the basis of the decision is emphasized by the subsequent decision in *Lochner v. New York,* . . . reviewing a state statute which restricted the employment of all persons in bakeries to ten hours in any one day. The court referred to *Holden v. Hardy, supra,* and, declar[ed] it to be inapplicable. . . .

In *Bunting v. Oregon,* . . . since the state Legislature and state Supreme Court had found such a law necessary for the preservation of the health of employees in these industries [mills, factories, and manufacturing establishments], this court . . . accept[ed] their judgment, in the absence of facts to support the contrary conclusion. . . .

In the *Muller* Case the validity of an Oregon statute, forbidding the employment of any female in certain industries more than ten hours during any one day, was upheld. The decision proceeded upon the theory that the difference between the sexes may justify a different rule respecting hours of labor in the case of women than in the case of men. It is pointed out that these consist in differences of physical structure, especially in respect of the maternal functions, and also in the fact that historically woman has always been dependent upon man, who has established his control by superior physical strength. . . . But the ancient inequality of the sexes, otherwise than physical, as suggested in the *Muller* Case . . . , has continued "with diminishing intensity." In view of the great — not to say revolutionary — changes which have taken place since that utterance, in the contractual, political, and civil status of women, culminating in the Nineteenth Amendment, it is not unreasonable to say that these differences have now come almost, if not quite, to the vanishing point. In this aspect of the matter, while the physical differences must be recognized in appropriate cases, and legislation fixing hours or conditions of work may properly take them into account, we cannot accept the doctrine that women of mature age, *sui juris*,[1] require or may be subjected to restrictions upon their liberty of contract which could not lawfully be imposed in the case of men under similar circumstances. To do so would be to ignore all the implications to be drawn from the present-day trend of legislation as well as that of common thought and usage, by which woman is accorded emancipation from the old doctrine that she must be given special protection or be subjected to special restraint in her contractual and civil relationships. In passing, it may be noted that the instant statute applies in the case of a woman employer contracting with a woman employee as it does when the former is a man.

The essential characteristics of the statute now under consideration, which differentiated it from the laws fixing hours of labor, will be made to appear as we proceed. It is sufficient now to point out that the latter ... deal with incidents of the employment having no necessary effect upon the heart of the contract; that is, the amount of wages to be paid and received. A law forbidding work to continue beyond a given number of hours leaves the parties free to contract about wages and thereby equalize whatever additional burdens may be imposed upon the employer as a result of the restrictions as to hours, by an adjustment in respect of the amount of wages. . . .

If now, in the light furnished by the foregoing exceptions to the general rule forbidding legislative interference with freedom of contract, we examine and analyze the statute in question, we shall see that it differs from them in every material respect. It is not a law dealing with any business charged with a public interest or with public work, or to meet and tide over a temporary emergency. It has to do with the character, methods, or periods of wage payments. It does not prescribe hours of labor or conditions under which labor is to be done. It is not for the protection of persons under legal disability or for the prevention of fraud. It is simply and exclusively a price-fixing law, confined to adult women (for we are not now considering the provision relating to minors), who are legally as capable of contracting for themselves as men. It forbids two parties having lawful capacity — under penalties as to the employer — to freely contract with one another in respect of the price for which one shall render service to the other in a purely private employment where both

---

[1] In their own right.

are willing, perhaps anxious, to agree, even though the consequence may be to oblige one to surrender a desirable engagement and the other to dispense with the services of a desirable employee. The price fixed by the board need have no relation to the capacity or earning power of the employee, the number of hours which may happen to constitute the day's work, the character of the place where the work is to be done, or the circumstances or surroundings of the employment, and, while it has no other basis to support its validity than the assumed necessities of the employee, it takes no account of any independent resources she may have. It is based wholly on the opinions of the members of the board and their advisors — perhaps an average of their opinions, if they do not precisely agree — as to what will be necessary to provide a living for a woman, keep her in health, and preserve her morals. It applies to any and every occupation in the District, without regard to its nature or the character of the work.

The standard furnished by the statute for the guidance of the board is so vague as to be impossible of practical application with any reasonable degree of accuracy. What is sufficient to supply the necessary cost of living for a woman worker and maintain her in good health and protect her morals is obviously not a precise or unvarying sum — not even approximately so. The amount will depend upon a variety of circumstances: the individual temperament, habits of thrift, care, ability to buy necessaries intelligently, and whether the woman lives alone or with her family. To those who practice economy, a given sum will afford comfort, while to those of contrary habit the same sum will be wholly inadequate. The cooperative economics of the family group are not taken into account, though they constitute an important consideration in estimating the cost of living, for it is obvious that the individual expense will be less in the case of a member of a family than in the case of one living alone. The relation between earnings and morals is not capable of standardization. It cannot be shown that well-paid women safeguard their morals more carefully than those who are poorly paid. Morality rests upon other considerations than wages, and there is, certainly, no such prevalent connection between the two as to justify a broad attempt to adjust the latter with reference to the former. As a means of safeguarding morals the attempted classification, in our opinion, is without reasonable basis. No distinction can be made between women who work for others and those who do not; nor is there ground for distinction between women and men, for, certainly, if women require a munimum wage to preserve their morals men require it to preserve their honesty. For these reasons, and others which might be stated, the inquiry in respect of the necessary cost of living and of the income necessary to preserve health and morals presents an individual and not a composite question, and must be answered for each individual considered by herself and not by a general formula prescribed by a statutory bureau. . . .

The law takes account of the necessities of only one party to the contract. It ignores the necessities of the employer by compelling him to pay not less than a certain sum, not only whether the employee is capable of earning it, but irrespective of the ability of his business to sustain the burden, generously leaving him, of course, the privilege of abandoning his business as an alternative for going on at a loss. Within the limits of the minimum sum, he is precluded, under penalty of fine and imprisonment, from adjusting compensation to the differing merits of his employees. . . . The law is not confined to the great and powerful employers but embraces those whose bargaining power may be as weak as that of the employee. It takes no account of periods of stress and business depression, of crippling losses, which may leave the employer himself without adequate means of livelihood. To the extent that the sum fixed exceeds the fair value of the services rendered, it amounts to a compulsory exaction from the employer for the support of a partially indigent person, for whose condition there rests upon him no peculiar responsibility, and therefore, in effect, arbitrarily shifts to his shoulders a burden which, if it belongs to anybody, belongs to society as a whole.

The feature of this statute, which perhaps more than any other, puts upon it the stamp of invalidity, is that it exacts from the employer an arbitrary payment for a purpose and upon a basis having no causal connection with his business, or the contract or the work the employee engages to do. The declared basis, as already pointed out, is not the value of the service rendered, but the extraneous circumstance that the employee needs to get a prescribed sum of money to insure her subsistence, health, and morals. The ethical right of every worker, man or woman, to a living wage may be conceded. One of the declared and important purposes of trade organizations is to secure it. And with that principle and with every legitimate effort to realize it in fact, no one can quarrel; but the fallacy of the proposed method of attaining it is that it assumes that every employer is bound at all events to furnish it. . . .

It is said that great benefits have resulted from the operation of such statutes, not alone in the District of Columbia but in the several states, where they have been in force. A mass of reports, opinions of special observers and students of the subject, and the like, has been brought before us in support of this statement, all of which we have found interesting, but only mildly persuasive. . . . No real test of the economic value of the law can be had during periods of maximum employment, when general causes keep wages up to or above the minimum; that will come in periods of depression and struggle for employment, when the efficient will be employed at the minimum rate, while the less capable may not be employed at all. . . .

It follows, from what has been said, that the act in question passes the limit prescribed by the Constitution, and accordingly the decrees of the court below are Affirmed.

Mr. Justice Brandeis took no part in the consideration or decision of these cases.

Mr. Chief Justice Taft, dissenting.

Legislatures in limiting freedom of contract between employee and employer by a minimum wage proceed on the assumption that employees, in the class receiving least pay, are not upon a full level of equality of choice with their employer and in their necessitous circumstances are prone to accept pretty much anything that is offered. They are peculiarly subject to the overreaching of the harsh and greedy employer. The evils of the sweating system and of the long hours and low wages which are characteristic of it are well known. Now, I agree that it is a disputable question in the field of political economy how far a statutory requirement of maximum hours or minimum wages may be a useful remedy for these evils, and whether it may not make the case of the oppressed employee worse than it was before. But it is not the function of this court to hold congressional acts invalid simply because they are passed to carry out economic views which the court believes to be unwise or unsound. . . .

The right of the Legislature under the Fifth and Fourteenth Amendments to limit the hours of employment on the score of the health of the employee, it seems to me, has been firmly established. . . . In *Holden v. Hardy* . . . it was applied to miners and rested on the unfavorable environment of employment in mining and smelting. In *Lochner v. New York* . . . it was held that restricting those employed in bakeries to ten hours a day was an arbitrary and invalid interference with the liberty of contract secured by the Fourteenth Amendment. Then followed a number of cases . . . beginning with *Muller v. Oregon* . . . sustaining the validity of a limit on maximum hours of labor for women to which I shall hereafter allude, and following these cases came *Bunting v. Oregon*. . . . In that case, this court sustained a law limiting the hours of labor of any person, whether man or woman, working in any mill, factory, or manufacturing establishment to ten hours a day with a proviso as to further hours to which I shall hereafter advert. The law covered the whole field of industrial employment and certainly covered the case of persons employed in bakeries. Yet the opinion in the *Bunting* Case does not mention the *Lochner* Case. No one can suggest any constitutional distinction between employment in a bakery and one in any other kind of a manufacturing establishment which should make a limit of hours in the one invalid, and the same limit in the other permissible. It is impossible for me to reconcile the *Bunting* Case and the *Lochner* Case, and I have always supposed that the *Lochner* case was thus overruled *sub silentio.* Yet the opinion of the court herein in support of its conclusion quotes from the opinion in the *Lochner* Case as one which has been sometimes distinguished but never overruled. . . .

However, the opinion herein does not overrule the *Bunting* Case in express terms, and therefore I assume that the conclusion in this case rests on the distinction between a minimum of wages and a maximum of hours in the limiting of liberty to contract. I regret to be at variance with the court as to the substance of this distinction. In absolute freedom of contract the one term is as important as the other, for both enter equally into the consideration given and received, a restriction as to one is not any greater in essence than the other, and is of the same kind. One is the multiplier and the other the multiplicand.

If it be said that long hours of labor have a more direct effect upon the health of the employee than the low wage, there is very respectable authority from close observers, disclosed in the record and in the literature on the subject quoted at length in the briefs that they are equally harmful in this regard. Congress took this view and we cannot say it was not warranted in so doing. . . .

. . . I respectfully submit that *Muller v. Oregon* . . . controls this case. . . .

I am not sure from a reading of the opinion whether the court thinks the authority of *Muller v. Oregon* is shaken by the adoption of the Nineteenth Amendment. The Nineteenth Amendment did not change the physical strength or limitations of women upon which the decision in *Muller v. Oregon* rests. The amendment did give women political power and makes more certain that legislative provisions for their protection will be in accord with their interests as they see them. But I do not think we are warranted in varying constitutional construction based on physical differences between men and women, because of the amendment. . . .

I am authorized to say that Mr. Justice Sanford concurs in this opinion.

Mr. Justice Holmes, dissenting.

The question in this case is the broad one. Whether Congress can establish minimum rates of wages for women in the District of Columbia, with due provision for special circumstances, or whether we must say that Congress had no power to meddle with the matter at all. To me, notwithstanding the deference due to the prevailing judgment of the Court, the power of Congress seems absolutely free from doubt. . . .

The earlier decisions upon the same words [the due process clause of the Fifth Amendment] in the Fourteenth Amendment began within our memory and went no farther than an unpretentious assertion of the liberty to follow the ordinary callings. Later that innocuous generality was expanded into the dogma, Liberty of Contract. Contract is not specially mentioned in the text that we have to construe. It is merely an example of doing what you want to do, embodied in the word liberty. But pretty much all law consists in forbidding men to do some things that they want to do, and contract is no more exempt from law than other acts. Without enumerating all the restrictive laws that have been upheld I will mention a few that seem to me to have interfered with liberty of contract quite as seriously and directly as the one before us. Usury laws prohibit contracts by which a man receives more than so much interest for the money he lends. Statutes of frauds restrict many contracts to certain forms. Some Sunday laws prohibit practically all contracts during one-seventh of our whole life. Insurance rates may be regulated. . . .

I confess that I do not understand the principle on which the power to fix a minimum for the wages of women can be denied by those who admit the power to fix a maximum for their hours of work. I fully assent to the proposition that here as elsewhere the distinctions of the law are distinctions of degree, but I perceive no difference in the kind or degree of interference with liberty, the only matter with which we have any concern, between the one case and the other. The bargain is equally affected whichever half you regulate. *Muller v. Oregon,* I take it is as good law today as it was in 1908. It will need more than the Nineteenth Amendment to convince me that there are no differences between men and women, or that legislation cannot take those differences into account. I should not hesitate to take them into account if I thought it necessary to sustain this Act. . . . But after *Bunting v. Oregon,* . . . I had supposed that it was not necessary, and that *Lochner v. New York* . . . would be allowed a deserved repose. . . .

I am of the opinion that the statute is valid and that the decree should be reversed.

12. THE WOMEN'S MOVEMENT IN THE EARLY 1920s

The National Woman's Party's drive for legal equality split the post–Nineteenth Amendment women's movement into embattled factions and made protective laws a focus of debate. To NWP members, who supported removal of women's legal disabilities, protective laws for women were a roadblock to equality. Such laws hindered women in competition for jobs, crowded them into low-paid occupations, and ensured their status as second-class citizens. In the NWP view, reformers who defended protective laws were meddling social workers and wooly-minded do-gooders. To reformers, who had long fought for protective laws, the proposed equal rights amendment was "pernicious," "insane," and "diabolical." In their view, the NWP represented the interests of a professional elite that knew nothing of the needs of working-class women. Compensatory laws were needed, the reformers claimed, to protect the least privileged workers. Although the reformers had numerical strength, they were forced to wage a defensive campaign; they had to defend not merely single-sex protective laws but sexual difference. NWP spokeswomen held an advantage in argument: They had nothing to lose.

The following documents suggest the tenor of the debate. Which faction of women activists has better arguments? Could the two factions have reconciled their differences and reached some sort of compromise, or did their conflict defy solution?

12a

A Debate in Life and Labor

Marguerite Mooers Marshall versus
Rose Schneiderman, 1920

Conflict over protection erupted in New York even before the National Woman's Party began its campaign for legal equality in 1921. At issue was New York's night work law, which prohibited women's work after 10 P.M. in factories (including newspaper plants). In 1919, women writers and reporters had won an exemption from the law, but a new bill — to limit office workers to a nine-hour day and ban women's night work in offices — loomed in the legislature. In 1920, as grievances mounted, an

argument over maximum-hours laws surfaced in the National Women's Trade Union League (NWTUL) journal Life and Labor.
In a letter to the publication, journalist Marguerite Mooers Marshall, an opponent of single-sex protective laws, attacked the NWTUL for its "anti-feminist" attitude. Protective laws, she claimed, kept women "from meeting men on the level ground of equality." To reformers, however, there was no level ground of equality. NWTUL leaders struck back at Marshall for her elitest myopia and ignorance of the needs of factory workers. Rose Schneiderman — former cap maker, founder of a women's local of the Cap Makers Union, activist in the International Ladies' Garment Workers Union, officer of the New York WTUL, and a prominent organizer for the league — proved an outspoken respondent.

Newspaper Woman Protests Against "Maternal Legislation"

To the Editor of *Life and Labor:*

Why is it that the National Women's Trade Union League chooses to assume in regard to special industrial laws affecting women, the *typical anti-suffragist, anti-feminist* attitude — i.e., that women must "be protected," that they must "shrink" from meeting men on the level ground of equality, that the dear, delicate creatures must be "shielded against themselves, if necessary, for their own welfare and that of the race"? It seems to me that anti-suffrage logic and nothing else supports the so-called *"welfare bills"* before the New York Legislature, and as a worker myself, with genuine respect for the League and its general aims, I am impelled to protest against what, from my point of view, is your unfair, old-fashioned, and distinctly short-sighted advocacy of special privilege for self-supporting women.

I feel that I have, in particular, the right to protest against the bill limiting women office workers to nine hours a day and no night work after 10 P.M. — although at present my own work would suffer little or no interference if the bill became law. (To be sure, it was 10:15 P.M. when I began this letter to *Life and Labor*, but, technically, I suppose, I am now in the role of friendly heckler, rather than of reporter or editorial writer!)

Night work, however, I have done for periods of a year or more at a time, since on a morning newspaper a woman works from 1 in the afternoon till midnight or thereabouts. I found that such work in no way injured my health, either physical or mental. Night after night I went home alone, through the streets of New York or Boston — and the later it was, the more infrequently was I addressed by impertinent gentlemen, who are not naive enough to expect to find a congenial acquaintance in a hurrying, preoccupied, plainly dressed woman encountered at midnight or later. At home I read myself to sleep and woke up as much rested as if I had retired at the conventional hour.

If I had quibbled about night assignments I simply should have given new life to a prejudice now becoming slightly moribund — that "a newspaper office is no place for women." Of course night work interferes with one's social life. But the stenographer, let us say, who prefers social enjoyment to professional advancement always can find her niche. She *won't* work overtime, or cut into her evenings to help out in an emergency. She needs no legislative protection to keep her in a rut. Why penalize, for her sake, the ambitious woman in newspaper or business office, who doesn't work with her eye on the clock, who is willing to do extra work, to stay after hours, to prove that she is a little bigger than her present job and so earn promotion to a better one?

I refuse to grant that, in office work or professional work where the chief demand is on intellectual energy, women are less fit than men to stand the gaff. If you will pardon, once more, the personal argument — in ten years I have lost exactly one day from my work through illness. I have known few men in my profession with a like record.

American women practically have won the fight for political equality with men. The struggle for economic and professional equality is still in the balance. To me and to others, it seems as if the National Women's Trade Union League, which should support us, were launching a flank attack at us! The ambitious young man working beside us, the conservative male employer, are our natural antagonists. But why should you, who are self-supporting women, stand back of a law which will so hobble and blindfold us that no man will give us any job that cannot be held by the cheapest of clock-watchers?

How can we — or you — ask for "equal pay for equal work," when the hours and conditions of our work are hedged about by taboos and thou-shalt-nots which do not apply to the young man with whom we are in competition?

It is with a sense of ironic despair that women like myself, who had hoped with the ballot to end the paternal legislation of the past, contemplate the spectacle of the women's trade unions, the consumers' leagues and *Life and Labor* all altruistically and determinedly beginning the *maternal* legislation of the future!

Yours regretfully,
Marguerite Mooers Marshall

Response from Rose Schneiderman

Dear Editor:

Reading Miss Marshall's letter in the March issue of *Life and Labor* . . . , one realizes that aside from being a strong individualist, Miss Marshall knows nothing about modern factory conditions.

Miss Marshall is one out of a number of highly paid professional women who insist that the legislation introduced at this session [of the New York State legislature] by the Women's Joint Legislative Conference of New York would hurt their progress, though time and time again we have tried to explain through newspaper articles, pamphlets, and public speeches that the eight-hour and Minimum Wage bills would only affect women in factories and mercantile establishments, and would in no way affect newspaper women, lawyers, physicians, authors, advertising women, or executives. . . .

I dare say that if Miss Marshall had to sort dirty linen for nine hours a day, instead of sitting in a nice, airy office, feeding the minds of working women with a lot of sob stuff, and if she had to go home and get her own dinner, wash and mend clothes, and had two or three children to take care of, and do it all on $12 per [week], she would be ready to be protected by legislation. Or if Miss Marshall had to dip chocolates in a temperature of 63 degrees, using her fingers a certain way, she would realize at the end of the day what a blessing an eight-hour law would be and her strong feminist principles would come into harmony with facts.

I think the whole mistake that Miss Marshall makes is in the idea that there is a career in industry or in the department store. Those of us who have worked in the factory or store know that there is only room for one at the top and the rest must struggle along until they get married or die.

Miss Marshall is shocked at the girl who watches the clock, but I dare say that if Miss Marshall thumped the typewriter for seven or eight consecutive hours and knew all the time that there was not a chance in a thousand of ever advancing toward anything else, she would find at the end of the day that she ached all over and would be glad when 5 o'clock came. . . .

Frankly speaking, the average working woman does not want a factory career, as there is no such thing. She is looking forward to getting married and raising a family. Perhaps Miss Marshall disapproves of such frivolity, but then, these are the facts, and girls will be girls even though they work for a living. And since labor statistics show us that the average work time of the woman in industry is between the ages of fifteen and twenty-five, it is our duty to see to it that the wages of the girls are big enough to make possible good, wholesome living conditions; clean, airy workrooms; and hours short enough to permit recreation and time to think. We want these things through organization wherever possible. Finding, however, that working women do not as yet realize the need of organization, it is the business of the State to protect the mothers of the future citizens, through legislation.

The salvation of the working woman does not lie in competing with her fellow worker, but in organization and amalgamation, and in standing shoulder to shoulder with him in the struggle for economic justice.

Rose Schneiderman
President, New York Women's Trade Union League

12b

Twenty Questions about the ERA

Florence Kelley, 1922

To Florence Kelley, who had fought for protective laws since the 1890s, the prospect of an equal rights amendment (ERA) was particularly offensive. In 1921, Kelley sent a critical list of questions about the ERA to an Ohio member of Congress, Simeon Fess, who had agreed to present the amendment to the House of Representatives. Kelley's pressure dissuaded him from doing so. The next year, the National Consumers' League published Kelley's impassioned attack as a pamphlet. The proposed ERA, Kelley pointed out, would destroy all legislative programs that benefited women, including mothers' pensions and the recent Sheppard-Towner Act of 1921. It would leave women open to new risks, such as conscription or loss of financial support from husbands. And it would invalidate existing protective laws for women, preclude further protective measures, and leave wage-earning women nothing "to compensate the disadvantages which they everywhere tend to suffer in competing with men." To Kelley, the ERA was a "dangerous experiment."

Which of Kelley's questions have been invalidated by the feminist legal revolution of the 1960s and 1970s? Which remain provocative or relevant?

Florence Kelley, *Twenty Questions about the Federal Amendment Proposed by the National Woman's Party* (New York: National Consumers' League, 1922), 3–7.

All modern-minded people desire, of course, that women should have full political equality and also be free from the old exclusions from the bench, the bar, the pulpit, the highest ranges of the teachers' profession, and of the civil service. Obviously all elective and appointive offices should be open to women and they should have every opportunity for jury duty and the right to equal guardianship of their children.

Ostensibly the National Woman's Party draft for an amendment to the United States Constitution is to assure to all women the foregoing rights — and many others. On first reading, its wording may seem adapted to this end.

The Proposed Amendment

Section 1. No political, civil, or legal disabilities or inequalities on account of sex, or on account of marriage unless applying alike to both sexes, shall exist within the United States or any place subject to their jurisdiction.

Section 2. Congress shall have power to enforce this article by appropriate legislation.

The Supreme Court of the United States Alone Can Give a Final Answer to Questions Raised by the Proposed Amendment

It is one of the gravest objections to the amendment that it will if enacted clog the courts for many years, from the magistrates' sessions to the Supreme Bench.

Endless confusion will ensue in the enforcement of existing laws, since their constitutionality may be in doubt for years. For instance:

MARRIAGE

1. Will husbands need to continue to support their wives?
2. Can deserting husbands be brought back and compelled to support wife and child? (They can now, in many states.)
3. Will it not be possible to compel mothers to work for the maintenance of their children, if the father must do so?
4. The payment of civilian widowed mothers' pensions is clearly an inequality on account of sex and of marriage, which does not apply alike to both sexes. Shall widowers have pensions — or shall widowed mothers be deprived of theirs? Will any third choice be possible under the amendment?
5. Will the amendment destroy the new law popularly known as the Sheppard-Towner bill, signed by the President on Thanksgiving

Eve under the title, "For the Promotion of the Welfare and Hygiene of Maternity and Infancy"? That federal law creates an inequality by reason of sex, in favor of women — maternity not applying alike to both sexes.

6. What becomes of the dower rights, that women now have in many states?

SEX

As to the merit of the following there is wide divergence. Questions 7 and 10c are within the domain of Congress. If section 2 of the proposed amendment were in force, all would be. Is this desirable?

7. Will women be subject to conscription?
8. a. What will be the effect upon the age for marriage?
   b. Will girls remain minors to the twenty-first birthday?
   c. Will all the age of consent laws be wiped out?
9. a. Will fathers become jointly responsible with mothers of illegitimate children?
   b. Will illegitimate children have the name of both father and mother?
   c. Will they inherit from both as legitimate children do?
10. What will become of
    a. The penalties for seduction?
    b. The penalties for rape?
    c. The Mann Act[1] which exists solely for the protection of women and girls?

(The penalties embraced under question 10 a and b obviously apply to men alone and constitute an inequality, civil and legal.)

WAGE-EARNING WOMEN

11. a. Will those women wage earners who now have the benefit of the statutory eight-hours' day, rest at night and one day's rest in seven, lose these advantages?
    b. How can they get an eight-hours' law for themselves — in a state where workingmen do not care to get it because they prefer negotiation backed by organization, to statutes?
    c. *Should* women be compelled to abandon protective legislation

---

[1] The Mann Act (1910) prohibited the interstate transportation of women for immoral purposes.

in their own behalf because workingmen do not prefer it for themselves?

d. *Why* should wage-earning women not be permitted to continue to get protective laws for their own health and welfare, and that of their unborn children, and to carry on labor unions too, if they so desire? Why should their activities be subordinated to the preferences of wage-earning men?

12. What safeguards will wage-earning women have to compensate the disadvantages which they everywhere tend to suffer in competing with men — i.e., longer hours and lower wages?

13. Is not this consideration one of great and growing importance for our Nation, when the number of women wage earners increases by leaps and bounds from one census to the next? And the industries involving exposure to poisons are increasing faster than ever before?

14. And when the overwork of mothers is one recognized cause of high infant mortality and the rising death rate of women in childbirth? (This is convincingly shown by the investigations of the Children's Bureau.)

THE POLICE POWERS

15. Proponents of the amendment contend that all laws now upheld by the Police Powers of the state will remain intact. Those who have struggled for years to secure beneficent laws to better the conditions of wage-earning women, view this amendment with great alarm. They are sincerely convinced that it would wipe out all regulatory legislation of this character now on the statute books, the constitutionality of which has been sustained by the United States Supreme Court after a decade of litigation. Why should these humane and progressive laws be subjected to this great hazard of complete nullification?

16. Whatever view may be entertained on this important point, it appears to be certain that, until the new amendment has been finally construed by the United States Supreme Court, and this would take years of litigation, not a single law for bettering the conditions of wage-earning women would be passed by any state. The present laws on this subject fall far short of sound industrial standards. Would not this amendment be a complete bar to any new laws needed by women to meet the changing industrial conditions of our time?

17. If there were no other way of promoting more perfect equality for

women, an argument could perhaps be sustained for taking these risks. But is the dangerous experiment necessary? Cannot every desirable measure attainable through the amendment be more easily attained without it?

18. The Nineteenth Amendment was necessary because, not having votes, women could not change forty-eight state constitutions. With votes, can they not change statutes, both state and federal, and state constitutions also, more quickly and far more safely than this amendment can be passed and ratified?

19. Are all the subjects mentioned above suitable for the congressional legislation prescribed in section 2 of the proposed amendment? When Congress undertakes "to enforce this article by appropriate legislation," will the rights of the separate states be unduly curtailed?

20. Will the National Woman's Party publicly answer the question — "Do you believe that the states should have the constitutional power to pass protective legislation affecting women if and when, in their judgment, it becomes advisable?" Yes? or No?

12c

A Debate in the Nation

Harriot Stanton Blatch versus Clara Mortenson Beyer, 1923

During the early 1920s, as the Adkins *case moved slowly through the federal courts, the feud among politicized women spilled into the popular press, which gave space to both factions. In the following excerpts from a debate in the* Nation, *two accomplished partisans exchanged recriminations — and views on protective laws. "[P]artial laws have not protected men and have thrown women out of employment," charged Harriot Stanton Blatch, prominent suffragist, founder of the Equality League (1907), a working women's suffrage organization, and stalwart of the National Woman's Party (NWP). "Legislatures would do more for children if adult women ceased to hang on their necks." To reformer Clara Mortenson Beyer, who disparaged "theoretical equality," protective laws brought*

"Do Women Want Protection?" *Nation,* January 31, 1923, 115–16.

women "*up to the point where industrial equality with men is more nearly possible.*" *The extension of protection to men, which the NWP claimed to endorse, was no different, she claimed, than the removal of protection for women. Beyer, who formerly taught economics at Bryn Mawr, served as the administrator of the Washington, D.C., Minimum Wage Board until it was dismantled by the* Adkins *decision in 1923. She later became assistant secretary of labor standards in the New Deal Department of Labor.*

Wrapping Women in Cotton-Wool

HARRIOT STANTON BLATCH

. . . Welfare workers always seem to think of industrial women as spavined, broken-backed creatures, and the sons of Adam as tireless, self-reliant, unionized supermen. Neither estimate is correct. Both need the protective aegis of the state. There are sex contrasts in susceptibility to occupational disease. Men are more open to tuberculosis, consequently, in processes where humidity is great, more men than women succumb. Excluding men from the linen industry is not the solution. Bend the industry to the need of the human being, not the human being to economy in safety devices. The average man is an overworked animal, and his fatigue tells on the race. A leading obstetrician in New York declares that in his practice nine times out of ten when he is called upon to diagnose the cause of sterility in the American family, he finds the trouble in the overwork of the professional or business man.

The objection to special legislation is not on the ground that no protection is necessary, but because partial laws have not protected men and have thrown women out of employment or crowded them into lower grades of work. Then, too, linking women with minors as is the rule in protective legislation forwarded by welfare workers has been a marked disadvantage in checking child labor. Legislatures would do more for children if adult women ceased to hang on their necks. . . .

Instead of wasting energy carrying on an internecine war, it might be well if those believing in protective legislation should unite on this program: First, the total exclusion of children from industry up to sixteen. Second, the drastic limitation of the hours of young people. Third, the raising of our code dealing with occupational diseases to the level of civilized communities. Fourth, the adoption of Mrs. Sidney Webb's recommendation in the Minority Report of the War Cabinet Committee, "the consolidation of the Factory Acts should be made the occasion of sweep-

ing away all special provisions of differentiating men from women."
Working women are ready for equality. It is the welfare worker who holds
up to them the inferiority complex.

What Is Equality?

CLARA MORTENSON BEYER

. . . The Woman's Party takes the position that industrial legislation for
women is discrimination against them in the field of industry. At present,
it does not consider it feasible to wipe out such legislation for women.
Therefore, in order to remove existing inequalities between the sexes, it
proposes to extend industrial legislation for women to men. For all
practical purposes, it might better work directly for the removal of such
legislation for women. The effect, in all probability, would be the same in
either case — women would be left without the safeguards which are
peculiarly necessary to their well-being and men would be in exactly the
same position as before. In the words of Dean Roscoe Pound, of the
Harvard Law School, "there is no surer method of repealing all legal
protection for women than to substitute for the laws now in force general
statutes covering all persons." . . .

. . . Working women have the world to lose and nothing to gain but
their chains. They have lost these chains all too recently to be willing to
be shackled again merely for the sake of a theoretical equality.

The Woman's Party, as a result of a recent questionnaire, is rapidly
proving, to its own satisfaction at least, that working women do not want
protective legislation. When convinced of that, how can it hope to prove
that working men want for themselves the legislation scorned by working
women and, if the Woman's Party so proves, would it, as an organization,
in the name of equality attempt to force the unwilling working women to
accept legal standards satisfactory only to their brothers? Does "equality"
deny women the right to differ from men?

Women cannot be made men by act of legislature or even by an
amendment to the United States Constitution. That does not mean
women are inferior or superior to men. Refusal to recognize the biological
differences between men and women does not make for equality. . . .
[W]omen will continue to bear children and certain physiological corol-
laries to this fact will continue to exist. Exposure to strain and overfatigue
in the child-bearing period, and wage-earning women are almost all in
this period of life, is reflected in higher morbidity of working women than
of working men, and in the excessive sickness and death rate of children
of working mothers. That long hours of constant standing or sitting are

more injurious to women than to men is another well-established fact. These actualities may not be pleasant to our feminist friends, but they will not be removed by playing ostrich. Students of industry recognize that women are an unstable factor in industry, that the majority enter industry to fill the gap between school and marriage. They are, on the whole, unskilled workers. Because of their instability, their lack of skill, and their extreme youth, trade union organization among women has been of slow growth, far slower than among men. Working conditions among women reflect this inability to organize. It was said at the woman's industrial conference that 1,000 men were working the eight-hour day to every one woman. Over one-half of the wage-earning women of the country are earning less than enough to live on. Trade union organizers familiar with these facts are advocating industrial legislation for women on the ground that unionism among them is too slow and has not reached the vast rank and file. They have further found that industrial legislation for women is a help rather than a hindrance to organization. We cannot expect overworked, undernourished women to have the energy or enthusiasm for joining a union and attempting to better their conditions. While the masses of women workers are so far down the industrial scale, it is ludicrous to talk of their freedom to choose their occupations, to bargain freely for their wages and hours of work. It would be more to the point to talk of the freedom of employers to exploit their workers.

By legislation an effort is being made to bring women up to the point where industrial equality with men is more nearly possible. The time undoubtedly will come when women will need less special legislation than they do now, but until that time it is little short of criminal to deny them the opportunity for reasonable leisure and a living wage, which legislation alone can obtain for them.

A Debate in the Forum

Doris Stevens versus Alice Hamilton, 1924

After Alice Paul presented her proposal for an ERA to Congress at the end of 1923, the debate over protective laws reached a crescendo. Doris Stevens, a founder of the National Woman's Party and one of its leaders, and Alice Hamilton, former Hull House resident and professor of industrial medicine at Harvard, summed up the arguments of their respective constituencies. The debaters agreed that protective laws were, in Stevens's words, "the heart of the whole controversy," but that was the only point on which they concurred. To Stevens, proponents of protection asked women "to set their pace with the weakest member of their sex." Hamilton, who conceded that legislation was a substitute for unionization, argued that women who were helped by protective laws far outnumbered those who were handicapped by them. (She also included many statistics about industrial hazards to workers' health, which are omitted in the following excerpt.)

Suffrage Does Not Give Equality

DORIS STEVENS

. . . When women finally got the right to vote, after seventy-five years of agitation in the United States, many good citizens sighed with relief and said, "Now that's over. The woman problem is disposed of." But was it? Exactly what do women want now? Just this. They ask the same rights, in law and in custom, with which every man is now endowed through the accident of being born a male. Frail and inadequate as these rights may be, compared to those rights we would like to see enjoyed by all men, women are nevertheless still deprived of many of them. To establish equality between men and women in law and in custom is the task undertaken by the National Woman's Party, an organization composed of women diverse in political, religious, and economic faith, but united on the platform of improving the position of women.

There is not a single State in the Union in which men and women live under equal protection of the law. There is not a State which does not in

"The Blanket Amendment — A Debate," *Forum* (August 1924), 124–60.

some respects still reflect toward women the attitude of either the old English Common Law or the Napoleonic Code. Woman is still conceived to be in subjection to, and under the control of the husband, if married, or of the male members of the family, if unmarried. In most of the States the father and mother have been made equal guardians of their children, but many of these States still deny the mother equal rights to the earnings and services of the children. Among the poor this is often a serious handicap to the mother. In New York, fathers are preferred to mothers as controllers of the services, earnings, and real estate of the children. In two States the father can still will away the custody of the child from the mother. In two States the earnings of the wife outside the home belong to the husband. In forty States the husband owns the services of his wife in the home. In most of these States this means that the husband recovers the damages for the loss of these services, should the wife meet with an injury. A wife then cannot collect for her own suffering, for in the eyes of such laws, it is not the wife who is injured, but the husband is assumed to be injured through the loss of her services to him. More than half the States do not permit women to serve on juries. Some legislators oppose jury service for women because of "moral hazard" of deliberating in a room with men. Other legislators favor jury service for women, for it means extending to women a service which men are seldom willing to perform. In only a third of the States is prostitution a crime for the male as well as the female.

With the removal of all legal discriminations against women solely on account of sex, women will possess with men:

Equal control of their children
Equal control of their property
Equal control of their earnings
Equal right to make contracts
Equal citizenship rights
Equal inheritance rights
Equal control of national, state, and local government
Equal opportunities in schools and universities
Equal opportunities in government service
Equal opportunities in professions and industries
Equal pay for equal work

. . . The plan of action is the next point to consider. The National Woman's Party, out of its experience in amending the national Constitution granting universal suffrage to women, proposes to secure the adoption of the further amendment now before Congress: "Men and women shall have equal rights throughout the United States and every place subject to its jurisdiction. Congress shall have power to enforce this article by appropriate legislation." . . .

In so far as opposition to the foregoing plan has crystallized at all, three main objections stand out. First, that change in the laws should come slowly, statute by statute. Our answer to this objection is found in the preceding paragraph on Federal action. Second, that maternity legislation and widows' pensions will be wiped out. Now maternity legislation is designed to assist a special group of women under special circumstances. It is not special legislation for *women*; it is for *mothers*. All women are not mothers. All mothers are not in constant need of maternity protection. That group of women whom this legislation is written to protect, will still be protected by such special legislation, just as workmen's compensation, written to cover special groups of men, and soldiers' bonuses and funds for invalided soldiers, are written to protect them. The amendment under consideration will in no way affect such special legislation, for the simple reason that it is not based on sex, but upon the special need of a given group under certain circumstances. The same is true of widows' pensions. . . . The final objection says: Grant political, social, and civil equality to women, but do not give equality to women in industry.

Here lies the heart of the whole controversy. It is not astonishing, but very intelligent indeed, that the battle should center on the point of woman's right to sell her labor on the same terms as man. For unless she is able equally to compete, to earn, to control, and to invest her money, unless in short woman's economic position is made more secure, certainly she cannot establish equality in fact. She will have won merely the shadow of power without essential and authentic substance.

Those who would limit only women to certain occupations and to certain restricted hours of work, base their program of discrimination on two points, the "moral hazard" to women and their biological inferiority. It is a philosophy which would penalize all women because some women are morally frail and physically weak. It asks women to set their pace with the weakest member of their sex. All men are not strong. Happily it has not occurred to society to limit the development of all men because some are weak. Would these protectionists be willing to say that because some men-members of the Cabinet had been suspected of moral frailty, no men should henceforth serve as Cabinet Ministers? This principle of penalizing the strong because some are weak, which has been abandoned by enlightened educationalists, now awaits rejection in the industrial field. Natural fitness, not "protection," will determine the extent of competition.

Dock work, dray work, and coal-heaving are occupations open to all men, and yet no one has ever seen the weakest members of the species rush into these occupations. Women will be quite as sensible and adroit at avoiding work beyond their strength as men have been, once they have a free choice. What reason is there to believe that if tomorrow the whole industrial field were opened to women on the same terms as men, women would insist on doing the most menial tasks in the world, the most difficult, the tasks for which they are the least fitted? May it not rather be that men know the reverse will be true, which has led some labor leaders to rush to the banner of "protection for women only"? Furthermore, if this argument were sound, then obviously women ought to have all the delightful office jobs, ought to be relieved of such tasks as scrubbing floors in office buildings, and ought to turn over this work to the stronger male members of the species. If it is only their physical strength that stands in their way, they should abandon drudgery by day and baby-tending by night, and, with the greatest possible speed, become railroad presidents, bank presidents, and other executive officers, whose weekly golf game is the chief physical tax.

No one really believes today that the morals of an adult grow stronger in the ratio that he is protected. Women as well as men become more responsible in the realm of morals only when all are free to behave according to the dictates of social conscience. And obviously, if the streets are unsafe at night for those women whose needs oblige them to work at night, the answer is most emphatically not to prevent women from earning their livelihood, but to make the streets safe for their coming and going.

But, it is argued, women are more easily exploited in industry than men. There are reasons for this outside of sex, not the least of which is the shocking neglect by men's labor organizations to organize women in their trades. When women first went from the home into industry, they carried with them, among other things, the psychology of unpaid workers. For as workers in the home they had always done the unpaid work of the world. They had their keep, but neither wages nor partnership profits. And so they shrank from asking adequate pay. They thought they should be grateful for being permitted to play in the big game at all. They were docile. They were exploited. Gradually they became bolder. Gradually they entered the better-paid trades and professions. Gradually they asked higher remuneration. It is only now that they are well on the road to matching their wits and their intelligences with men, that women are told they must be "protected." Protection is a delusion. Protection, no matter how benevolent in motive, unless applied alike to both sexes, amounts to actual penalization.

The Woman's Party is not an industrial organization and therefore does not presume to say whether workers shall work eight or four hours a day, or what wages shall be paid for such work; whether more leisure for the masses shall be got by legislation or unionism. In the best interests of women, it stands against restrictions which are not alike for both sexes, and which, therefore, constantly limit the scope of women's entry into the field of more desirable and better paid work. It believes that no human being, man or woman, should be exploited by industry. As firmly it believes that just so long as sex is made the artificial barrier to labor-selling, merit can never become the criterion of an applicant for a job. . . .

The National Woman's Party conceives women to be important, continuing, self-governing units of society. It conceives them to be possessed of talents and intelligences, of beauties and creative possibilities heretofore unfathomed. It proposes to do its uttermost to lift women from their present position of subjection and to put no human limits on the possibilities of their development.

To this end it seeks, as the next step, the equality of women in the law.

Protection for Women Workers

ALICE HAMILTON

There is a difference of opinion between two groups of women in this country with regard to the best way to secure for women freedom from discriminatory laws which hamper them as women and which survive as anachronisms in a modern society. The goal of all feminists is the same, the securing for women of as great a degree of self-determination as can be enjoyed in complex community life without detriment to others, and freedom from handicaps in the industrial struggle. The method whereby this is to be secured is the point of controversy. I belong to the group which holds that the right method is to repeal or alter one by one the laws that now hamper women or work injustice to them, and which opposes the constitutional amendment sponsored by the Woman's Party on the ground that it is too dangerously sweeping and all-inclusive. If no legislation is to be permitted except it apply to both sexes, we shall find it impossible to regulate by law the hours or wages or conditions of work of women and that would be, in my opinion, a harm far greater than the good that might be accomplished by removing certain antiquated abuses and injustices, which, bad as they are, do not injure nearly so many women as would be affected if all protective laws for working women were rendered unconstitutional.

It is a pity that words of general significance are used to describe this measure, for the result is a confusion which might be avoided by more precise terms. For instance, it is not really accurate to call this an amendment for "equal rights" for both sexes, when practically it forbids one sex to proceed along lines already tried and approved unless the other sex will come too. Organized working men in the United States long since adopted the policy of seeking improvement in hours, wages, and conditions of work through their unions and not by legislation. Women, whose labor organizations are young and feeble, have sought to secure reforms through legislation. This amendment would make it impossible for them to do so. The usual retort to that assertion is, that then the women must organize strongly, as men have done, but why? Trade unionism is a valuable weapon for the workers but it is not the only one. Women have never been strong in the trade union movement, not even in those industries which are overwhelmingly feminine, such, for instance, as the textile. Whatever be the reason for this, it is an indisputable fact, and it seems strange that women of the professional and leisure classes should wish to make it impossible for wage-earning women to use any method of procedure for their own betterment except one which they have shown themselves unable to use with any real power.

The advocates of the amendment quote in its favor working women who have lost their jobs because of laws prohibiting night work or overtime, and of course such cases do occur. Unfortunately there are always some individuals who lose out in any group action. The bitterest opponent of trade unionism is the highly skilled, exceptionally capable workman with an individualistic outlook on life, who resents any control from the group and wants to be let alone to work when and how he pleases. That his grievances are often real, nobody can deny, but if we are to live in a community, the greatest good to the greatest number must outweigh the rights of the individual. For every woman linotypist who wishes to take night work on a newspaper, there must be hundreds of textile mill operatives who suffer from the compulsion to work on the night shift. For one supervisor or forewoman who wishes to work overtime, there must be hundreds of saleswomen and telephone girls who long to be freed from the necessity of so doing. It would seem that the safer, if slower, way would be to work out exemptions, so far as possible, in such legislation, to provide for those women who really do wish for entire freedom in making their bargains and are entitled to it.

We are told by members of the Woman's Party that if we "free" the working woman, allow her to "compete on equal terms with men," her industrial status will at once be raised. She is supposed now to be suffering from the handicap of laws regulating her working conditions and hours of labor and longing to be rid of them. But such a statement could never be made by anyone familiar with labor. It assumes that the present protective laws have always been in force and that the passage of the blanket amendment would usher in a new era of freedom and equality. Of course the reverse is true. Laws protecting women workers are of comparatively recent origin and are still far from universal throughout the country. It is not necessary to try the experiment of identical laws for the two sexes; we have been watching that experiment for decades and we can still observe it in many States. Compare for instance . . . pairs of States lying side by side. Will anyone say that it is better to be a woman wage earner in Indiana where hours are practically unrestricted than in Ohio where a woman is sure of a nine-hour day and a six-day week? . . .

The advocates of the blanket amendment say that they do not oppose laws designed to protect the child, that they are ready to favor protection of "pregnant persons" and "nursing persons." This is, of course, an important concession. But the damage done by an industrial poison may antedate pregnancy. Women who have worked in a lead trade before marriage and still more women who work in lead after marriage are more likely to be sterile than women who have worked in other trades; if they conceive they are less likely to carry the child to term; and if they do they are less likely to bear a living child and their living children are less able to survive the first weeks of life. There are many proofs of this in the literature. . . .

The belief in the "equality of the sexes," interpreted to mean their essential identity, is very attractive to many people. When I first entered the labor field my inclination was in that direction, for I come of a family of suffragists; my grandmother was a close friend of Susan B. Anthony, and I had certainly never wished for any sort of privilege or special protection during my own career as a professional woman. During the first years of my study of the poisonous trades I was filled with impatience because I could get no hearing when I urged the necessity of safeguarding the ignorant, unorganized, foreign laborers in our dangerous lead trades, while at the same time I saw protective laws passed for women who were employed in far less dangerous work. But experience is a thorough if hard teacher, and I have learned now to take what I can get and be thankful. The American legislator cannot be aroused to much indignation over descriptions of poisonous, dusty, heavy, hot, and filthy work if it is done by men. The pioneer spirit which scorns "paternalism," the Nordic spirit which holds southern European labor in contempt, stand in the way and are hard obstacles to overcome. But this same hard-boiled legislator has a soft side when it comes to women workers. . . .

In Holland, I am told, the two sexes have recently been put on an equality in industry, not by taking privileges away from the women, but by extending them to the men. Holland is an old country, which has long been used to labor legislation. I cannot believe that we in the United States are nearing that point very fast, though I should like to think so. Meantime, until we reach it, I must, as a practical person, familiar with the great, inarticulate body of working women, reiterate my belief that they are largely helpless, that they have very special needs which unaided they cannot attain, and that it would be a crime for the country to pass legislation which would not only make it impossible to better their lot in the near future but would even deprive them of the small measure of protection they now enjoy.

13

West Coast Hotel Co. v. Parrish (1937)

The Adkins *decision of 1923, which upset the federal minimum-wage law for women workers in Washington, D.C., discouraged further legislation and provided a precedent for invalidating minimum-wage laws in subsequent cases. In 1937, however, the Supreme Court suddenly reversed itself. In another close, 5–4 decision, it overruled* Adkins *and upheld a Washington State minimum-wage law for women. Only the year before, the same justices had rejected a similar law from New York. But the impact of the Depression, the pressure of critical public opinion, and, more immediately, the threat of Franklin D. Roosevelt's court-packing plan spurred the Court to shift gears. Justice Owen J. Roberts, who had come close to changing his mind in 1936, now joined the Court's liberals and provided the swing vote.*

In the Stettler *and* Adkins *minimum-wage cases of 1917 and 1923, workers, along with employers, had challenged the minimum wage. In the 1937 case, however, a worker — Elsie Parrish, a hotel chambermaid —*

*sued to recover wages owed her under the minimum-wage law. At the
start of the majority opinion, Chief Justice Charles E. Hughes dispensed
with freedom of contract ("The Constitution does not speak of freedom of
contract"). In the following segment of the opinion, he offered the Court's
reasons (including "recent economic experience") for upholding the minimum wage for women workers.*

Compare the Adkins *and* Parrish *decisions. Which is more persuasive?*

Mr. Chief Justice Hughes delivered the opinion of the Court.

This case presents the question of the constitutional validity of the
minimum wage law of the state of Washington. . . .

The appellant conducts a hotel. The appellee Elsie Parrish was employed as a chambermaid and (with her husband) brought suit to recover
the difference between the wages paid her and the minimum wage fixed
pursuant to the state law. The minimum wage was $14.50 per week of 48
hours. The appellant challenged the act as repugnant to the due process
clause of the Fourteenth Amendment of the Constitution of the United
States. . . .

The appellant relies upon the decision of this Court in *Adkins v.
Children's Hospital.* . . .

The Supreme Court of Washington has . . . refused to regard the
decision in the *Adkins* Case as determinative and has pointed to our
decisions both before and since that case as justifying its position. We are
of the opinion that this ruling of the state court demands on our part a
re-examination of the *Adkins* Case. . . .

. . . [R]egulation which is reasonable in relation to its subject and is
adopted in the interests of the community is due process.

This essential limitation of liberty in general governs freedom of
contract in particular. . . .

The point that has been strongly stressed that adult employees should
be deemed competent to make their own contracts was decisively met
nearly forty years ago in *Holden v. Hardy,* . . . where we pointed out the
inequality in the footing of the parties. . . .

And we added the fact "that both parties are of full age, and competent
to contract, does not necessarily deprive the state of the power to interfere, where the parties do not stand upon an equality, or where the public
health demands that one party to the contract shall be protected against
himself." "The state still retains an interest in his welfare, however
reckless he may be. The whole is no greater than the sum of all the parts,

and when the individual health, safety, and welfare are sacrificed or neglected, the state must suffer."

It is manifest that this established principle is peculiarly applicable in relation to the employment of women in whose protection the state has a special interest. That phase of the subject received elaborate consideration in *Muller v. Oregon* (1908) . . . , where the constitutional authority of the state to limit the working hours of women was sustained. . . . Again in *Quong Wing v. Kirkendall,*[1] . . . in referring to a differentiation with respect to the employment of women, we said that the Fourteenth Amendment did not interfere with state power by creating a "fictitious equality." We referred to recognized classifications on the basis of sex with regard to hours of work and in other matters, and we observed that the particular points at which that difference shall be enforced by legislation were largely in the power of the state. In later rulings this Court sustained the regulation of hours of work of women employees. . . .

This array of precedents and the principles they applied were thought by the dissenting Justices in the *Adkins* Case to demand that the minimum wage statute be sustained. The validity of the distinction made by the Court between a minimum wage and a maximum of hours in limiting liberty of contract was especially challenged. . . . That challenge persists and is without any satisfactory answer. . . .

We think that the . . . *Adkins* Case was a departure from the true application of the principles governing the regulation by the state of the relation of employer and employed. Those principles have been reenforced by our subsequent decisions. Thus in *Radice v. New York,* . . . we sustained the New York statute which restricted the employment of women in restaurants at night. . . .

. . . What can be closer to the public interest than the health of women and their protection from unscrupulous and overreaching employers? And if the protection of women is a legitimate end of the exercise of state power, how can it be said that the requirement of the payment of a minimum wage fairly fixed in order to meet the very necessities of existence is not an admissible means to that end? The Legislature of the state was clearly entitled to consider the situation of women in employment, the fact that they are in the class receiving the least pay, that their bargaining power is relatively weak, and that they are the ready victims

---

[1] In 1912, Quong Wing, who ran a hand laundry in Montana, challenged a state law that imposed a licensing fee on all persons engaged in the laundry business except those involved with steam laundries and women who worked alone or in pairs. He charged that the law discriminated on the basis of sex. The Supreme Court upheld the law; it contended that distinctions based on sex had precedents and were constitutional.

of those who would take advantage of their necessitous circumstances. The Legislature was entitled to adopt measures to reduce the evils of the "sweating system," the exploiting of workers at wages so low as to be insufficient to meet the bare cost of living, thus making their very helplessness the occasion of a most injurious competition. The Legislature had the right to consider that its minimum wage requirements would be an important aid in carrying out its policy of protection. The adoption of similar requirements by many states evidences a deepseated conviction both as to the presence of the evil and as to the means adapted to check it. Legislative response to that conviction cannot be regarded as arbitrary or capricious and that is all we have to decide. Even if the wisdom of the policy be regarded as debatable and its effects uncertain, still the Legislature is entitled to its judgment.

There is an additional and compelling consideration which recent economic experience has brought into a strong light. The exploitation of a class of workers who are in an unequal position with respect to bargaining power and are thus relatively defenseless against the denial of a living wage is not only detrimental to their health and well being, but casts a direct burden for their support upon the community. What these workers lose in wages the taxpayers are called upon to pay. The bare cost of living must be met. We may take judicial notice of the unparalleled demands for relief which arose during the recent period of depression and still continue to an alarming extent despite the degree of economic recovery which has been achieved. It is unnecessary to cite official statistics to establish what is of common knowledge through the length and breadth of the land. While in the instant case no factual brief has been presented, there is no reason to doubt that the state of Washington has encountered the same social problem that is present elsewhere. The community is not bound to provide what is in effect a subsidy for unconscionable employers. The community may direct its lawmaking power to correct the abuse which springs from their selfish disregard of the public interest. The argument that the legislation in question constitutes an arbitrary discrimination, because it does not extend to men, is unavailing. This Court has frequently held that the legislative authority, acting within its proper field, is not bound to extend its regulation to all cases which it might possibly reach. The Legislature "is free to recognize degrees of harm and it may confine its restrictions to those classes of cases where the need is deemed to be clearest." If "the law presumably hits the evil where it is most felt, it is not to be overthrown because there are other instances to which it might have been applied." . . . This familiar principle has repeatedly been applied to legislation which singles out women, and particular classes of women, in the exercise of the state's protective power. . . . Their relative need in the presence of the evil, no less than the existence of the evil itself, is a matter for the legislative judgment.

Our conclusion is that the case of *Adkins v. Children's Hospital, supra,* should be, and it is, overruled. The judgment of the Supreme Court of the state of Washington is affirmed.

14

United States v. Darby (1941)

Four years after the Parrish *decision, the "entering wedge" strategy worked once more. In* United States v. Darby, *the Supreme Court upheld the Fair Labor Standards Act of 1938, which set maximum hours and minimum wages for men and women involved in the production of goods for interstate commerce. The* Darby *decision had much in common with the* Bunting *decision of 1917, which had extended maximum hours to men. Both decisions were made by liberal panels of justices (FDR made seven Supreme Court appointments between 1937 and 1941). In both cases, the majority opinions dwelled on issues other than whether a protective policy for women could be extended to men. In* Darby, *most of the decision involved the interstate commerce clause. The crucial section on protection, reprinted here, simply states that "the fixing of a minimum wage is within the legislative power," that it violated neither the Fifth nor the Fourteenth Amendment, and that it could apply to men as well as women. This statement signified the long-awaited triumph of the progressive campaign for protective labor legislation.*

. . . Since our decision in *West Coast Hotel Co. v. Parrish,* . . . it is no longer open to question that the fixing of a minimum wage is within the legislative power and that the bare fact of its exercise is not a denial of due process under the Fifth more than under the Fourteenth Amendment. Nor is it any longer open to question that it is within the legislative power to fix maximum hours. *Holden v. Hardy,* . . . *Muller v. Oregon,* . . . *Bunting v. Oregon,* . . . *Baltimore & Ohio R. Co. v. Interstate Commerce Comm'n.* . . . Similarly, the statute is not objectionable because applied to both men and women. Cf. *Bunting v. Oregon.* . . .

312 U.S. 100 (1941).

Chronology:
Major Hours and Wages Cases
1895–1941

U.S. Supreme Court cases appear in boldface type.

1895

Ritchie v. People, 155 Ill. 98. Illinois Supreme Court invalidates the state's eight-hour law of 1893 for women in factories.

1898

Holden v. Hardy, 169 U.S. 366. U.S. Supreme Court upholds, 7–2, a Utah law of 1896 limiting mine workers' hours to eight a day.

1900

Commonwealth v. Beatty, 15 Super. Ct. (Pa.) 5. A Pennsylvania court upholds a state law of 1897 limiting women's working hours to twelve a day and sixty a week.

1902

Wenham v. State, 65 Neb. 394; *State v. Buchanan* 29 Wash. 602. Nebraska and Washington Supreme Courts uphold ten-hour laws of 1899 (Nebraska) and 1901 (Washington) for women workers in factories and laundries.

1905

Lochner v. New York, 198 U.S. 45. U.S. Supreme Court strikes down, 5–4, New York's ten-hour law of 1896 for bakery workers.

1907

People v. Williams, 189 N.Y. 131. New York Court of Appeals strikes down 1899 law prohibiting night work (10 P.M. to 6 A.M.) for women workers.

1908

Muller v. Oregon, 208 U.S. 412. U.S. Supreme Court unanimously upholds Oregon ten-hour law of 1903 for women workers in factories and laundries.

1910

Ritchie v. Wayman, 244 Ill. 509. Illinois Supreme Court upholds ten-hour law of 1909 for women workers in factories.

1915

People v. Schweinler Press, 214 N.Y. 395. New York Court of Appeals upholds 1913 law prohibiting night work (10 P.M. to 6 A.M.) for women workers in factories.

1917

Bunting v. Oregon, 243 U.S. 426. U.S. Supreme Court upholds, 5–3, an Oregon ten-hour law of 1913 for all workers in factories. The law limits overtime to three hours a day at one and one-half times the regular wage.

1917

Stettler v. O'Hara, 243 U.S. 629. U.S. Supreme Court upholds, 4–4, an Oregon law of 1913 providing minimum wage for women workers. The companion case is *Simpson v. O'Hara.*

1923

Adkins v. Children's Hospital, 261 U.S. 525. U.S. Supreme Court strikes down, 5–4, a federal minimum-wage law of 1918 for women workers in the District of Columbia. The companion case is *Adkins v. Lyons.*

1924

Radice v. New York, 264 U.S. 292. U.S. Supreme Court unanimously upholds New York law of 1917 extending the state's ban on night work (10 P.M. to 6 A.M.) to women workers in restaurants in large cities.

1937

West Coast Hotel Co. v. Parrish, 300 U.S. 379. U.S. Supreme Court upholds, 5–4, a Washington State minimum-wage law of 1913 for women workers.

1941

United States v. Darby Lumber Co., 312 U.S. 100. U.S. Supreme Court unanimously upholds the Fair Labor Standards Act of 1938, which provides maximum hours and minimum wages for workers producing goods for interstate commerce.

In Search of *Muller*:
Suggested Reading

The exploration of *Muller v. Oregon* involves a journey through women's history, constitutional history, and studies of the Progressive era. This selective bibliography offers some starting points; additional sources appear in the notes to part 1.

The rise of women's history in the past generation has impelled extensive scholarship on protective laws, the women's reform network, and the origins of the welfare state. For women's labor history, see Leslie Woodcock Tentler, *Wage Earning Women: Industrial Work and Family Life in the United States, 1900–1930* (New York: Oxford University Press, 1979), and Alice Kessler-Harris, *Out to Work: A History of Wage-Earning Women* (New York: Oxford University Press, 1982). For protective legislation for women workers, older sources include Elizabeth Faulkner Baker, *Protective Labor Legislation* (New York: Columbia University Press, 1925); Clara M. Beyer, *History of Labor Legislation in Three States,* Bulletin No. 66, pt. 1, Women's Bureau, U.S. Department of Labor (Washington, D.C.: Government Printing Office, 1929); Elizabeth Brandeis, "Labor Legislation," in John R. Commons, ed., *History of Labor in the United States,* vol. 3 (New York: Macmillan, 1935), 399–697; and Elizabeth Brandeis, "Protective Legislation," in Milton Derber and Edwin Young, eds., *Labor and the New Deal* (Madison: University of Wisconsin Press, 1957), 195–237. Recent studies of protective laws include Kessler-Harris, *Out to Work,* ch. 7; Susan Lehrer, *Origins of Protective Labor Legislation for Women, 1905–1925* (Albany: State University of New York Press, 1987); Claudia Goldin, *Understanding the Gender Gap: An Economic History of American Women* (New York: Oxford University Press, 1990), ch. 7; Theda Skocpol, *Protecting Soldiers and Mothers: The Political Origins of Social Policy in the United States* (Cambridge: Harvard University Press, 1992); Eileen Boris, *Home to Work: Motherhood and the Politics of Industrial Homework in the United States* (New York: Cambridge University Press, 1994); and Ulla Wikander, Alice Kessler-Harris, and Jane Lewis, eds., *Protecting Women: Labor Legislation in Europe, the*

United States, and Australia, 1880–1920 (Urbana: University of Illinois Press, 1995), which provides a comparative perspective.

For Florence Kelley, see Josephine Goldmark, *Impatient Crusader: Florence Kelley's Life Story* (Urbana: University of Illinois Press, 1953); Dorothy Rose Blumberg, *Florence Kelley: The Making of a Social Pioneer* (New York: A. M. Kelley, 1966); Kathryn Kish Sklar, "Hull House in the 1890s: A Community of Women Reformers," *Signs* 10 (Summer 1985): 658–77, which presents the roots of *Ritchie v. People* (1895); Kathryn Kish Sklar, ed., *Notes of Sixty Years: The Autobiography of Florence Kelley* (Chicago: Charles H. Kerr, 1985); Kathryn Kish Sklar, "The Historical Foundations of Women's Power in the Creation of the American Welfare State, 1830–1930," in Seth Koven and Sonya Michel, eds., *Mothers of a New World: Maternalist Politics and the Origins of Welfare States* (New York: Routledge, 1993), 43–93; and Kathryn Kish Sklar, *Florence Kelley and the Nation's Work: The Rise of Women's Political Culture, 1830–1900* (New Haven: Yale University Press, 1995).

For the National Consumers' League, see Maud Nathan, *The Story of an Epoch-Making Movement* (New York: Doubleday, Page, 1926), which understates Kelley's role, and Clement E. Vose, "The National Consumers' League and the Brandeis Brief," *Midwest Journal of Political Science* 1 (November 1957): 267–90. Two major primary sources are Florence Kelley, *Ethical Gains in Legislation* (New York: Macmillan, 1905), and Josephine Goldmark, *Fatigue and Efficiency: A Study in Industry* (New York: Charities Publication Committee, 1912). For the Women's Trade Union League, see Nancy Shrom Dye, *As Equals and as Sisters: Feminism, Unionism, and the Women's Trade Union League of New York* (Columbia: University of Missouri Press, 1987), and Diane Kirkby, "'The Wage-Earning Woman and the State': The National Women's Trade Union League and Protective Labor Legislation, 1903–1928," *Labor History* 28 (1987): 54–74. Scholarship on the women's reform network includes William L. O'Neill, *Feminism in America: A History,* 2nd rev. ed. (New Brunswick, N.J.: Transaction, 1989); Linda Gordon, ed., *Women, the State, and Welfare* (Madison: University of Wisconsin Press, 1990); Robyn Muncy, *Creating a Female Dominion in American Reform, 1830–1930* (New York: Oxford University Press, 1991); Noralee Frankel and Nancy S. Dye, eds., *Gender, Class, Race, and Reform in the Progressive Era* (Lexington: University of Kentucky Press, 1992); and Koven and Michel, eds., *Mothers of a New World,* cited above.

Discussions of the *Muller* case have proliferated since the 1970s. For primary documents, see Louis D. Brandeis and Josephine Goldmark, *Women in Industry,* introduction by Leon Stein and Philip Taft (1908;

reprint, New York: Arno Press, 1969), which includes the Brandeis brief and the *Muller v. Oregon* decision. *Landmark Briefs and Arguments of the Supreme Court of the United States,* ed. Philip B. Kurland and Gerhard Casper (Arlington, Va.: University Publications of America, 1975), vol. 16, includes the two briefs for Oregon and the brief for Curt Muller. For the Oregon context, see Ronald K. L. Collins and Jennifer Friesen, "Looking Back on *Muller v. Oregon,*" *American Bar Association Journal* 69 (March 1983): 294–98, and (April 1983): 472–77. Robert Johnston's work-in-progress on Portland, Oregon, in the Progressive era will further illuminate the local roots of the *Muller* case.

Judith A. Baer, *The Chains of Protection: The Judicial Response to Protective Labor Legislation* (Westport, Conn.: Greenwood, 1978), a detailed study of women's labor laws and the courts, includes critiques of the Brandeis brief and the *Muller* decision. Informed discussions of the *Muller* case and protective laws in general include Ann Corinne Hill, "Protection of Women Workers and the Courts: A Legal Case History," *Feminist Studies* 5 (Summer 1979): 247–73; Nancy Erickson, "Historical Background of 'Protective' Labor Legislation: *Muller v. Oregon,*" in D. Kelly Weisberg, *Women and the Law: A Social Historical Perspective,* vol. 2 (Cambridge: Schenkman, 1982), 155–86, which discusses the public response to *Muller* in 1908; Nancy Erickson, "*Muller v. Oregon* Reconsidered: The Origins of a Sex-Based Doctrine of Liberty of Contract," *Labor History* 30 (Spring 1989): 228–50; and Lise Vogel, *Mothers on the Job: Maternity Policy in the U.S. Workplace* (New Brunswick: Rutgers University Press, 1993), ch. 2.

Surveys of women's legal history and casebooks also offer much on *Muller* and on the controversy over single-sex protective laws; see Barbara Allen Babcock, Ann E. Freedman, Eleanor Holmes Norton, and Susan C. Ross, eds., *Sex Discrimination and the Law: Causes and Remedies* (Boston: Little, Brown, 1975), ch. 1; Deborah L. Rhode, *Justice and Gender: Sex Discrimination and the Law* (Cambridge: Harvard University Press, 1989), ch. 2; Leslie Friedman Goldstein, *The Constitutional Rights of Women: Cases in Law and Social Change* (Madison: University of Wisconsin Press, 1989), ch. 1; Joan Hoff, *Law, Gender, and Injustice: A Legal History of U.S. Women* (New York: New York University Press, 1991), chs. 5, 6. Frances E. Olsen's articles include "From False Paternalism to False Equality: Judicial Assaults on Feminist Community, Illinois, 1869–1895," *Michigan Law Review* 84 (June 1986): 1518–41, on the *Bradwell* and *Ritchie* cases; and "The Family and the Market: A Study of Ideology and Legal Reform," *Harvard Law Review* 96 (May 1983): 1497–1578. For the minimum-wage battle, see Alice Kessler-Harris, "Law and a Living: The Gendered Content of Free 'Labor,'" in Frankel and Dye, eds., *Gender, Class, Race, and Reform,* 87–109; Sybil Lipschultz, "Social Feminism and Legal Discourse, 1908–1923," *Yale Journal of Law and Feminism* 2 (Fall 1989): 131–60; Joan G. Zimmerman, "The Jurisprudence of Equality: The Women's Minimum Wage, the First Equal Rights Amendment, and *Adkins v. Children's Hospital,* 1905–1923," *Journal of American History* 78 (June 1991): 188–225; and Vivien Hart, *Bound by Our Constitution: Women, Workers, and the Minimum Wage* (Princeton: Princeton University Press, 1994).

A large body of scholarship on Louis D. Brandeis presents the *Muller* case in a positive light. For the laudatory view of Brandeis (and of *Muller*) that prevailed for decades, see, for instance, Thomas Alpheus Mason, *Brandeis: A Free Man's Life* (New York: Viking, 1946), ch. 16, and "The Case of the Overworked Laundress," in John A. Garraty, ed., *Quarrels That Shaped the Constitution,* 2nd ed. (New York: Harper and Row, 1987), ch. 12. More recent studies in the appreciative mode include Melvin I. Urofsky, *A Mind of One Piece: Brandeis and American Reform* (New York: Scribner's, 1971); Leonard Baker, *Brandeis and Frankfurter: A Dual Biography* (New York: Harper and Row, 1984), ch. 1 of which discusses *Muller;* and Philippa Strum, *Louis D. Brandeis: Justice for the People* (Cambridge: Harvard University Press, 1984), especially ch. 8, on the *Muller* case, which takes account of recent criticism of single-sex protective laws. A more critical view of Brandeis has also emerged, as in, for instance, Thomas K. McCraw, *Prophets of Regulation: Charles Francis Adams, Louis D. Brandeis, James M. Landis, Alfred E. Kahn* (Cambridge: Harvard University Press, 1984), chs. 3, 4. For the Brandeis brief, see Marion E. Doro, "The Brandeis Brief," *Vanderbilt Law Review* 11 (1958): 784–99, and David P. Bryden, "Brandeis's Facts," *Constitutional Commentary* 1 (Summer 1984), 281–326, which analyzes the *Muller* brief and the subsequent *Stettler* brief. For a sample of Brandeis's articles, see "The Opportunity in the Law," *American Law Review* 39 (July–August 1905): 555–63; "The Living Law," *Illinois Law Review* 10 (February 1916): 461–71; and "The Constitution and the Minimum Wage" *Survey,* February 6, 1915, 490–94, 521–24. Also of interest is Felix Frankfurter, "Hours of Labor and Realism in Constitutional Law," *Harvard Law Review* 29 (February 1916): 353–73.

For protective laws and the courts, see Melvin I. Urofsky's overview in *A March of Liberty: A Constitutional History of the United States,* vol. 2 (New York: Knopf, 1988), ch. 24, and Urofsky, "State Courts and Protective Legislation during the Progressive Era: A Reevaluation," *Journal of American History* 72 (June 1985): 63–91. For changes in jurisprudence, see Arnold M. Paul, *Conservative Crisis and the Rule of Law: Attitudes of Bar and Bench, 1887–1895* (Ithaca: Cornell University Press, 1960); Howard Gillman, *The Constitution Besieged: The Rise and Demise of Lochner Era Police Powers Jurisprudence* (Durham: Duke University Press, 1993); and Owen M. Fiss, *Troubled Beginnings of the Modern State, 1888–1910* (New York: Macmillan, 1993). For labor unions and the courts, see William E. Forbath, *Law and the Shaping of the American Labor Movement* (Cambridge: Harvard University Press, 1991), ch. 2. For sociological jurisprudence and legal realism, see G. Edward White, "From Sociological Jurisprudence to Realism: Jurisprudence and Social Change in Early Twentieth Century America," *Virginia Law Review* 58 (September 1972): 999–1028; Morton Horwitz, *The Transformation of American Law, 1870–1960: The Crisis of Legal Orthodoxy* (New York: Oxford University Press, 1992), chs. 3, 4; William W. Fisher III, Morton J. Horwitz, and Thomas A. Reed, eds., *American Legal Realism* (New York: Oxford University Press, 1993); and Laura Kalman, *Legal Realism at Yale, 1927–1960* (Chapel Hill: University of North Carolina Press, 1986). For the Supreme Court in the 1930s, see William Leuchtenberg, *The Supreme Court Reborn: The Constitutional Revolution in the Age of Roosevelt* (New York: Oxford University Press, 1995).

For background on business, labor, reform, and ideas in the Progressive era, see, in order of publication, Morton White, *Social Thought in America: The Revolt against Formalism* (1957; 2nd ed., London: Oxford, 1976); Robert H. Wiebe, *Businessmen and Reform: A Study of the Progressive Movement* (Cambridge: Harvard University Press, 1962); Gabriel Kolko, *The Triumph of Conservatism: A Reinterpretation of American History, 1900–1916* (New York: Free Press, 1963); Robert H. Wiebe, *The Search for Order, 1877–1920* (New York: Hill and Wang, 1967); James Weinstein, *The Corporate Ideal in the Liberal State, 1900–1918* (Boston: Beacon Press, 1968); John W. Chambers II, *The Tyranny of Change: America in the Progressive Era, 1900–1917* (New York: St. Martin's, 1980); Robert M. Crunden, *Ministers of Reform: The Progressives' Achievement in American Civilization, 1889–1920* (New York: Basic Books, 1982); Arthur S. Link and Richard L. McCormick, *Progressivism* (Arlington Heights, Ill.: Stanley Davidson, 1983); and Christopher L. Tomlins, *The State and the Unions: Labor Relations, Law, and the Organized Labor Movement in America, 1880–1960* (New York: Cambridge University Press, 1985).

Index